The Grover E. Murray Studies in the American Southwest

FINDING THE GREAT WESTERN TRAIL

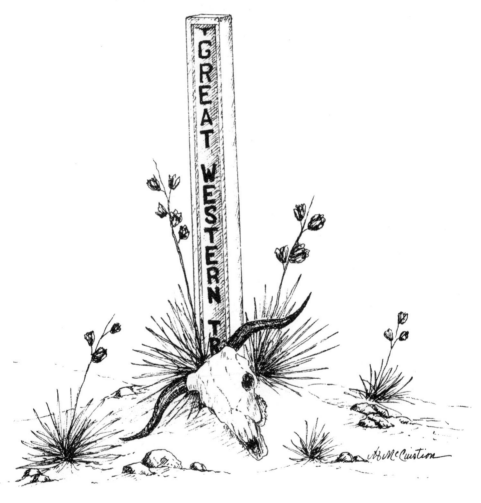

Image courtesy of Mary Ann McCuistion, Vernon, Texas.

FINDING THE GREAT WESTERN TRAIL

SYLVIA GANN MAHONEY

FOREWORD BY RAY KLINGINSMITH

Texas Tech University Press

This book is typeset in Minion Pro. The paper used in this book meets the minimum requirements of ANSI/NISO Z39.48-1992 (R1997). ∞

Designed by Kasey McBeath
Cover illustration courtesy Western History Collections, University of Oklahoma Libraries, Forbes 129.

Library of Congress Cataloging-in-Publication Data
Mahoney, Sylvia Gann, 1939-
    Finding the Great Western Trail / Sylvia Gann Mahoney ; foreword by Ray Klinginsmith.
        pages cm. — (The Grover E. Murray studies in the American Southwest)
        Summary: "Follows the recovery and marking of the Great Western Trail from northern Mexico through the US just passed the Canadian border"—Provided by publisher.
    Includes bibliographical references and index.
    ISBN 978-0-89672-943-8 (hardback : alkaline paper) — ISBN 978-0-89672-944-5 (e-book) 1. Great Western Scenic Trail—History. 2. Historical markers—Great Western Scenic Trail—History. 3. Great Western Scenic Trail—History, Local. 4. West (U.S.)—History, Local. I. Title.
        F590.7.M34 2015
        978—dc23   2015024147

15 16 17 18 19 20 21 22 23 / 9 8 7 6 5 4 3 2 1

Texas Tech University Press
Box 41037 | Lubbock, Texas 79409-1037 USA
800.832.4042 | ttup@ttu.edu | www.ttupress.org

Vision—Bob Klemme

Challenge—Dennis Vernon & John Yudell Barton

Project—Rotary Club of Vernon, Texas

Historian and Project Co-Chair—Jeff Bearden

National & International Rotary Leadership—Ray Klinginsmith

District Rotary Leadership, Going the Extra Mile—Jim Aneff & David Mason

Marker Makers—Phil McCuistion, Rick Jouett, Paul Hawkins

Museum Trail Collection & Art—Red River Valley Museum & Mary Ann McCuistion

GWT Music, Poetry, & Video—Dr. Michael Babb & Leroy Jones,
original GWT songs; Sherri Grant, original GWT poem; J. L. Courtney, video of trail
events; Jerry McClain, GWT video

Permanent Trail Collection & Oral Interviews—Texas Tech University
Southwest Collection/Special GWT Collection: Dr. Monte Monroe & Dr. Tai Kreidler

National Historic Trail Designation Efforts—National Park Service,
Congressional Feasibility Study:

Dr. Arron Mahr & Dr. Frank Norris

Hundreds of research volunteers from nine US states, Mexico, Canada

Of the things we think, say or do:
> *Is it the Truth?*
> *Is it Fair to all concerned?*
> *Will it build Good Will and Better Friendships?*
> *Will it be Beneficial to all concerned?*

> > —The Four-Way Test
> > Rotary International's Ethics Guide
> > for personal and professional relationships

Tell the truth, Be tough but fair
Keep your word, Finish what you start
Work hard, Be loyal

> —A Cowboy Code of Ethics

CONTENTS

ILLUSTRATIONS

MAPS

Thank you to cartographer and Great Western Trail historian Gary Kraisinger of Halstead, Kansas, for permission to use the GWT maps he produced.

Herd with cowboys, c. 1880s. Courtesy Western History Collections, University of Oklahoma Libraries, Forbes 129.

FOREWORD

It was a lucky day for me when I had the good fortune to meet Sylvia Mahoney! I was in Abilene, Texas, for a Rotary fundraising event for polio eradication efforts on October 22, 2009, and I was strongly encouraged by my longtime friend, PDG Jim Aneff, to meet Sylvia and learn about the Rotary trail marking project for the Great Western Trail. I did so with some reluctance because the promoters of Rotary projects often want assistance from Rotary International to encourage other clubs to adopt their projects and/or want to request money from the Rotary Foundation to subsidize such projects. That was not the case with Sylvia!

It took less than thirty minutes for Sylvia and her PowerPoint presentation to convince me that the Great Western Trail is a significant segment of Western culture that needs to be preserved. I also liked the fact that most of the Rotary clubs along the GWT are located in small towns, which appealed to my rural roots. By marking the GWT near their respective towns, the Rotary clubs are not only enhancing the history and heritage of each town, they are creating local tourism sites. It is truly a win-win situation for everyone involved in marking the trail.

Of course, during our initial meeting in Abilene, I didn't know that Sylvia is a former college rodeo coach and the author of an authoritative book about college rodeo. I also learned later that she is a gifted and studious writer as well as a promoter *par excellence*. She is a tireless worker, and if she decided to reopen the Great Western Trail for a few cattle drives, I would not bet against her ability to do so. In fact, I would happily sign on as a drover for the first drive!

Sylvia chooses her projects carefully, and I think she chose wisely in her project to validate and publicize the Great Western Trail by marking its route from Mexico to Canada. Americans admire the Western culture of cowboys and cattle ranches, particularly the cattle drives from Texas to the north, which called for the highest level of skill and fortitude. Dozens of Western movies have featured cattle drives, and the television show *Rawhide* was so popular that one of its stars, Clint Eastwood, went on to fame and fortune in countless movies. Cattle drives were also featured with a lighthearted touch in the popular *City Slicker* movies with Billy Crystal and Jack Palance.

After learning about the Rotary project to mark the GWT, I asked a singer-songwriter friend, Dr. Michael Babb, to consider writing a song about the GWT, and I was delighted to learn from Mike that he was born and reared near the trail in Oklahoma. He then wrote an outstanding song named "The Great Western Cattle Trail," which is available for purchase on both iTunes and Amazon.com, and he has become a strong supporter for Sylvia's project. In the closing verse of his song, the cowboy singer laments that now "The trail will be,—but a memory,—in the heart of every cowboy." Mike's song sweeps us away to the thrill of riding high in the saddle, and with Sylvia's book, the GWT will be a pleasant memory for all of us who learn and appreciate the history and significance of the trail.

Toni Morrison once said "If there is a book that you really want to read, but it hasn't been written yet, then you must write it." Sylvia has clearly accepted that challenge, and I now look forward to receiving her book, which I really want to read. Thanks, Sylvia, for your book—and for making the Great Western Trail come alive for all of us who have always wanted to be cowboys!

Ray Klinginsmith
President 2010–2011, Rotary International
Kirksville, Missouri

PREFACE

The prodigious grassroots research project presented in this book, *Finding the Great Western Trail*, started with the goal to recover evidence to verify the route of the Great Western Trail (GWT). The trail had almost faded from history for several reasons, which will be explained in the course of the book. The trail, more than two thousand miles long, lacked documentation to correct inaccurate theories and research to replace popular fiction that continued to be passed along as truth. People asserted that the GWT was the longest trail, lasted more years, and carried more cattle than any other cattle trail originating in Texas. This contradicted the assertions surrounding other, more famous, trails. The project became a record of the work by communities to recover primary sources, original materials that had not been altered or distorted, that document the authenticity of the route. The sources showed that the Great Western Trail was indeed the longest cattle trail originating in Texas, that its longevity was unsurpassed, and that it carried more cattle than any other trail. This narrative, which includes nineteenth-century trail history and a twenty-first-century research project that made trail history, necessitated an unusual organizational style.

The intellectual design required a convoluted style; therefore, this book differs from other books. The dual aspect of volunteers being both researchers and participants in making new trail history complicated the writing of the narrative. The complexity of writing about several periods of time interlaced with examples and reasons for misinformation and myths further complicated it. The narrative also became, in part, a personal history to remedy the confusion surrounding the trail's name. The first-person recounting of on-site visits to trail sites and the burial sites of trail entrepreneurs offers the visual and emotional descriptions so often effective for visual learners. Transitions between nineteenth-century cattle-trail history and the making of twenty-first-century cattle-trail history necessitated a shift between third person and first person. Much like a drover's journal that reported new trail history, the first-person narrative is a primary source about the twenty-first-century history-making journey up the trail. The nineteenth-century trail history is extracted from primary sources and secondary sources such as magazine articles, histories, criticisms, commentaries, and encyclopedias.

The research procedure became a standard approach for the members of the GWT project. Researchers examined county records, contacted descendants of drovers, and reviewed correspondence and photos from ranchers and others who settled there during the trail days. They recovered letters, journals, and personal family histories from the trail days that supported the length and longevity of the GWT. County historical societies, county history books, and local historians were rich resources. The local museums were repositories for trail history, including longtime executive directors, exhibits, and archival information.

With no designated place to archive primary sources at the time nor any on-site time to gather, copy, and identify the sources, the monumental task of recording and collecting all the primary sources recovered was not possible. At times, two dedication ceremonies were held on one day, so trail teams often moved on to another location in haste. Apart from this brevity, family records are family treasures and had to be treated with care. The names of some sources, for which I am greatly indebted, are included in endnotes. In addition, the Sources and Further Readings include an extensive list of sources used and titles of books and articles collected along the way.

The narrative of each community's volunteers to recover evidence where the trail crossed their county or state could fill the pages of several books. The more than seven hundred volunteers, their dedication to the completion of the project, and the many others they enfolded into the project were worthy of being included in the narrative—but it is a narrative limited by length. The length, the focus, and the flow required that titles and names be included in the Appendix, a list of Trail Team Volunteers, following the chapters. This list, to honor the self-funded, selfless contributions of many individuals, many Rotarians, will be a valuable tool for research resources.

The organization for the narrative begins with an introductory chapter that sets the stage for the book. It relates influences, errors, and myths that shaped trail history. To connect the trail era to the trail project era, the chapter briefly reviews three major trail components: the longhorns, the cowboys/drovers, and the legend. The cultural, political, and transformative times following the Civil War broadened the scope of the influences of the trail era on today's culture. Reasons for the proliferation of errors about the trail follow the overview. Related effects on the trail, such as its many names, the mixing of major cattlemen/trail bosses' names and trails, and the effects of time and memory are provided. A surprising part of the trail research was the discovery that the most persistent myth originated with a man who tried to change its name.

The chapters following the introductory chapter are organized using several points. Each chapter starts with a trail map for that segment of the trail. The first map shows the complete length of the trail. Each map segment of the trail includes communities that dedicated a marker. The narrative for the journey gives a vignette of each community or county, the site for a GWT post dedication, and related trail-era people, events, and historical influences. Specific aspects of the trail era that surfaced include women's roles on the plains and the growing conflict between ranchers and homesteaders. If trail history remained usable, if trail memories had faded, if erroneous trail history was discovered, reasons are included. The final chapter assesses the sustainable results of an extraordinary grassroots research project.

The narrative includes the dates for the marker dedications but follows the path of the trail from Mexico to Canada with two exceptions. The first Texas dedication was at Doan's Crossing followed by one in Bandera. After these two ceremonies, the narrative moves to Matamoros, Mexico, the origin of the trail. It documents thirty-seven dedication ceremonies held in eight of the nine US trail states and Saskatchewan. To help correct historical errors and enhance memory about the length of the trail, this narrative follows the same path the drovers traveled.

To determine which communities to contact, project leaders studied GWT maps that showed various trail lengths. Some maps pinpointed the trail as originating at San Antonio, Texas, and terminating at Ogallala, Nebraska, or even Dodge City, Kansas. Other maps showed its origin and terminus at various places beyond the three limited versions. Rather than arbitrarily selecting a shorter version, leaders selected the longest trail because preliminary research supported this view. It originated along the border in South Texas and terminated in Canada. Eventually, evidence verified that the trail branched, with one segment going as far north as North Dakota and the other branch through eastern Wyoming and Montana into Saskatchewan and Alberta provinces. The research was not based on volume of cattle, which was subjective, but on movement of longhorns up the trail to a final destination point.

One hundred forty years had passed since drovers defined the new western route north to railheads, to supply government buyers, and for open-range ranchers. Many grassroots volunteers validated their own credentials by being direct descendants of drovers and pioneers. The researchers also used other ways to verify its path. They searched for evidence of trail requirements, such as rivers and infinite expanses of unencumbered grassland. They looked at the terrain for bluffs, sand hills, and other elements that obstructed the movement of cattle. The millions of longhorns, found only in South Texas, helped verify the origin of the trail there. With their unique body structure, colors, and long horns, they also identified the northern terminus. Other trails had been short-lived for several reasons, especially the absence of water or the presence of a steady stream of homesteaders. The researchers searched for other names used for the GWT, for habits of cattle being trailed, and for political and cultural issues that affected the path of the trail. Local historians also noted the number of years that cattle passed through their area, which helped in determining the approximate number of cattle and horses that went up the trail.

Beyond local information, the search continued for books and articles and even academic authorities on GWT history. The search uncovered limited evidence specific to the trail. Some books had a few paragraphs about the subject. Community history books proved to be the best collections of information. Two major sources were found, a thesis and a book published in 2004, the year this project started (endnotes cite and credit these valuable sources). Newspaper and magazine articles and online information tended to be repetitive and cursory, often filled with errors. The challenge of the GWT volunteers was to correct vast inaccuracies about the trail and to add to the history of the trail . . . accurate history.

The two major sources mentioned above proved to be valuable for directing and corroborating the grassroots research. Jimmy M. Skaggs's 1965 master's thesis, "Great Western Cattle Trail to Dodge City, Kansas," was a vital find. Although the complete length of the trail was not included, the manuscript provided documented details about the terrain and the route of the trail. *The Western: The Greatest Texas Cattle Trail, 1874–1886*, the first documented GWT book, came on the market in 2004, the same year this project began. A Kansas cartographer-historian and his wife, Gary and Margaret Kraisinger, traveled the route of the trail checking local courthouses and museums, interviewing descendants, and checking other resources for their book. The timing for their book expedited the research for the trail in Texas, Oklahoma, Kansas, and Nebraska. The Kraisingers continued their research, focusing on the northern part of the trail. They completed the research in time to draw the maps used in this book.

The project sounded easier to accomplish than it proved to be. During the seven years that it took to complete the project, 2004 to 2011, it acquired new dimensions and challenges. Rotary, an international service organization for businesspeople, was the key to its success. Hundreds of Rotarians joined the search for verification of the path the trail took through their areas. Without the Rotarians' vast network, the project would not have been possible.

The project spread from local research efforts in two states to include seven more states and two other countries, Mexico and Canada. Its methods and approach spread as well. Of preeminent importance to the Vernon, Texas, Rotary trail team—the first Rotary club to become involved—was the network of Rotarians ranging from Matamoros, Mexico, to Regina, Saskatchewan. This network made it possible to contact and enlist business leaders in communities along the trail.

For the Rotarians involved, the search for trail history often highlighted a strong commonality between the drovers' and the members' ethics. Rotarians and cowboys/drovers are and were businesspeople. The analogous relationship between Rotary's Four-Way Test and the Code of the Cowboy was a set of shared values. The Four-Way Test asks, "Of the things we think, say or do: Is it the Truth? Is it Fair to all concerned? Will it build Good Will and Better Friendships? Will it be Beneficial to all concerned?" The legendary cowboy/drover's code of ethics includes tell the truth, be tough but fair, keep your word, and be loyal to the trail boss. Business, ethics, and an international nonprofit service organization unified the volunteers searching for trail verification.

Whether you can call it coincidence, good timing, or a response to a need, Rotary International President Ray Klinginsmith selected the theme of cowboy ethics and cowboy logic for his presidential year, 2010–2011. Rotary's ethics statement, cowboy ethics, and cowboy logic were woven into his presentations during his international tour. Klinginsmith brought recognition to the project on the Great Plains by attending dedication ceremonies and requesting a photo shoot at a marker on the Texas-Mexico border.

The team leaders started the project, after reviewing the map of the trail, by contacting community leaders in Texas towns, usually the county seat. The Vernon Rotary trail team presented an overview plan for the project to communities that were possibly on the path of the GWT. If local research provided evidence that the trail passed through their county, the county trail team scheduled a dedication ceremony to publicize their trail history. The Oklahoma model showed a marker every six miles. Most Texas counties followed the Oklahoma model, which required six or seven markers per county. Vernon Rotarians donated the first marker to be used by each county for its dedication.

In preparation for the dedication ceremonies, volunteers had to be found to make the posts. Finding someone to make 225-pound, seven-foot cement posts that required painting and moving was problematic. Three men, cited and thanked in Chapter 2, volunteered to do this yeoman's job without compensation and made it possible for the project to move forward. The coordination of hauling posts some 620 miles across Texas and to other states' dedication ceremonies was another logistic that seemed insurmountable, but, as always, GWT volunteers solved the problem. The Vernon Rotarians donated a post and a mold to each state to make posts. These posts and molds were transported to a central location, Ogallala, Nebraska, where contacts from the other states picked them up. More about this is included in the chapters.

Trail dedication ceremonies were designed to combine and display patriotism and oral trail history; to recognize descendants of drovers, elected officials, dignitaries, and visiting Rotarians; to further promote the trail research project; and to bring recognition and publicity to the obscure trail. The capstone experience during each ceremony was an invitation for everyone to join in the dedication ritual using Red River water poured from a Mason jar jointly with water from a local river. The Vernon group took Red River water to the ceremonies for three reasons: the river's name was Hollywood famous, it ritually symbolized the necessity of water for the herds, and it actively involved the audience in the dedication. Often, local sheriff's posses, Boy Scouts, folklore dancers, fiddle players, cowboy poets, or singers added color to the ceremonies. Each ceremony started with the presentation of the US flag and the Pledge of Allegiance. For the ceremonies in Mexico and Canada, the Vernon Rotary project team followed the protocol for joint presentations of allegiance and friendship among the participating countries.

The smaller towns along the GWT readily embraced the proposal for marking the trail within their counties. With the growing mobility of their citizens, many of the towns faced the prospect of declining populations and closing businesses. The heritage of cowboys/drovers going up a trail pushing longhorns could be marketed to regional, national, and international tourists. A small town, designated as a GWT town with related events, could become a tourist destination. Heritage tourism, once limited to the affluent population, is a growing industry worthy of small towns partnering along the trail to tap that market.

Perhaps this method of community involvement is the best way, maybe the only way, to inspire research to verify the two-thousand-mile-path of the GWT. In verifying its path, efforts were made to extract it from long-standing history that has been distorted and even manipulated. This project is possibly the only way a cattle trail of this length, age, and complexity could have been liberated from its sometimes arbitrary and often inaccurate historical confinements.

As told in these chapters, the GWT *project* took a surprising path. One discovery was learning that there is no substitute for visiting a site for primary sources, for seeing the location from which the information sprang. At the conclusion of a seven-year effort, the goal was accomplished, verification for the physical route of the Great Western Trail across some two thousand miles was established. The endeavor reflected the commonality and cohesion among the people whose ancestral records documented the trail. Equally mirrored was the cooperation and camaraderie that grew among the participants in this remarkable event to identify the trail with tangible evidence—the markers. In addition, the establishment of national and state trail organizations and the approval of a Congressional Feasibility Study to determine the desirability and feasibility for designating the trail as National Historic Trail added permanency to the project.

The grassroots research venture produced a large amount of important, new historical information. The evidence was not always perfect; some of it may still be disputable. The evidence, nonetheless, is considered fact, so it must be dealt with as the current best set of data. It is no less valuable in how it compels historians to reevaluate before they dismiss any of it. In addition, evidence to be considered is the way this book documents the spirit of the GWT that is alive in the communities. Marking the trail galvanized communities in their joint efforts to uncover documents and other primary trail evidence heretofore unavailable to the public. The book is a record of those who gave selflessly to verify the origin and terminus of the two-thousand-mile GWT trail. What we hope most of all for this seven-year grassroots research project is that it will result in the somewhat obscure past history of the trail becoming a verified living history.

ACKNOWLEDGMENTS

The Great Western Trail research project involved hundreds of volunteers from three countries along the path. These volunteers were the main characters, the stars of the project. It is my privilege to cite their names and titles on the Trail Volunteers list (in the Appendix) for their invaluable contributions to this twenty-first-century recovery of a legendary and celebrated part of American history, the Great Western Trail. The Dedication page was designed to show the process by which a grassroots project originated by one person is then encompassed by many people with a variety of skills to support it and sustain it. Here, I would like to acknowledge others who contributed to the content and to the preparation of this manuscript.

The GWT maps drawn for this book by cartographer Gary Kraisinger were a major contribution to authenticating the path of the trail and to giving readers of this book an accurate visual image of the path the trail traversed in each chapter. Gary and Margaret Kraisinger's definitive book, *The Western: The Greatest Texas Cattle Trail,* has added evidence needed to correct errors about the history and the name of the GWT that have been perpetuated because of the lack of academic research.

Thanks to Dr. Frank Norris for corroborating segments of the trail in South Texas and providing documentation recovered and discovered for the congressional study.

Thanks to my colleague and classmate Uyless Black, author of some forty books, whose roots originated in the cowboy culture on the high plains of the Southwest. He understood the challenge of writing a book whose goal was to verify as well as correct the history of a nineteenth-century cattle trail, one seen through the eyes, the efforts, and the research of hundreds of twenty-first-century volunteers. With this insight, he read the manuscript and offered wise suggestions that helped my narrative weave the past with the present. Thanks to Dr. Paul Carlson who read the manuscript and gave knowledgeable, insightful suggestions.

Thanks to Mary Ann McCuistion, artist and Red River Valley Museum retired executive director, for her artistic rendition of the signature component of the project, the GWT marker.

A
C
K
N
O
W
L
E
D
G
M
E
N
T
S

·XXVIII·

Thanks to Ray Klinginsmith, Rotary International past-president, for the Foreword and for his friendship, vision, and leadership. He demonstrated that the code of the cowboy continues to unify people across the Great Plains as well as nationally and internationally.

Thanks to my editor, Judith Keeling, editor-in-chief (now retired) at Texas Tech University Press, for her belief in the merit of this book, her discerning direction, and her kind considerations. Thanks to my new editor, Joanna Conrad, for stepping up to continue astute support for my manuscript as it moved forward successfully to publication. Thanks to Kathy Clayton for her skills that added the final polish to the manuscript.

Thanks to the readers whose suggestions were used to polish the manuscript. One's suggestion that there is "great material here to explore history and memory" helped broaden the scope of the narrative to include evidence of collective memories that shaped current events along the trail.

Thanks to my friend Susan Couch, whose constant support motivated me to move forward with my writing. Thanks to my sister Susie Potter, who traveled with me up and down the trail. Thanks to my daughter Lesli Laughter for her support, political contacts, and ideas. Thanks to my grandson Ross Laughter and my son-in-law Steve Laughter, who gave technical support. Thanks to everyone who helped recover the almost forgotten history of the Great Western Trail and to identify its influence on the economy and culture today.

FINDING THE
GREAT WESTERN
TRAIL

CANADA

MONTANA
TERRITORY

Milk River

Missouri River

DAKOTA
TERRITORY

Ft. Buford

Medora • Dickinson

Missouri River

Yellowstone River

Miles City

Powder River

WYOMING
TERRITORY

Deadwood

Ft. Laramie

Bridgeport

NEBRASKA

Cheyenne

Ogallala

Platte River

Omaha

Denver

COLORADO

KANSAS

Kaw River

Kansas
City

Missouri River

St. Louis

MISSOURI

Arkansas River

Wichita

Cimarron River

Santa Fe

NEW MEXICO
TERRITORY

Canadian River

Red River

Brazos River

Doan's
Crossing

INDIAN
TERRITORY

Ft. Smith

Ft. Worth   Dallas

Colorado River

TEXAS

Waco

Pecos River

Rio Grande River

Houston

Rio Grande River

MEXICO

Matamoros

Brownsville

Gary Kraisinger

Scale
100 Miles

N

GREAT WESTERN TRAIL

Great Western Trail from Mexico to Canada. Courtesy of Gary Kraisinger

CHAPTER 1
Longhorns, Drovers, Legends, Confusion

Volunteers searching for evidence to verify the route of the Great Western Trail faced several formidable challenges. Confusion about the very name of the Great Western Trail, about the major trails that famous trail bosses traveled, and confusion about events caused by memory and time complicated the research. The failure of historians and others to corroborate and closely examine evidence about the path has led to the perpetuation of errors. Adding to the confusion was a major discovery that one man had attempted to change the trail's name. The attempt was so convincing that even in towns that have worked to correct it, some local citizens continue to publicize the erroneous history as truth. Volunteers working to validate the route of the trail had to carefully sift through the evidence to achieve their goal of documenting the trail accurately.

To place trail history into perspective, the following sections offer background information about the longhorns, the trail era, and the cowboy, all of which continued to influence residents along the trail as this project was undertaken. To help correct long-standing trail-name confusion, the narratives of on-site visits to a trail boss/cattleman's ranch headquarters—John Chisum—whose name is often confused with Jesse Chisholm, and to the burial sites for men whose names are used for the names of trails, Oliver Loving, Charles Goodnight, and Jesse Chisholm, are included to create descriptive visualization of historically correct locations. The most persistent challenge was to overcome past attempts to manipulate trail history. Myths live on in the presence of truth. These problems permeated the research efforts, so they are also addressed in this first chapter.

The Reason for the Trail: The Longhorn

The longhorn, an American icon of the trail era, comparable to the cowboy/drover, contributed to the legend of the cowboy. The longhorn had the adaptability and physical durability sufficient to trod some two thousand miles, if necessary, across endless grassy plains. On occasion, the longhorns were pushed without water to limits that seemed impossible, but they endured. Because of their distinctive abilities and features, the presence of longhorns along the trail can be considered a visible resource for identifying links to South Texas, where they originated.

Herds were typically composed of 2,500 to 3,000 head of longhorns. The trail boss and eight to ten drovers moved the cattle twelve to fifteen miles a day. The cook drove the chuck wagon, and the wrangler took care of the remuda, the extra saddle horses. To stay well mounted for the arduous trip, each drover required at least four or five horses. If a horse became lame, got hurt or sick on the trail, the cowboy had to have a backup. He also changed horses to give them rest. The drovers had specific positions: two at the front, or point; two or more on each side, or flank; and two or more at the rear, or drag. The dusty rear position motivated the drovers to work hard to be promoted to flank or point positions.

The Longhorn

The longhorn's history echoes the history of settlement and the blending of cultures in South Texas and northern Mexico. The huge number of longhorns populating South Texas following the Civil War evolved from cattle that had arrived with Spanish explorers. The first domesticated animals arrived in 1493 when Christopher Columbus brought Iberian long-horned cattle, horses, hogs, and sheep on his second trip to the West Indies, or Greater Antilles Islands (Puerto Rico, Cuba, Jamaica, and Española). In the 1520s, other Spanish colonists brought horses, cattle, hogs, and sheep to sustain their move north to establish new settlements on the Gulf Coast region of Mexico. Some settled at Veracruz, and others went as far north as Tampico, less than two hundred miles south of the future Texas border.

During the next three centuries, open-range cattle ranching spread northward through the Mexican state of Tamaulipas and into Texas. In these areas, cattle-raising traditions blended with those from the East Coast, Louisiana French, and Tejanos (Texans of Mexican descent).[1] Drovers from a diversity of ethnic backgrounds adapted Mexican equestrian skills for long trail drives across the Great Plains. The history of cattle brought to the Americas is a small entry in history books. Research, however, shows that "origins of western ranching were more complex and ethnically diverse than has been supposed."[2]

In the New World, the long-horned cattle flourished by adapting through survival of the fittest. The original Spanish cattle were solid colors ranging from tan to cherry red with a few being black or brindle (grayish with darker flecks). By the seventeenth and eighteenth centuries, Spanish explorers, settlers, and mission priests started moving them north into the area that would become Texas. The cattle were used for breeding stock as well as for food, hides, and tallow.

By the nineteenth century, the Spanish horned cattle had interbred with feral English cattle, producing an ideal animal that gained weight while on the trail, withstood extreme heat or cold, and adapted to the terrain. They were able to subsist on very little feed and could travel long distances without water. The cows were fertile, reproduced easily and often, and protected their young. After centuries of adapting to life and circumstances in northern Mexico and South Texas, this American icon became famous during the Texas cattle trail days.[3] In the late nineteenth century, groups of mostly young Texans and Mexicans mounted horses, gathered longhorns, and formed herds from the millions of free-roaming South Texas longhorns. They trailed the cattle north across the Great Plains, but this time they were used for turning a profit, not merely for consumption.

As the trail days ended and the twentieth century started, the longhorns had almost disappeared. Millions of longhorns had been sold for meat, used for tallow, or were even destroyed. Cattle owners started cross-breeding the lanky longhorn with other breeds to accommodate the demand for a higher fat content needed for tallow and desired in beef. Tick fever also contributed to the declension of the longhorn. The longhorn's lean meat had not yet been recognized as heart-healthy beef.

An effort to save the longhorns from extinction began in 1927. With the help of a transplanted Texas cowboy, US Senator John B. Kendrick of Wyoming, a federal herd of purebred Texas Longhorns was established at the Wichita Mountains Wildlife Refuge in Cache, Oklahoma.[4] Will C. Barnes and other US Forest Service rangers found twenty cows, three bulls, and

Texas Gold, **Bronze, Fort Worth Stockyards, Texas**
At the Fort Worth Stockyards, *Texas Gold* is a larger-than-life bronze sculpture of seven longhorns cast by sculptor T. D. Kelsey, representing the original seven Longhorn herds.

four calves that were, in their opinion, "purebred Texas Longhorns."[5] Another seed herd was established by native South Texas historian J. Frank Dobie, author of *The Longhorns,* who joined former range inspector Graves Peeler and oilman Sid W. Richardson in assembling a herd. That herd's descendants, now cared for under the auspices of the Texas Parks and Wildlife Department, can be seen today at Fort Griffin State Historical Park.

By the 1930s, the future of the Longhorn breed was secured. Seven groups of longhorns of different origins and genetic bases were assembled by six families and one organization: Marks, Phillips, Butler, Wright, Yates, Peeler, and the Wichita Refuge. To verify the breed's bloodline, the Cattlemen's Texas Longhorn Registry (CTLR) inspected the cattle (and later used blood type and DNA analyses) to prove or disprove their sightings.[6] In 1964, the Texas Longhorn Breeders Association of America (TLBAA), headquartered at the Fort Worth Stockyards, established the seven groups as authentic pure Longhorns.[7]

Two other Longhorn associations solidified the future of the breed. In 1990, the International Texas Longhorn Association (ITLA) created the first library of Texas Longhorn Research and Information Bulletins.[8] In 2007 the new Texas Longhorn Marketing Alliance (TLMA) started the Longhorn World Championship competition with prestigious awards for length and circumference of horns.[9] Today at the entrance to the Fort Worth Stockyards, *Texas Gold*, a larger-than-life bronze of seven longhorns cast by sculptor T. D. Kelsey of Rama, Colorado, represents the seven official Longhorn herds.[10]

The Trail Era

Initially, Easterners' taste for beef following the Civil War contributed to the partnership between the longhorns and the cowboys/drovers. After the war, Texas veterans returned home to face another crisis: unemployment without benefits. Soon, entrepreneurs with considerable initiative and a willingness to take risks provided solutions for both unemployed Americans and a surplus of millions of longhorns in South Texas. One of these entrepreneurs, Joseph G. McCoy of Illinois, first recognized economic potential within the Pacific Railroad Acts of 1862 and 1864. The Union Pacific and the Central Pacific Railroads drove the "golden spike" on May 10, 1869, that completed the transcontinental railroad, thus reducing travel time and cost from the West to the East Coasts.

Taking advantage of this new rapid transportation to supply beef to Easterners, McCoy negotiated with Kansas Pacific (Union Pacific, Eastern Division) railroad to establish a railhead at Abilene, Kansas. He sent flyers to South Texas inviting unemployed Civil War veterans and others willing to take a risk to gather herds of 2,500 to 3,000 longhorns and trail them to Abilene, Kansas, on the east side of that state. Other railroad lines took advantage of the lucrative cattle market and other markets in Kansas and other Great Plains states. The Atchison, Topeka, and Santa Fe Railway Company (shortened to Santa Fe Railroad) followed the ruts of the Santa Fe Trail, which included a line to Dodge City, Kansas, a major Great Western Trail railhead. The Union Pacific built lines into Nebraska and Colorado. Ogallala, Nebraska, and the northeastern corner of Colorado at Julesburg also became railhead destinations for GWT herds.

Dovetailing with the growth of railroads and advent of Texas cattle drives were acts of infamy that became notorious parts of America's history:

the destruction of the buffalo and the forced relocation of the Plains Indians onto reservations. The results of those two infamous acts left vast expanses of unoccupied grasslands that became available for open-range ranching while leaving a nefarious stain on the history of the American West. To help the railroads raise money for construction, the federal government gave grants of land to railroads, which encouraged sales of land to settlers. With these changes on the Great Plains, the economy boomed and the settlement of the American West surged with a large movement of people seeking land and a new life.

During this post–Civil War time, entrepreneurs vied to purchase Texas longhorns and horses to stock new open-range ranching enterprises in the northern Great Plains states. As the flow of cattle and horses moved from south to north, the booming cattle industry provided an abundance of new jobs for many different skill levels. With the addition of open-range ranching enterprises to the burgeoning Eastern markets for Texas beef, the depressed economy recovered in Texas and across the Great Plains states.

The Cowboy/Drover Legend

As the drovers journeyed across the Great Plains seeking easy passage for their large herds of cattle, their images acquired the aura of legend. Traveling across the vast plains area, the cowboys/drovers were isolated from supplies, law enforcement, medical help, religious support, families, and other things conducive to their well-being.

The relative isolation of the cowboys/drovers inspired writers who generated volumes about the new business lifestyle and its inherent risks. Even more, it resulted in the creation of the legend of the cowboy through popular accounts and novels based on the glimpses others had of the cowboy/drover lifestyle. The cowboys/drovers, matured by war, were partially unrestricted by political, religious, and social rules for two to three months or more at a time. From this singular experience, they learned to be self-reliant, innovative, trustworthy, and adaptable to changing, often deadly situations. Business opportunities abounded. Some became trail bosses and even ranchers. Drovers learned the necessity of being loyal to the trail boss, which seems a contradiction to being independent; however, responsibility melded loyalty and independence together. Drovers also learned the merits of having a strong work ethic and the importance of practicing integrity among their drover companions and others along the trail. More than cattle went up the trail. Along the way, the drovers also mixed their cultures from south to north and north to south. The cowboy became the symbol of a lifestyle that had a usable range of values. Those values inspired and continued to foster a cultural commonality among residents in towns along the trail.

During this brief period, the common man in America's Southwest experienced fewer restrictions than those levied onto the common man living elsewhere. As the newly employed trail hands stepped up into the saddle, a position once reserved for kings and military, their perspective from the back of a horse evolved while traveling up the trail. The optimism of economic recovery joined with captivating tales of young employees experiencing life on the trail. The drovers' newly found freedom from restrictions became the basis of the image of the iconic cowboy. Fiction writers, especially the early Western dime novels written for eastern readers during the 1870s and 1880s, capitalized on the new lifestyle of freedom from political, religious, and social traditions depicted by major characters displaying legendary attributes. Thus, the legend grew to symbolize a way of life directed by values that defined Americans in a new way. Wild West shows, novels, songs, and art depicted the cowboys' trail experiences in ways that captured the imagination of the international community. On the trail, the old hierarchies separating men fell away in the face of work responsibilities, loneliness, danger, or possibly death. Through the years, cattle- and horse-related enterprises and commemorative trail-related events have contributed to the trail residents' collective memories that continue to reinforce the values attributed to the cowboy legend.

Memories of the Trail Era Contributed to the Grassroots Research Project

As the citizens in trail communities extended their hospitality to the trail research teams, it was evident that the cowboy lifestyle and values were an ongoing part of their lives. The ranch families continued to conform to the ranch-founder patriarch's original work ethic, practices, and traditions in their day-to-day ranch operations. Volunteers, invited to watch the cowboys work, witnessed cowboys gathering, sorting, working, and branding cattle and horses, following practices similar to those used during the trail days. Most founders established their ranches as the result of trail-driving profits. In many communities, individual ranches have continued as family businesses from the trail days to the owners being participants in this twenty-first-century research project. The current ranch owners with their

almost continuous replication of the past in their daily working-ranch practices provided substantial Great Western Trail primary-source materials.

Along the route, trail traditions rewarded loyalty to the status quo. Particularly in smaller towns, annual events such as cattle and horse shows and
rodeos (especially ranch rodeos) held fast to traditions used in the trail days.
Ranch teams competed in various contests for bragging rights among the
ranches. Crowds of neighbors and friends of the cowboys and cowgirls filled
the stands. Along with rodeo events, other contests contributed points to
the ranch-team competition. Equally competitive were the chuck-wagon
cook-offs, photography and art contests (often specific to a ranch), and music talent contests. Western symposiums and conferences, cowboy poetry
events, and Western dances claimed attendance for two primary reasons: to
visit with friends and to reinforce this way of life. These types of interactions
helped set the stage for the GWT research project.

Confusion Regarding the Name of the Great Western Trail

The path followed by the Chisholm Trail, first used in 1867, ran into obsta-
cles caused by the flow of homesteaders into Kansas, longhorns carrying tick
fever, Kansas legislation to limit the passageway for cattle, and the increasing
use of barbed wire. The result was that the trail's shortest route to railheads
on the eastern side of Kansas were closed to cattle moving in from Texas
by 1884. The Great Western Trail's path remained usable for some nineteen
years, 1874 through 1893. Grassy open-range land, strategically located rivers, and the lack of settlers made the GWT the most accommodating path
going north across the Great Plains, which is also called the High Plains in
some northern states. Political and cultural influences, however, affected the
path of the trail in some areas, such as the violence in the South Texas Nueces Strip, a subject for Chapter 3.

When research on this project was under way, some citizens along the
trail disclosed that their towns had retained only minimal connections to
their trail history. Although the main streets had been beaten out by the
hoofs of thousands of cattle going north, their trail history had faded. Some
towns had focused on other historical events or famous people from their
towns. However, research volunteers in these towns joined the grassroots
effort because they recognized the benefits of a project that focused on their
town and county.

Research started with the names used for the Great Western Trail in their towns. Drovers tended to use the name of the next supply point for the name of that segment of the trail. Some names for segments were Matamoros Trail, Western Trail (used when leaving San Antonio), Fort Griffin Trail, Doan's Crossing, Fort Supply, Dodge City Trail, Ogallala Trail, and Texas Trail. The last segment name was the most common name used for the trail into Canada. Slowly, and with mixed results, these piecemeal names gave way to the use of a name for the complete trail—the Great Western Trail. Another possible reason for the GWT's obscurity was the use of a direction in its name. Trails named for famous cattlemen or trail bosses, such as Goodnight and Loving, gained easy recognition. Initially, the Chisholm Trail was called the Eastern Trail until it left Texas at Red River Station near Nocona. In Oklahoma, known then as Indian Territory, the Eastern Trail followed freighter Jesse Chisholm's wagon ruts to Kansas. As time passed, the Eastern Trail acquired the more usable name, Chisholm Trail—a name attached to a persona rather than a direction. The only segment called the Western Trail during trail days was the path that went west, not east, from San Antonio. When it turned north, it became known as the Fort Griffin Trail. A few early novels used the Western Trail's generic name in relation to the Eastern Trail. Although fiction promoted the name *Western Trail*, that name for the complete length of the trail had not been verified in an academic study.

In 1965, the first definitive academic study for the Great Western Trail was Texas Tech University historian Jimmy M. Skaggs's thesis, "The Great Western Cattle Trail to Dodge City, Kansas." In the preface, Skaggs wrote, "The *Great Western Cattle Trail*, the last of the major Longhorn cattle trails, has been conspicuously overlooked as a research topic. The reasons for its beginning, its route and problems, the experiences of the drovers, the story of the towns that grew up alongside it, and the reasons for its decline have been dealt with separately in letters, memoirs, and literature, but no synthesis of all of these various aspects has ever before been combined into a single story. It is the purpose of this thesis to provide such a synthesis from the materials accessible at Texas Technological College."[11] Since Skaggs's academic study used *Great Western Trail*, that name was apparently in common usage or was the most logical name to use for a trail with many names.

The lack of documented research saddled the history of the Great Western Trail in inaccuracies. Skaggs said that he used material to verify the history of the GWT, which was available at Texas Tech University.[12] Another Texas historian made note of the academic research void about the cattle trail era. Located near a Great Western Trail marker in George West, Texas, on the Live Oak County Courthouse lawn, a state marker honors historian and folklorist J. Frank Dobie, who avidly promoted in the academic world (without success for years) his belief that longhorns, cattle, horses, and trails were worthy of scholarly study. Dobie's belief identifies a reason for Skaggs's statement in 1965 that the Great Western Trail, the last of the major longhorn cattle trails, had not been the subject of an academic study. In addition, the name *Western Trail* was often used for other trails that went west of a previous route. Skaggs states, ". . . from there we went [up] the extreme Western Trail [probably the Potter-Bacon route] across the plains to Trail City, Colorado."[13] However, no other trails were called *Great Western Trail*, another reason to use this name for the longest Texas cattle trail.

Skaggs also wrote, "The heritage of the *Great Western Cattle Trail* persists, but its story is largely forgotten. . . . The *Great Western*, unlike the *Chisholm Trail*, has been allowed to pass into oblivion with no song immortalizing its unique and colorful past nor hithertofore scholarly study recording its incalculable contributions. Nevertheless, so long as man occupies the towns that sprang up along its dusty path and so long as cattle constitute a major product of the Southwest, the *Great Western Cattle Trail* will be remembered as a significant factor in the western march of American civilization."[14]

In 2004, the timing was perfect for Great Western Trail scholars Gary Kraisinger and Margaret Kraisinger to publish their book: *The Western: The Greatest Texas Cattle Trail*. Skaggs's thesis and the Kraisingers' book were invaluable to the "marking the trail" project. Also, while the project was in process, Gary Kraisinger, a cartographer, designed documented Great Western Trail maps that followed the trail from the Rio Grande on the Mexican border across nine US states into two provinces of Canada. Skaggs's and the Kraisingers' works, both restricted to the study of the Great Western Trail, are the two documented, research-based sources. Other sources have brief accounts with limited research on the trail, and some tend to be generic, repetitious, and even inaccurate.

The Chisholm Trail's name, however, was so well known that its Hollywood-famous name has almost become a generic name for all cattle trails. Researchers found that they had to check sources to see whether Chisholm Trail history had been reshaped through the years to include parts of the GWT and/or its history. The proximity of the parallel trails certainly contributed to the confusion. In some places in Texas, only ninety miles separated the two trails. Both crossed the Red River but at different locations. When Kansas legislators closed the passageway of the Chisholm Trail on the eastern side of the state to herds of cattle from Texas, trail bosses moved their herds west. The Great Western Trail filled the void left by the Chisholm Trail.

The Chisholm Trail's name continued to be used long after its closure, especially in South Texas. One reason could be that, for a brief time, both the GWT and Chisholm Trail used a common trail once called the Matamoros Trail. Following the closure of the Chisholm Trail's path in Kansas, trail bosses tried other routes. Some traveled westward from Fort Worth, Oklahoma, and Kansas to intersect with the GWT. These re-routes added more miles and more expense, so these new routes for the Chisholm Trail were eventually abandoned. During the active years for the Great Western Trail, documents show that large numbers of longhorns left the area near the border towns of Brownsville and Matamoros and ended their journey in Canada. It was the only trail continuously active from 1874 to 1893.

Members of one of the Rotary clubs in South Texas said that Great Western Trail was not the name that they had heard. The confusion of the two trails' names as well as the varied routes required Rotary researchers to seek additional sources of information. Local trail teams, nonetheless, recovered evidence that verified the path of the GWT through their counties. Since each county was responsible for verifying the trail's route in that county, all the counties eventually became stakeholders in our project.

An additional search for evidence in South Texas supported the trail teams' documented conclusions. In May 2009, President Obama signed the Congressional bill for a Feasibility Study to determine the significance, feasibility, suitability, and desirability for designating the Chisholm Trail and the Great Western Trail as National Historic Trails. Dr. Frank Norris, the lead historian for the study, credits "outstanding research done" by Texas A&M University history professor Dr. Armando Alonzo in 2010 and 2011 that documented the route of the Chisholm and Great Western Trails as originating in South Texas near the Texas-Mexico border. Dr. Norris said,

> What [Dr. Alonzo] found confirmed what our collective "hunches" had been previously. . . . Between 1867 and the mid-1870s, the vast majority of those ranches resulted in cattle heading north along the Chisholm Trail: to Abilene [KS] (1867–71), and later to Ellsworth and several minor destinations as well. Those same ranches, starting in the mid-1870s and up into the

mid-1880s, took most (though certainly not all) of their cattle up the Great Western Trail. . . . We've done our best to "tease out" which of those southern routes were primarily Chisholm routes and which were Great Western routes. But several of the major (meaning nationally significant) routes served both purposes.[15]

The Chisholm Trail's name is entrenched in the collective memory of so many that its claim to paths also taken by the GWT is secure. At the Cattle Raisers Museum in Fort Worth, a large cattle trails map highlights the origin of the Chisholm Trail at the Mexico border between Brownsville and Matamoros. It followed the old Matamoros Trail to San Antonio. This part of the map is accurate. On the same museum map, the GWT, the later trail, used the same route from South Texas, yet the beginning of its pathway is marked at San Antonio. With limited sources for documented GWT history, inaccuracies continue to be perpetuated.

If a cattle trail was mentioned in folklore, legend, fiction, or movies, it was usually the Chisholm Trail. In later years, entrepreneurs recognized the marketability of the famous name, so, especially in Fort Worth, advertising for daily displays of cowboys herding longhorns in the Fort Worth Stockyards and toll roads borrow the name Chisholm Trail. For most foreign visitors, every cowboy is John Wayne; every cattle trail is the Chisholm Trail; every river is the Red River. In discussing the phenomena, Norris said "I'm not sure why (historically), but the name 'Chisholm' has until lately, I hope! been considered synonymous with all cattle trails heading northward from Texas."[16]

Creators of Fiction and Film Caused Confusion

Confusion led to more confusion when the creators of fiction and movies inculcated their fantasies into the minds of an unwary public. Western-themed dime-novel authors, during the 1860s to 1890s, and filmmakers capitalized on action-packed, contrived plots that rearranged trail history. As the legend of the cowboy and the trail made its way into the media, the audience chose fiction over fact. The positive side to these historical infractions was that fiction and film helped generate and publicize the legend and lore of the cowboy. The heroes such as John Wayne often rode up an invented trail and settled into "authentic history" in the minds of the general public.

Did these fictional heroes distort the realities of those times? To an extent, yes. They expanded the truths about the cowboy. They embellished facts with fiction. But they did not incorrectly represent the persona of the American cowboy. In those past times, the cowboy visibly embodied many qualities we Americans hold dear: independence, self-reliance, and integrity. Occasionally, the Great Western Trail was mentioned in a movie or novel. Unfortunately, in one novel, a herd goes up the Chisholm Trail, but it crosses the Red River at Doan's Crossing, not Red River Station. These influences on memory added credence to popular trail history, rather than skepticism.

Occasionally an author, such as Texas writer Elmer Kelton, noted for his detailed and authentic portrayal of cowboys, would mention Doan's Crossing in a novel. In Kelton's *The Good Old Boys,* Doan's Crossing is used. In the movie of the same name, actor Tommy Lee Jones as Hewey Calloway said at the funeral of an old drover, "Whether you knowed him or not, you all know the breed. He was followin' the mossyhorns up the trail when most of us was still followin' our mothers around the kitchen. It was him and his kind that beat out the trails and shot at the Yankees and fought off the Indians. It was them old fellers that taken the whippin' so me and you could have the easy life we're livin' today."[17] Calloway, an old-time cowboy himself, was "a long way from Doan's Crossing on the Red."[18] The GWT was not mentioned, but Doan's Crossing was. Even more significant, Kelton promoted the idea that the legend of the cowboy that had become firmly embedded in American culture grew from hard work and perils experienced by the trail drovers. Kelton demonstrated the role that time played in allowing society's collective memory to arrange and rearrange history to perpetuate the legend to accommodate current cultural needs. As the grassroots research efforts continued, our libraries grew with history books from trail communities that, although limited to a few paragraphs or sometimes to a chapter, supported respect for the continuing contributions to the economy and the culture of the communities that originated with the GWT drovers.

Effects of On-Site Visits to Trail-Related Locations

With only two documented sources focused on finding the path of the Great Western Trail, the trail's history remained obscure. Accurate information was further impeded by confusion between names of famous trail people, which trails the famous trail bosses traveled, and the moving of facts from one trail to another in fiction and movies, especially the made-for-TV movie *Lonesome Dove.* Confusion can often be corrected by on-site visits to help visualize physical facts related to historical places or people. For this purpose, I visited the first ranch headquarters in New Mexico of trail boss/ cattleman John Chisum and visited the burial sites of Charles Goodnight, Oliver Loving, and Jesse Chisholm as well as the hotel where the fictional character Gus from *Lonesome Dove* died.

Reading history is one thing, but visiting a historical site (such as John Chisum's first New Mexico ranch headquarters) can create a powerful personal connection, especially when joined to an emotional experience. John Chisum was a major cattle dealer and rancher for some thirty years. Although he trailed herds to New Mexico, he never considered himself a trail driver. Chisum joined Charles Goodnight, known for the Goodnight-Loving Trail, to move cattle from Texas to New Mexico in 1866. In 1872 Chisum relocated to New Mexico (before the first herd went up the GWT in 1874) and established a ranch near Roswell on the Pecos River, where he continued open-range ranching.[19] In spite of that history, Chisum's name is often interchanged with Chisholm for that trail's name. Evidence of this is given in Chapter 5.

On the first morning of my visit to Roswell, New Mexico, rancher Larry Wooton suggested to his wife, Waynette, that she take me to Pioneer Plaza in Roswell to see the larger-than-life bronze statue of John Chisum on horseback alongside his lead steer, Ruidoso. Larry had tacitly displayed his deep-rooted cowboy code; his pain and his promise to show me the ranch were at odds.

Larry's lung cancer had brought him to the end of the trail. By suggesting the side trip, Larry bought himself a little time in the morning to "cowboy-up" to make the twenty-mile trip to Chisum's headquarters. Larry was the sort of cowboy who, when he said he would take me to the ranch, he meant *he* would drive to the ranch, located on the Bosque Grande Draw, which feeds into the Pecos River. We went; Larry drove. In spite of his use of an oxygen apparatus, Larry was able to tell the history of Chisum, the Lincoln County War, and Chisum's partnership with Charles Goodnight. At the ranch, we visited a historical marker designating the site as Chisum's first headquarters. That day was the last time I saw Larry.

At Larry Wooton's funeral, the overflow crowd of people from every lifestyle was evidence that those whose lives exhibit legendary cowboy traits continue to have widespread influence on the people who encounter them. With that visit, John Chisum's trail history and his relocation from Texas to New Mexico before the path of the Great Western Trail crossed land where

Oliver Loving Burial Site, Weatherford, Texas

Author Larry McMurtry, in *Lonesome Dove*, used the death of Goodnight-Loving trail boss Oliver Loving as inspiration for the death of Augustus "Gus" McRae, who followed the GWT route to Miles City, Montana.

Chisum once ranched became an indelible part of my personal memory and identified reasons for the mixing of various trails' histories.

After visiting John Chisum's first ranch headquarters in New Mexico and learning of his work with Charles Goodnight, I visited Goodnight's burial place in North Texas. A sign on Highway 287, which connects Amarillo and Vernon, directed the way north to the village of Goodnight. There, a smaller sign pointed the way northeast up a dirt road to a small cemetery on a knoll. The prominent monuments for Goodnight and his wife, Molly, were surrounded by family members' stones. With no other humans in sight, I stood and observed the rolling plains, felt the ever-present wind, listened to the distant train whistle, and overlaid my book memories about the trail days by reading the inscriptions on the monuments, viewing the vast landscape, and listening to the sounds.

After visiting Charles Goodnight's burial site, I visited the burial site of Oliver Loving, his partner on the Goodnight-Loving Trail. Loving's burial site at Weatherford, Texas, connects with the Great Western Trail through the death of fictional character Augustus "Gus" McRae, whose character had been inspired by Loving. Rotarian Janet Holland invited me to speak to the Mineral Wells Rotary Club about the Great Western Trail research project. Afterward, she, her husband, Mike, and I visited the Oliver Loving homestead and bedding grounds for his herds. Loving's land was about ten miles northwest of town.

At the site, a barbed-wire fence and tall, rounded cedar trees obscured a large granite monument standing about five feet inside the fence. In Texas, a person knows not to cross a fence onto private property. We were glad we did not. As we leaned forward against the fence trying to read the inscription on the historical monument, a man stepped out from behind a cedar tree. The gun in the holster across his chest and his reflective sunglasses stopped us in our tracks. After hearing our explanation, Gary Shaw, the owner of the Loving homestead and land, opened the gate and invited us for a tour. So much could be told, but the most chilling reminder of life back then was a tunnel that started under the house and surfaced on the other side of a small rise. It provided a secret escape route if the house was burned, a possibility during those violent times. The house was gone, but the tunnel stood as a grim reminder of those times.

In 1989 the award-winning TV-movie *Lonesome Dove*, based on Larry McMurtry's novel of the same name (1985), helped revitalize the public's interest in the Western genre. It used two thematic episodes based on Loving's ill-fated cattle drive with Charles Goodnight. The real-life Loving was seriously injured during an Indian attack when he and a scout had gone ahead of Goodnight and the herd, up a route later known as the Goodnight-Loving Trail. Loving eventually made it to Fort Sumner, New Mexico, but he died there of gangrene. Goodnight had given his word to his friend, Loving, that he would bury him at his home in Texas. Goodnight delivered the herd to Colorado and then, returning to Fort Sumner, had Loving's body exhumed and returned it to Texas. Stories differ as to who accompanied the body back to Weatherford, but Loving was reburied there in Greenwood Cemetery on March 4, 1868.[20]

In McMurtry's work, Woodrow Call promised and honored Gus's request to be buried in Clara's Grove in Texas. To keep his word, Call had to transport his friend's body some two thousand miles. McMurtry sent Gus up the Great Western Trail to Ogallala, Nebraska, and on to Miles City, Montana, where he died at the Olive Hotel (built in 1899), which is on the

Olive Hotel, Miles City, Montana
Although trail boss Oliver Loving died in New Mexico, the Olive Hotel in Miles City, Montana, became famous when the death scene for *Lonesome Dove*'s Gus McRae, whose character was based on Loving, was filmed there.

National Register of Historic Places. While standing in front of the Olive Hotel and having seen *Lonesome Dove* at least five or six times, it was difficult to separate the fiction from the facts. The well-known movie characters seemed more intimate than the little-known real-life people. Some questions came to mind: Does the retelling of Loving's life through fiction promote Goodnight's ethics of keeping his word to his friend? Does fiction immortalize Loving's desire for his permanent home on his homeland? How much do fiction and fact shape our personal ethics and memories, especially for those living on the land with an analogous lifestyle?

The history of the famous Chisholm Trail name became more vivid when I visited Jesse Chisholm's burial site at Left Hand Spring, Oklahoma, which is near the town of Geary. Chisholm Trail historian Bob Klemme recounted Chisholm's life. While we sat on the iron rail around the Chisholm memorial, Klemme's details created an image of Chisholm. The Oklahoma Historical Society had erected the monument near Chisholm's burial site in 1976. It said that Chisholm had died "after eating bear meat cooked in a copper kettle." On April 4, 1868, he was "buried near Left Hand Spring Allotment of his old friend Chief Left Hand." On Chisholm's small tombstone, the inscription said, "No one ever left his home cold or hungry."

Effects of Manipulated Trail History

The names of major trail bosses and cattlemen are known to have been manipulated by time and fiction; however, a man from Elk City, Oklahoma, P. P. Ackley, *avidly* worked to change the name of the Great Western Trail to the Longhorn Chisholm Trail. One of Ackley's methods was to mark the GWT with granite monuments and metal markers inscribed with "Going up the [Longhorn] Chisholm Trail." He convinced the State of Texas to approve his placing the markers along the Chisholm Trail on courthouse lawns, city squares, roadside parks, and historical sites. These signs were historically correct. He, however, placed the same metal signs along the Great Western Trail, which were historically incorrect.

P. P. Ackley's name is inscribed on a five-foot red-granite monument at a roadside park about eight miles north of Vernon. The inscription says, "Going Up the Chisholm Trail" with a longhorn graphic over the word *Chisholm* along with the name P. P. Ackley and the date, 1878. Ackley, according to current citizens, convinced the donors of the land that he was correct, so his monument has remained in the park since the 1930s. To set the record straight, the Vernon Rotary trail team placed a GWT white post near the Ackley monument at the roadside park. The conflicting markers reflect the complexity of historical research and the difficulty in trying to correct myths.

P. P. Ackley has left an ingrained mark on Great Western Trail history. He grew up in the Dodge City, Kansas, area and went up the GWT in 1878 from Dodge City to Ogallala, Nebraska. After a time as a deputy trail-brand inspector, he found financial success in the oil business. With money enough, he started a commendable project to mark the route of the Great Western Trail. He, however, tried to change the name of the trail to the Longhorn Chisholm Trail. He had several reasons for the fabrication. The early twentieth century, when Ackley started his project, saw the dawning of a new means of transportation—the age of the automobile. With his fascination for motor transportation, Ackley envisioned an international highway designated as the Longhorn Chisholm Trail International Highway. He persuaded the Oklahoma State Legislature to designate Highway 34 as the

GWT Marker, Near P. P. Ackley's Longhorn Chisholm Trail Monument, Vernon, Texas

Although the Chisholm Trail never went through Vernon, Texas, nor did it cross the Red River at Doan's Crossing, in the 1930s major donor P. P. Ackley attempted to change the name of the Great Western Trail to the Longhorn Chisholm Trail. Today, a Great Western Trail marker, set by Vernon Rotarians (l-r) Mark Reynolds, Curtis Johnson, Jeff Bearden, Larry Crabtree, Paul Hawkins, and Terry Graf, stands to refute the erroneous trail name on the granite Longhorn Chisholm Trail monument in a roadside park north of Vernon.

"Longhorn Chisholm Trail Highway." A more subtle reason for the renaming was Ackley's self-aggrandizement: he planned to be named the "daddy of the Longhorn Chisholm Trail."[21]

Ackley's efforts to change the name coincided with legitimate efforts being made in the 1930s to preserve cattle-trail history. His project conflicted with those of Corwin E. Doan's daughters, Bertha Doan Ross and Mabel M. Igou; George W. Saunders, president of the Old Time Trail Drivers' Association (OTTDA); and Will Rogers. Saunders recognized the value of capturing trail history from drovers. Many of them were headed to the back gate of their lives. With the help of J. Marvin Hunter, Saunders directed a monumental, successful effort to interview drovers. His efforts resulted in a lengthy tome titled *The Trail Drivers of Texas*. The collection of some 350 oral interviews reflected an era through the eyes and memories of trail drivers grown old but still passionate about those years.

With significant efforts being made by Saunders, the OTTDA, and the interviews of drovers for the book, it seemed that the record of trail days would be as authentic as possible. Historical remembrances, however, tend to change through the years without conscious effort. When the trail drovers were interviewed (late in their lives), they did not change trail history on purpose. Some were beset by selective remembering reshaped during their sunset years.

P. P. Ackley's efforts agitated those who were working to preserve trail history as accurately as possible. In 1931, after the Seventh Annual Old Time Trail Drivers' Association Reunion, Saunders and some members decided to set the record straight. Their Texas effort was supported by Oklahoma House Bill No. 149. The legislation approved funding to locate, trace, and map the "Chisholm and Texas Cattle Trails." H. S. Tennant of the Oklahoma State Highway Department interviewed C. F. Doan's daughters, Bertha and Mable. They said their father called the trail the Fort Griffin–Dodge City Trail. They emphasized it had never been called the Chisholm Trail.[22] Although the Chisholm Trail preceded the GWT, except for overlapping for a brief time, the paths of the two trails ran parallel from Brownsville, Texas, approximately 90 to 150 miles apart. The OTTDA passed a Resolution in 1931 that ". . . a marker shall be placed on the banks of the Red River, where the trail crossed, bearing the words 'Trail Crossing on Red River' at Doan's Crossing."[23]

The OTTDA Resolution, passed in 1931, started a fund-raising effort to preserve trail history. On August 4, 1931, Bertha Doan Ross received a donation and a letter from Will Rogers. He said,

My Dear Mrs. Ross, Was glad to get your invitation. Now, there is no where I would rather go, but you see I am in the Movies, and we are supposed to be right in the middle of a Picture about that thime [sic]. But you write me later on and kinder keep me posted. I want to see Mr. Tom Waggoner, and all the San Antonio bunch, and also Tom Burnett. I am sending you fifty bucks to add to the Pot. Taint much, but you don't need much monument if the cause is good. Its those monuments that are for no reason at all that have to be big. Good luck to you all anyhow, Yours, Will Rogers.

P. P. Ackley's 1931 Monument, Doan's Crossing
A ten-foot granite monument near Doan's Crossing erected in 1931 is also associated with P. P. Ackley. A blank strip across the monument indicates where an inscription (P. P. Ackley's attempt to change the GWT name to Longhorn Chisholm Trail) was removed. The other side of the monument includes sixty-two brands used by trail bosses who crossed cattle at Doan's Crossing. Corwin Doan's adobe home can be seen in the background.

This letter, exhibited in the Red River Valley Museum in Vernon, Texas, frames the circumstances, a fund-raiser for a large marble monument designated to set the record straight.

Instead, the ten-and-a-half-foot granite monument created havoc. In the fall of 1931, George S. Saunders, other members of the OTTDA, and the Doan sisters gathered to dedicate the monument near Doan's Adobe. When the inscription was unveiled, it read, "In honor of the trail drivers who freed Texas from the yoke of debt and despair by their trails to the cattle markets of the far north, we dedicate this stone, symbol of their courage and fortitude, at the site of the old Doan's Store, October 20–21, 1931. The Longhorn Chisholm Trail and the Western Trail, 1876–1895. This monument built of Texas Granite, by G. W. Backus." The monument, in fact, angered the Doan sisters, Saunders, and everyone except Ackley.[24]

Ackley's $1,000 donation for the monument gave him access to the inscription that was placed on the monument. One side is historically significant, with sixty-one names of drovers and their brands, many of which were major ranch brands. The other side is equally significant with its bronze bas relief by noted Panhandle-Plains artist H. D. Bugbee. It features two cowboys, one near and one at a distance, herding nineteen head of longhorns down the bluffs into the Red River. At the bottom of the bronze plaque, P. P. Ackley's name with 1876–1895 was on one corner and H. D. Bugbee's name on the other. The nineteen steers are said to represent the nineteen years that cattle crossed the Red River at Doan's Crossing.[25] Other errors were embedded in the bronze. The dates of 1876–1895 have been documented to be 1874 to 1893.

When the inscription on the monument was unveiled, the incorrect dates did not cause the fury. It was the words, "Longhorn Chisholm Trail." George W. Saunders wrote University of Texas professor J. Frank Dobie, an authority on Texas cattle trails, that he had confronted Ackley in a letter. Ackley responded, "If we protested, he had a right to ask Mrs. Ross to return his $1,000." Saunders responded to Ackley, "He had a right to put what he pleased on the monument, but he would be ignoring Texas history."[26]

Today, the large granite monument near Doan's Adobe stands mum like the Sphinx. It harbors a secret that stands as a tribute to someone who, surreptitiously, found a way to set the record straight and make the two Doan sisters happy. As is typical in the West, silence shrouds the name of the perpetrator of the solution. The solution is not obvious to a casual observer. A strip of text about four lines wide that included the name *Longhorn Chisholm Trail* has been neatly sliced out of the granite. An inscription was added at the end: "The Western Texas–Kansas Trail 1876–1895. This Monument erected by Texans." Ackley was from Oklahoma.

Nearby, another granite monument, placed five years later, stands as a tribute to keeping the record straight and to the man who led the way. The monument, titled *Doan's Crossing on Red River*, is "dedicated to George W. Saunders, president of the Old Trail Driver's Assn. 'Who kept the trail records straight.'" It was "Erected by the State of Texas, 1936." These two granite monuments stand side-by-side near Doan's Adobe as sentinels to the secret heralding the covert efforts that resulted in truth.

The reason for the inaccurate dates on the monument remains unknown. The nineteen years have been verified as 1874 to 1893. In 1874 John T. Lytle drove the first documented herd up a trail to the west of populated

DOAN'S CROSSING
ON RED RIVER

BY HERDS ON THE WESTERN TEXAS-
KANSAS TRAIL, 1876-1895 · SIX MILLION
CATTLE AND HORSES CROSSED HERE ·
"YOU DON'T NEED MUCH MONUMENT
IF THE CAUSE IS GOOD · IT'S ONLY
THESE MONUMENTS THAT ARE FOR NO
REASON AT ALL THAT HAS TO BE BIG ·
GOOD LUCK TO YOU ALL ANYHOW
YOURS,
WILL ROGERS"

DEDICATED TO GEORGE W. SAUNDERS,
PRESIDENT OF THE OLD TRAIL DRIVER'S
ASSN., "WHO KEPT THE TRAIL RECORDS
STRAIGHT."

Erected by the State of Texas
1936

Doan's Crossing on Red River, **Near Doan's Crossing, Vernon, Texas**
In 1935, the monument *Doan's Crossing on Red River* was erected by the State of Texas to honor George W. Saunders, president of the Old Time Trail Drivers' Association, "Who Kept the Trail Records Straight." It is adjacent to the ten-foot monument donated previously by P. P. Ackley.

areas. He crossed the herds at a place on the Red River that would become known as Doan's Crossing and trailed the cattle on to Red Cloud Indian Agency at Fort Robinson, Nebraska. This route to the west proved to be a shorter route than the Eastern/Chisholm Trail.[27]

The last documented herd of significance that used the GWT went to Deadwood, South Dakota, in 1893. For some twenty years, John R. and Bill Blocker trailed cattle to Colorado, Nebraska, Wyoming, the Dakotas, and Montana. On their final trip up the GWT, the Blocker brothers moved approximately nine thousand head for Harris Franklin to a buyer in Deadwood. John Blocker later joined in the efforts to preserve trail history by helping to organize the Old Time Trail Drivers' Association and served as its first president.[28]

P. P. Ackley Metal Sign at Donna, Texas

One of the metal [Longhorn] Chisholm Trail signs stands in Donna, Texas, near the Texas-Mexico border, where P. P. Ackley spent his winters. In 2006, the PBS History Channel's *History Detectives* pursued an answer to the question, "Is the Ackley marker authentic in its location in Donna, Texas, and did both the Chisholm and Western Trails originate as far south as the Mexican border?" Their research was timely as it coincided with the GWT grassroots research project. Laura Lincoln, executive director of the Donna Hooks Fletcher Historical Museum in Donna, called me seeking information about P. P. Ackley and the GWT. She said that a metal sign in the town plaza had Ackley's name on it and a longhorn with "Chisholm Trail" written under it. It had been there as long as anyone could remember. She was seeking documentable facts about the sign for the episode, so we were both interviewed for the program.

Great Western Trail Marker, Placed Near P. P. Ackley's Longhorn Chisholm Trail Marker, Donna, Texas

In the 1930s, P. P. Ackley placed a metal Longhorn Chisholm Trail sign in the town of Donna, Texas, near the US-Mexico border. Laura Lincoln, executive director of the Donna Fletcher Museum, and television program *History Detectives* worked together to verify that a GWT marker should also be placed at the South Texas location where both trails originated.

The Fort Worth, Texas, campus of Texas Christian University was the filming site. *History Detectives* started with the Laura Lincoln interview. Their researchers had recovered evidence that supported the origin of *both* trails in South Texas. With this verification, Lincoln invited the Vernon Rotary trail team to dedicate a GWT post in Donna and cement it in place next to Ackley's Chisholm Trail sign. On June 2, 2006, at the town plaza, museum board members and community leaders joined the Vernon trail team in recognizing the GWT marker as a worthy partner to the preexisting Chisholm Trail sign. Both trails had used the same route, but at different times.

Ackley's metal signs and granite monuments, like tombstones, have been convincing and still are. Even as late as March 28, 2012, in the Wichita Falls, Texas, *Times Record News*, an article with a photo of Ackley's metal sign corroborated that some local historians persist in supporting Ackley's attempt to change the name of the GWT. The headline stated, "Historian: Great Western really part of Chisholm Trail." Those signs have relentlessly protected the incorrect information. Chisholm Trail continues to show up on maps, historical plaques, in books, on websites, and in the names of businesses on the route of the GWT. History errors embedded in the minds of citizens remain as facts in spite of newly documented truth.

Some trail information is vague enough that it can easily cause errors in interpretation. A bronze plaque erected in 1967 at the Red River Valley Museum in Vernon proclaims, ". . . tracing history of early man along the Red River, before Chisholm Trail Days, when thousands of cattle crossed Red River at nearby Doan's Crossing." It does not mention the GWT, which is the only major cattle trail to cross at Doan's Crossing. To help correct the oversight, a granite monument was located near the plaque that explains that the path of the Chisholm Trail ran some ninety miles to the east. An article, "Chisholm Trail," on The Handbook of Texas website, states, "The Chisholm Trail was the major route out of Texas for livestock."[29] With the change of one word, "*a* major route out of Texas," the statement would be valid.

With the legacies of the cowboys, the entrepreneurs, and even the opportunists as a foundation, the story of the research for placement of the GWT markers preserves a rich history. The research teams along the trail sifted through the different names, overlapping history, faded memories, and other common divergences that affect history—a daunting task. The facts have been verified, but the granite monuments and metal signs bearing the name Chisholm Trail have had enormous influence. Myths survive even when confronted by truth. On-site visits to burial sites and historical trail locations provided visualizations to help sort the fact from fiction. The Congressional Feasibility Study professional historians verified the South Texas route with research. A constant along the trail were drover descendants, who supported the route with family documents that became primary sources. Volunteers are redefining ambiguous, erroneous trail history so that when academic historians and others closely examine trail evidence, they will document it accurately.

CHAPTER 2
First Two GWT Markers in Texas

T he Great Western Trail (GWT) has long been celebrated in two communities: Vernon, Texas, and Altus, Oklahoma. The towns share a state
border defined by the Red River, a river that cattle drovers feared, or at
least respected, as they forded it with their northbound longhorn herds. This
river, with annual trail celebrations on both banks, helped keep alive the
two communities' trail-era memories. Trail exhibits at the local museums,
ongoing narratives from residents and descendants of drovers, ranches purchased with trail gold, and historical monuments and structures maintain
the communities' living trail presence. Residents of both places responded
almost without pause to the suggestion that the Great Western Trail's path
should be marked across the two states.

The research venture originated with a proposal by Oklahoma Chisholm
Trail historian Bob Klemme. He offered to provide metal molds for making seven-foot cement posts to commemorate the path of the GWT across
Oklahoma. Klemme had previously established a model for identifying the
path of a cattle trail by marking the Chisholm Trail, which passed about
ninety miles east of the two GWT communities. Two Oklahoma men accepted Klemme's offer and agreed to follow his model: mark the route every
six miles across the state. Then, the idea was brought across the Red River to
challenge a community-service organization of businesspeople in Vernon.

The concept had first taken shape at the National Cowboy Symposium
and Celebration in Lubbock, Texas, an event that promotes the Western way
of life. At this event, Klemme proposed that Western Trail Historical Soci-

ety board members Dennis Vernon, a banker with ties to agriculture, and John Yudell Barton, a retired pharmacist, both of Altus, launch the project in Oklahoma. Having been party to the discussion, I invited them to present the trail idea to the Vernon Rotary Club, which they did in April 2003. Chris Jefferies, executive director of the Chisholm Trail Museum at Duncan, Oklahoma, joined them. On September 16, 2003, Vernon and Barton returned to issue a challenge to the Vernon Rotarians to mark the trail across Texas. The Oklahomans sweetened the challenge with an offer to donate the first post for Texas.

The Vernon Rotary Club did not hesitate to commit to such a daunting project. The path under consideration in Texas would be 620 miles long. That did not deter club members. I was pressed into service as a co-chair with Jeff Bearden, who was an authority on Doan's Crossing history. He was also a Davy Crockett reenactor, not to mention the owner of a chuck wagon and two mules. He and Ann Huskinson, a previous Red River Valley Museum executive director, had collaborated to restore the small town of Doan's near the river crossing to its 1880s cattle-trail days. However, they discovered that the privately owned land needed for the project was not for sale.

A little Texas pride sealed the deal, a deal made without benefit of research on the amount of time and expense it would require. No one could have known that the project started in 2004 would continue at a steady pace for some seven years. This ambitious research project began with two dedications in Texas. The first took place at Doan's Adobe near the Red River. Shortly thereafter, the citizens of Bandera, a trail town in South Texas, requested the second one.

Doan's Crossing: Annual Doan's Picnic Preserved Memories of Trail Days

For more than 120 years, in Vernon, Texas, local citizens have maintained vivid trail memories in an unusual way. An annual commemorative event, the Doan's May Day Picnic, is staged at Doan's Adobe, a designated historic home built during the trail days. Drovers' wives started the event in 1884 as a traditional May Day picnic. After watching their husbands cross the Red River with their herds into Indian Territory, now the state of Oklahoma, the wives decided to celebrate May Day. At a nearby area called Watt's Grove, they had a picnic, an event that has continued without interruption for more than a century. In 1911, the annual event became the Doan's May Day Picnic and Crowning of Royalty. Community citizens decided to honor drover and pioneer families. With remembrances from European traditions, they initiated the crowning of a young queen with an attendant royal court. A young king was added in 1939. Today, some members of the royal court are sixth-generation representatives of drover and pioneer families. This celebration, an important but little-known part of Great Western Trail history, has kept trail history viable in the community of Vernon.

During the trail days, Doan's trading post was the drovers' last major source for supplies for many days. Drovers sometimes spent a month at the trading post preparing for the long trip north. On occasion, following a storm at Doan's Crossing, drovers would have to wait for the Red River to subside before they attempted to cross their herds. A weather-created backlog of herds would further complicate crossing the river. One time ten herds of 2,500 to 3,000 longhorns in each herd were waiting their turn to use the low-water crossing. An electrical storm caused a stampede. It took 120 cowboys ten days to separate the cattle into their respective herds. This arduous task, requiring an immense amount of skill from horse and rider alike, could not have been accomplished if the cattle had not been marked with their owners' herd brands.[1]

With numerous herds passing through, Doan's settlement soon became a bustling, growing town, one whose citizens lived at peace with the Comanches. The community was founded in April 1878 when Jonathan Doan, a member of the Religious Society of Friends (Quakers), moved from near Fort Sill, Oklahoma. Chief Quanah Parker and other Comanches had advised him to establish a trading post near a shallow-water crossing on the Prairie Dog Fork of the Red River. The Quakers, known as peacemakers, did not wear guns. They made efforts to befriend the Indians. Some family members learned to speak the Comanche language. The Indians often set up teepees nearby. On occasion, places were raided on the trail, but the Doans were never bothered.[2]

The history of the community, one that thrived on trade from the drovers going north, gives insight into life in other small trail communities. Soon after arriving in 1878, Jonathan Doan built a dual-purpose picket house. With a dirt floor, prairie-grass roof, and a buffalo-robe door, the 20-by-30-foot room served as a store on one end and a home on the other. In the fall of 1878, widower Jonathan Doan had his family from Ohio join him. His nephew, Corwin Doan and his wife, Lide, brought their small daughter, Bertha, and Jonathan's two daughters, Emma and Eva, to Doan's. In 1879, they added a post office to Doan's store, with Corwin serving as the postmaster. With

Doan's Store, 1880s, Near Vernon, Texas

In the 1880s, Doan's Store, near a low-water crossing on the Red River, was built by Jonathan Doan. His store was the last place to buy supplies before crossing into Indian Territory, now Oklahoma. Image courtesy of Red River Valley Museum, Vernon, Texas.

the establishment of Wilbarger County in 1881, Jonathan Doan became the first county judge. By 1885, Doan's community could boast of a population of approximately three hundred residents.[3]

Two commercial changes occurred that caused the demise of the town of Doan's. In 1886, the Fort Worth and Denver City Railroad tracks reached Vernon, one segment of the plan to build tracks northwest through the Texas Panhandle to eventually connect Fort Worth and Denver, Colorado, which it did.[4] In 1893, the last large herd crossed the Red River at Doan's Crossing, which eliminated the small settlement's major flow of revenue. With these changes, Doan's Adobe was the lone structure to survive from the trail days. However, the event that originated in 1884, Doan's May Picnic, continued to be held annually near Doan's Adobe. Vernon residents and drovers' descendants produced the annual celebration. Jonathan Doan's great-granddaughter Regina Doane [spelling changed] and Corwin's great-grandson Tip Igou have helped maintain a living history by supporting the annual event and donating memorabilia to the local museum.

Doan's Crossing, First GWT Marker Dedication in Texas

The Vernon Rotary Club comprised the first Texas GWT research team. The Western Trail Historical Society of the Museum of the Western Prairie in Altus comprised the Oklahoma research team. These two teams held many meetings to plan the first dedication ceremony, set for May 1, 2004. The dedication was added to the picnic festivities. Planning for this kickoff event created a protocol that was used for other commemorative GWT ceremonies in towns along the trail. Some of the records specific to community events provided primary resources for the research project. In this case, the Crowning of the Doan's Queen and King booklet of biographies documented family histories (some dating back six or more generations).

An unexpected part of the project was the readiness of people to accept jobs such as making the more than one hundred posts needed to mark the route in Texas. This was a physically rigorous, time-consuming, weather-dependent project. It was amazing. Not one but two men volunteered: Phil McCuistion and Rick Jouett. Both were retired Vernon firefighters who had worked together for many years. To round out this bedrock team, Bob Klemme of Enid, Oklahoma, provided the foundry-made Great Western Trail letters used in the metal molds. They also embedded a Rotary wheel in the cement posts. They made concrete, poured it into the seven-foot mold, with rebar included to strengthen it, and let it cure for thirty days. The moisture content responded negatively to cold or to heat, so the marker makers also had to be weather watchers.

A marker weighed 225 pounds. Four markers were made in each production cycle. After the markers were made and lifted out of the mold, they were furbished with a steel brush to remove the rough parts. Then the thirty-day seasoning took place. Afterward, Rotarians were recruited to load and move the markers to a warehouse. When asked why he would do so much labor-intense volunteer work, McCuistion said, "Someday one of my grandsons might say, 'My grandpa made this marker.'"[5]

The time-consuming painting of the posts required another volunteer. Paul Hawkins, retired Vernon city manager and Rotarian, stepped up to meet that critical need. This task was also an arduous undertaking. The white posts with indented letters of red required many hours of meticulous painting. Paul said, "My principle contribution to the project involved painting the posts and coordinating the moving of the posts both in our local production process, and in the distribution of the finished product to the various post-setting locations up and down the trail."[6]

GWT Marker Makers Paul Hawkins, Rick Jouett, and Phil McCuistion of Vernon, Texas

Phil McCuistion and Rick Jouett made more than one hundred 225-pound, seven-foot, cement posts to mark the Great Western Trail across Texas. Paul Hawkins painted them white with red letters, stored, and dispensed them.

When posts were moved to the city warehouse, Hawkins started painting. Five painting steps were required in a cycle, and each step required up to two hours to complete. After each step, the paint cured overnight before the next step could take place. The entire painting cycle required a period of six days. On the seventh day, instead of resting, the cycle would begin again. After he painted the posts, they were stored on sawhorses until needed for a dedication ceremony. When asked if he would do it again, Hawkins said, "Most certainly! The historical significance, the camaraderie, and the friendships developed were both immeasurable and very rewarding. To be a part of history is both unimaginable and humbling."[7]

Yet another person volunteered to join the project at the right time: the Red River Valley Museum Executive Director Mary Ann McCuistion, a noted artist. Her creativity and her position at the museum gave the Rotary

Corwin F. Doan's Adobe Home, 1881
Widower Jonathan Doan sent for his two young daughters and his nephew, Corwin F. Doan, to move to Doan's Crossing to help him with his store for drovers. Corwin's adobe home, a Texas Historic Landmark built in 1881, stands today north of Vernon.

GWT project visibility and a home. When the museum hired Mary Ann for the half-time position, they acquired two people—her husband Phil, a post maker, provided a strong arm and artistic talent.

Many citizens supported, in various ways, the first GWT dedication ceremony in Texas. The *Vernon Daily Record* publisher, Larry Crabtree, and editor, Jimmy Carr, frequently headlined the GWT project on the front page. They also printed a twenty-page insert that reaffirmed trail history for the local community. In a letter, Texas Governor Rick Perry said, "To all who worked tirelessly to make today a reality, I applaud you. Together, you highlight the best of the Lone Star State."[8] The governor's stamp of approval for "the best of the Lone Star State" strengthened the trail team's efforts to enlist Texas towns on the trail to join the project.

Twelve miles north of Vernon, at the 120th Doan's Picnic and the first dedication of a GWT post, a large group of people made twenty-first-century trail history. The cold weather reminded the participants of drovers from the past working the trail under various circumstances. Wind blew twenty miles an hour, making the 49 degrees at 7:00 a.m. in May seem like

First GWT Marker Dedicated in Texas, Doan's Adobe, 2004

On May 1, 2004, the first Great Western Trail marker in Texas was dedicated near Doan's Adobe, built in 1881. Vernon Rotarians accepted Oklahoma's challenge to mark the trail every six miles through Texas (across 620 miles). Texas co-chairs Sylvia Mahoney (left) and Jeff Bearden partnered on the project with Oklahoma co-chairs Dennis Vernon and John Yudell Barton (right). Texas State Representative Rick Hardcastle (center left) and Oklahoma Senator Robert Kerr were instrumental to the success of the project.

zero-degree weather. The local participants discussed the harsh trail conditions for the cowboys/drovers more than a century before—they had no tents, no sleeping bags, and no air mattresses, just hard, cold ground and a few horse blankets.

At the dedication, trail descendant Gary Chapman served as a lead cook for the cowboy breakfast. His period clothing created a visual image of Great Western Trail days. The crowd watched him and other Rotarians cooking breakfast through the door of the white cook tent as it flapped in the cold wind. In spite of the harsh conditions, the crowd gathered for a feast of eggs, ham, hash-brown potatoes, tortillas, and cowboy coffee boiled in a pot on a campfire. All the while they talked about cattle trails, horses, and great-grandfathers and -uncles who were drovers. Gary, whose home was across the road from Doan's Adobe, also owned ranch land along the Red River where drovers had once forded their longhorns. Other Chapman family members had lived nearby since their drover ancestors settled there.

After the breakfast, the Oklahoma and Texas groups started the dedication ceremony. Oklahoma Senator Robert Kerr, on horseback, set the pace for a horse-drawn buggy that carried the seven-foot post. The senator, wearing a frock coat harking back to the cattle-trail era, carried an Oklahoma flag. Horse and rider moved between an honor guard formed by the Texas Ambassadors on Horseback, also called Vernon's Santa Rosa Palomino Club. As the wagon passed between the mounted Club riders, they moved in behind the wagon to follow it, two-by-two, each rider carrying a Texas flag. Texas State Representative Rick Hardcastle, wearing a black frock coat, rode from the south carrying a Texas flag. The two met and rode toward the GWT marker location together.

As the wagon that brought the post moved away, Doug Tolleson of College Station, Texas, sang his original song, "Crossing the Red at Doan's." Guitarist Mark Reynolds and James Streit and his Fiddlers finished the ceremony with "Oh, Bury Me Not on the Lone Prairie." Tradition holds that this song originated in 1879 at Doan's when a dying cowboy asked his friends, Pink Burdette and Jesse James Benton, not to bury him there on the lonely prairie. This cowboy, who had accidentally shot himself at a dance, was buried north of Doan's Adobe.[9] Rancher Grady Stowe reflected on his childhood memories for the possible location of the unmarked burial site, which is on land he now owns.

After the introduction of out-of-town trail descendants from Oklahoma, Kansas, and South Texas, and other dignitaries, master of ceremony Ann Huskinson reviewed the history of Doan's Crossing and the trail days. Vernon and Altus trail teams jointly carried the post from the wagon to its permanent location by Doan's Adobe, where it was cemented into place. Senator Kerr and Rep. Hardcastle read state proclamations. Then the two men dedicated the post with Red River water poured from a Mason jar. People in the audience, one-by-one, poured water on the post, thus making them active participants in commemorating trail history. Participants often had their photos made while dedicating the post. Grant Smith, whose family had called the Doan's area home for generations, became the official collector of Red River water for identical ceremonies at all thirty-seven dedications.

The crowning of the 2004 Doan's King and Queen followed the GWT

Doan's May Picnic and Crowning of King and Queen, 2004
In 2004, the first GWT marker in Texas was dedicated on the same day as the annual Doan's May Picnic, which included the crowning of Queen Alice Tate Smith and King Nicholas Rea Lehman at Doan's Adobe. The Picnic, started in 1884, added the crowning of a queen in 1911 and a king in 1939 to commemorate a new freedom: ownership of land without allegiance to a national royalty.

dedication. Approximately eighty lords, ladies, princes, and princesses, along with the trainbearers and royal crown bearers, served in the ceremonial crowning of the young king and queen. The ceremony took place in the shade of a large tree that sheltered Doan's Adobe, the home Corwin Doan built in 1881. This historical, beautiful, and unusual event, like the trail, was relatively unknown outside the community. Despite that, former queens, such as Mary and Christy Bearden, wife and daughter of trail co-chair Jeff Bearden, acknowledged this honor with pride. After the crowning, participants moved to tables under another large tree where the picnic was held.

That day, a sixth-generation descendant of farmers/ranchers of Wilbarger County was crowned King Nicholas Rea of the House of Lehman. Nicholas lived with his parents Mark and Deana Lehman on his paternal family's original homestead, which was settled in 1859. This was fifteen years before the first drover traveled through going north. The original Lehmans came from France to Texas seeking rich farmland. South of what would be Vernon, the Lehmans broke out land to start their farming enterprise. Nearby, they had made their first home in a dugout.[10]

A fifth-generation Wilbarger County resident was crowned Queen Alice Tate of the House of Smith, another quaint title, but one befitting the culture it was honoring. A star monogrammed on the queen's coronation dress represented the Lone Star of Texas and "the pride we feel in being Texan." It was a "reminder of the song, 'The Yellow Rose of Texas,' the queen's favorite lullaby song." Two family ranch brands on the dress, a bar-two and an S bar, belonged to the paternal and maternal families of the queen's parents, Jim and Julie Smith.[11]

The crowning of royalty as a trail event relates to the generational connections between drovers and farmers, some of whose descendants had lived on the same land since before trail days. Ownership of land, once the domain of the gentry, became available to the commoner—both drover and farmer—in the American West. The crowning of royalty symbolically celebrated the cultural shift that occurred during the trail era. No longer must average people pay homage to a national king and queen. They celebrated owning land and being good stewards of it, being responsible and self-supporting, being independent, and being free to pursue happiness.

Again, a chance meeting started another GWT project. Previously, Oklahoman co-chair John Yudell Barton had traveled south to Bandera, Texas, a town near San Antonio, in search of trail documentation. Bandera and San Antonio, along with Castroville, served as supply and gathering points for herds from South Texas and Mexico. In Bandera, at the Frontier Times Museum, Barton met area GWT historian Peggy Tobin, president of the Bandera Historical Society. Barton and Tobin connected readily as Tobin had lived in Altus. Barton told Tobin about the Oklahoma GWT project, and she stirred local interest in the project. Soon, Bandera citizens were planning a trail ride to Dodge City, Kansas.

January 18, 2004, Three GWT Groups Gather at the Red River Valley Museum in Vernon

The Barton-Tobin chance meeting initiated a gathering that took place in Vernon on January 18, 2004, at the Red River Valley Museum. Altus, Vernon, and Bandera trail enthusiasts met prior to the dedication of the first marker in Texas. The group assembled in the Waggoner Room, home to

GWT Planning Groups, Waggoner Room, Red River Valley Museum

In 2004, Vernon, Texas, trail volunteers hosted volunteers from Altus, Oklahoma, and Bandera, Texas, to initiate GWT events. The group gathered in front of artist Adrian Martinez's mural of the history of the W. T. Waggoner Ranch in the Waggoner Room at the Red River Valley Museum, in Vernon.

a fittingly symbolic representation of the Great Western Trail: artist Adrian Martinez's wall-size mural of the history of the W. T. Waggoner Ranch. The artist exhibited the ranch's history, established during the trail era, using images of generations of Waggoner ranchers and some of their friends, such as Quanah Parker, Theodore Roosevelt, and wolf hunter Jack Abernathy. Images common to the prairie ecosystem of the vast 530,000-acre ranch, the largest Texas ranch under one fence, include tall grasses, mesquite, scrub oaks, buffalo, prairie dogs, coyotes, rattlesnakes, and birds, including a turkey.

During this meeting, the three groups explained their GWT vision and plans. The Oklahoma group planned to mark Oklahoma. The Vernon Rotarians planned to enlist citizens in the twenty counties to verify the path of the trail and mark it across 620 miles in Texas. The Bandera group, headed by David Burell and Dan Wise, announced their plans for a forty-eight-day trail ride from Bandera to Dodge City, Kansas. Burell's great-grandfather, originally from Alsace-Lorraine, settled at Castroville; he was one of the first seventeen settlers there. Each settler received an incentive of 1,200 acres. Given his family ties, Burell responded enthusiastically when Tobin gave him a copy of Marvin Hunter's book, *Trail Drivers of Texas,* and told him about the marking-the-GWT project. On a napkin at a restaurant, David and Dan began planning the trail ride to Dodge City.[12] The group decided to dedicate the second Texas GWT marker at Bandera on Labor Day, September 6, 2004. The finale of the dedication ceremony would be the exodus of the Bandera trail riders to Dodge City.

Bandera, Texas, First Road Trip for the GWT Vernon and Altus Teams

History-making trips to dedications started with the Vernon and Altus trail teams' trip to Bandera—a six-hour drive. One of the group made reservations at a dude ranch where he had stayed some ten or fifteen years earlier. When the group arrived at the headquarters of the LH7 Ranch, we learned one of the lessons of relying on memories. Instead of a dude ranch, the place had become a popular fishing camp. With the overflow Labor Day crowds in Bandera, the self-named Cowboy Capital of the World, we knew that the LH7 cabins, offering just the basics of four walls, a roof, running water, and "indoor plumbing," were preferable to the limited alternatives.

Maudeen Marks, LH7 Ranch Owner, an Authority on Longhorns

The ranch owner, Maudeen Marks, proved to be an unexpected primary source for our research. Our first view of the place was one of aged longhorns grazing around the small cabins. Reminiscent of a small-town museum, the cabin headquarters reflected the owner's life. The sprightly eighty-two-year-old noted her slow pace in trying to register us. She requested our patience, to which we readily acceded—the space was filled with photos and other memorabilia. She was also interested in our trail project as her family history encompassed trail history.

Maudeen's business style, her hospitality, and her clothing reflected a persona that recalled traits of the trail era. When we registered (actually we wrote our names on a piece of paper), one of our group asked for keys. Maudeen said, "Keys, what do you need keys for? Just go knock on the cabin doors—if no one answers, you can have that cabin." She sent us off to find our cabins, saying that she would deliver "Happy Hour" refreshments.

This modern example of trail-era hospitality, we learned, also provided her an audience to give a lesson about longhorns. Maudeen brought an ample supply of cowboy libations to the cabins. Dressed to perform for her audience, she wore a white hat shaped with a rounded top and flat, three-inch brim, much like a Navajo-style hat. Maudeen called it her party hat; she said her identical pink hat was for formal occasions. Her outfit did not distract from the fact that her discussion proved to be a primary source for the history of the longhorn's evolution to becoming a recognized breed.

Moving her chair to face the group, Maudeen became the center of attention. With animation, she told tales of the hearty, survivor Longhorn breed of cattle. She gave reasons for raising them and loving the breed. Maudeen had inherited the original LH7 Ranch near Houston when her father, E. H. Marks, died. With the city encroaching on it, Maudeen sold the land and bought her ranch near Bandera. She said that her dad was one of the first Texas cattlemen to cross Brahman bulls imported from India and Brazil with the longhorn. However, she emphasized that her dad had selected specific longhorns to protect the foundation stock of the LH7 and to protect the longhorn (a mixed breed) from extinction. His five hundred head of longhorns became one of seven groups selected to become the foundation for future purebred herds.[13]

Maudeen's passion for longhorns showed in her gestures indicating the curvature of the horns. She encouraged everyone to join in imitating the patterns she was creating in the air as she explained the reasons for their curves. Soon, we were all undulating our arms trying to mimic Maudeen's horn patterns. According to Maudeen, the bulls' horns curve up and forward to provide protection and augment procreation. Using his horns, a bull would drive off competitors for the females he selected for his herd harem. The females have long horns that curl out from the head to the sides. The steers had the same pattern for horn curves as the females. However, she mentioned that ideas were changing about the horns. Some owners were now breeding the curves out of the horns to enhance the length to compete for championships.

Since Maudeen's father was one of the seven founders for purebred Longhorns, her vivid portrayal of longhorn traits and history rang with authenticity. Staying at the LH7 Ranch introduced the trail team to the first of many unexpected discoveries of descendants with personal knowledge of trail history.

September 6, 2004, Second GWT Dedication in Texas, at Bandera

Bandera, a town that actively promoted its cowboy culture heritage, had been a supply and entertainment point for drovers herding longhorns from Laredo and Eagle Pass, two major feeder routes originating on the Mexi-

GWT Marker Dedication, Bandera, Texas
On Labor Day 2004, Bandera, Texas, held the second GWT dedication in Texas. It coincided with the start of the Bandera Trail Riders' forty-eight-day trip to Dodge City, Kansas. Working together on marking the GWT project were (l-r) Rick Jouett, John Yudell Barton, Sylvia Mahoney, Bandera historian Peggy Tobin, Bandera Trail Riders president Dave Burell, Dennis Vernon, and Jeff Bearden. Maudeen Marks's (front) father owned one of the seven original Longhorn foundation herds used for the breed registry.

can border. The use of the word *feeder* implies that they were lesser-than the main trails. However, the premise for this project was not the volume of cattle, but the contribution of longhorns to the GWT. One route came from Mexico through Laredo across four counties to Castroville in Medina County. Farther west, drovers used a low-water crossing on the Rio Grande near Eagle Pass. The herds crossed three counties from there to reach Castroville.[14] From Castroville, the herds forded the Medina River going to Bandera. At Castroville and Bandera, after cattle were branded and herds configured, the drovers continued through Bandera Pass.[15] From Bandera, the herds moved north along the west bank of Bandera Creek. South Texas cattle from San Antonio, following the larger Matamoros segment of the GWT, converged at Kerrville with the Bandera route.[16] Drovers called the second segment of the trail the Fort Griffin Trail, which led to the next major supply and entertainment point at Fort Griffin (north of Interstate 20, near Albany).

In 2004 in Bandera, horses stood tied to a hitching post at the local saloon on the main street. Sunday was still "ride your horse to town day." The Great Western Trail dedication day and the annual Labor Day festivities had filled the town with locals, tourists, and trail fans. They witnessed two history-making events: the GWT marker dedication ceremony followed by the Bandera Trail Riders leaving on a forty-eight-day trip to Dodge City, Kansas. The chairs at the Bandera city plaza across from the Bandera County Courthouse filled quickly with folks from many states. They listened to the Almost Patsy Cline Trio while waiting for the 10:00 a.m. ceremony to begin.

After introductions of numerous dignitaries, Texas Senator Frank Madla and Texas Representative Carter Casteel spoke and emphasized the importance of preserving trail history. Bandera Historical Society President Peggy Tobin was recognized as the local authority on GWT history and the initiator of the GWT project in their community. Local longhorn authority Maudeen Marks, wearing her pink hat, joined the group in the ritual of simultaneously pouring Red River water and Medina River water from Mason jars onto the marker.

Friends of the Western Trail President David Burell provided details about the planned ride to Dodge City, a trip worthy of a book itself. Following the post dedication, the Bandera Trail Riders, with some fifty wagons and one hundred riders from fifteen states, paraded by the dedication site. They timed it to be the finale of the day's trail celebration: a tribute to bygone days of rugged cowgirls and cowboys, good horses, and colorful wagons. Trail boss Suzie Heywood and assistant trail boss Richard Burney led the entourage. They headed north with plans to enter Dodge City on October 23, 2004. A photographer from Germany traveled with them to capture their trail experience and send photos to newspapers throughout his home country. Thus, the once-unknown GWT, with modern media coverage in Europe, was not so unknown.

With the first two dedication ceremonies completed, the Vernon trail team started calling citizens in each of the twenty Texas counties to clarify any possible ambiguity about the GWT crossing their county. Fifteen of the twenty counties had Rotary clubs. The trail team contacted chambers of commerce in the other five counties. Letters went to the president of each club or chamber. A follow-up call helped to explain the project. To enlist

Bandera Trail Riders Leave for Dodge City

A commemorative event reinforced collective memories of the GWT era. The Bandera Trail Riders, with some fifty wagons and one hundred riders, left Bandera, Texas, on Labor Day 2004 for a forty-eight-day ride to Dodge City, Kansas. Led by trail boss Suzie Heywood and assistant trail boss Richard Burney, the riders arrived in Kansas on October 23, 2004.

club volunteers to join the unique project, the trail team realized that a personal visit to each club was necessary. I agreed to go.

Rotary clubs scheduled appointments or programs for me in Brownsville, Edinburg, Falfurrias, Alice, and George West. North of San Antonio, Rotary clubs scheduled programs in Brady, Coleman, and Abilene. Chambers of commerce executive directors scheduled appointments in Menard, Baird, and Seymour. The newspaper editor in Throckmorton was the contact point. Later, the Amity Club in Moran requested a dedication. San Antonio had so many Rotary clubs that instead of being easy, it was difficult to interest a club in a cattle trail when they had the historic Alamo at their doorsteps. Despite this potential diversion, they fielded a dedication worthy of the historic city.

Vernon is fifteen miles from the Oklahoma border; the 620-mile-drive to Brownsville on the Mexican border took ten hours. To keep us from succumbing to doubts about our ability to complete this project, the trip south to visit clubs or chambers in twelve of the twenty counties committed us to finishing the project. The enthusiastic support by club members and chamber executives for verifying the path of the GWT increased our level of commitment. The narrative about my successful first journey south (my sister accompanied me) is included in Chapter 3. Just as drovers made many trail trips, North Texas–based trail team leaders made three trips to South Texas with additional trips to Corpus Christi and San Antonio.

As the days passed and the project progressed, it seemed to take on a life of its own. The markers were being made; the path of the trail was being authenticated. Rotarians, local historians, and chambers of commerce along the trail had committed to join the project. The first two dedication ceremonies had been completed. Had we known how much physical labor was required, how complicated corroborating the path of the trail would be, how many years the project would take, and how much time would be required to travel—more than once—from Mexico to Canada, we might have reconsidered.

Nonetheless, the project seemed to be fated to succeed. With every need, a volunteer stepped up to help. The project would reach proportions, distances, and successes beyond anything anyone had imagined. Why did so many people volunteer to help with this time-consuming job? This answer might be debatable, but the spirit of the GWT and the need to honor it with an authentic history seemed to galvanize each community's trail team. The history of the GWT was the history of their land, of their grandparents and great-grandparents, of the origin of their businesses and competitions, of their culture, and of their values. The search for GWT documentation was a reminder to the communities of their roots, of their heritage.

CHAPTER 3
Mexico and South Texas

The record of the journeys of millions of longhorns and horses from South Texas and Mexico would be more accurate if the three South Texas routes had had trail names rather than the vague terms, *gathering places* or *feeder trails*. Research teams for the six South Texas counties documented the Matamoros Trail, or southernmost portion of the Great Western Trail, as the route for thousands of cattle from Matamoros to San Antonio. Two other South Texas trails from Laredo and Eagle Pass also provided cattle for the GWT. However, due to lack of time for contact with those areas, local research teams were not available to provide primary sources for the trails. The six counties on the Matamoros Trail scheduled dedications to reclaim the almost-forgotten trail history.

The name *Matamoros Trail* was identified by the research teams as a name for the segment of trail between Matamoros and San Antonio that was active prior to its use to deliver cattle up the Chisholm and then the Great Western Trails. The name contradicted the typical pattern used for naming a segment of trail going north, which was commonly based on the next supply town. This and other segment names (or lack thereof) complicated the research. Another variance that caused problems was that some maps were based on the volume of cattle that traveled between San Antonio and Dodge City, Kansas, or Ogallala, Nebraska. Those maps, focused on delivery of cattle to railheads, identified the beginning of the GWT at San Antonio. No standard for volume of cattle to qualify a GWT segment of trail was found. Although most longhorns originated in South Texas and

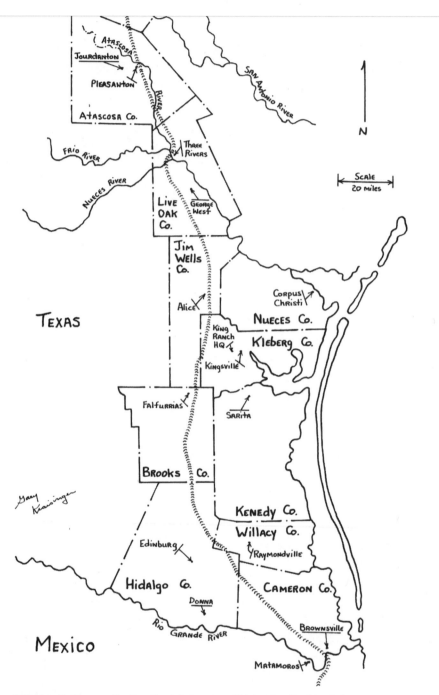

GWT from Matamoros, Mexico, through Cameron, Hidalgo, Brooks, Live Oak, and Atascosa Counties

Mexico, the three trails used to deliver cattle to the next supply town have not been fully recognized for their contributions. Plagued by misconstrued or missing trail names south of San Antonio, the South Texas and Mexico trail teams worked diligently to overcome questions about the GWT as it passed through their six Texas counties and one Mexican state.

Rotarians at Statue of General Lucio Blanco, Museo del Agrarismo Mexicano
In Matamoros, Mexico, in front of a statue of Mexican Revolutionary General Lucio Blanco at Museo del Agrarismo Mexicano, members of Club Rotario Matamoros Profesional joined Rotary district leaders Jorge and Olga Verduzco of Laredo and Bill Huskinson of Vernon.

June 3, 2006, Matamoros, Mexico, Dedication, Club Rotario Matamoros Professional

The dedication ceremony at Matamoros, Mexico, on June 3, 2006, marked twenty-first-century international trail history. Mexico became the first of two participating countries that joined the United States in recognizing shared cattle-trail history. Matamoros trail-team members verified that longhorns from their area went north up the Matamoros Trail, the first part of the GWT. The Matamoros Trail, called by its place of origin, was significant to the research study. Noted historian Jimmy Skaggs said the Matamoros Trail carried more cattle than any other trail that moved cattle north from South Texas.[1] The Matamoros Trail, as a vital supply route for the GWT, was part of the most direct route for trailing South Texas cattle to railheads on the west side of Kansas and the northern open-range ranching states.

With verification completed that the GWT moved longhorns north from Matamoros, the eight-member Texas trail team made the eleven-hour trip to participate in two border-area dedication ceremonies. At Brownsville, Melida Buentello and other members of the Club Rotario Matamoros Profesional met the team and escorted everyone across the border to the Museo del Agrarismo Mexicano (known as the Land Reform Movement Museum), which would host the first dedication in Mexico. The museum site was selected because of its historical commonality to the trail drivers.

Both the trail experience and the Land Reform Movement elevated the common person in these areas to a more prominent position in the business world. The Land Reform Movement in Mexico, the first distribution of land to people other than gentry, began on August 30, 1913, at the site of the museum. After taking Matamoros, revolutionary General Lucio Blanco decided to distribute the land to eleven farmhands who were being exploited in the hacienda Los Borregos. This event had national impact, as it was echoed throughout the Mexican Revolution.[2] Thus, the choice of this site to celebrate the past had more than one cause for commemoration.

At the GWT dedication ceremony, Matamoros Rotarians, historians, and museum and city officials celebrated the occasion with a vivid display of Mexican culture. Folk dancers twirling to the music displayed their native, multicolored costumes. The Charreada Riding Group carried the flag of the state of Tamaulipas, Mexico, and the national flags of Mexico, the United States, and Canada, paying tribute to the three countries crossed by the GWT. A certificate of official recognition from Texas Governor Rick Perry was presented to Nancy Estrada Ayala, secretary of the Fomento Economico y del Empleo and a representative of the mayor of Matamoros. Each document presented at the ceremony was read in English by Jorge Verduzco of Laredo and in Spanish by David Mason of Abilene, both Rotary leaders in their districts. Speakers recognized the major contributions made by Mexico to the cattle, the horses, and the skills needed by the cowboys to push longhorns north some two thousand miles.

Museum Director Lie Monica Robles and Professor Andres Cuellar, di-

GWT Marker Dedication, Matamoros, Mexico

On June 3, 2006, in Matamoros, Mexico, at the Museo del Agrarismo, the first Great Western Trail marker in Mexico was dedicated. A large group of local historians, museum personnel, elected officials, and Texas trail team members joined Edith Mercedes Angulo, club president, and the Club Rotario Matamoros Profesional members in a celebration of the shared history of Texas and Mexico linked by the Great Western Trail.

rector of history, both emphasized the importance of preserving the two countries' shared trail history. On display, a large map of the trail stated, "La Gran Ruta del Ganado del Viejo Oeste," and illustrated the path of the trail from Mexico to Canada. Professor Cuellar spoke about the origin of the trail and its economic and cultural impact. He said for those still doing research, additional trail evidence could be found in the late 1800s section of the city newspaper archives.

At the ceremony, Edith Mercedes Angulo, Rotary president, said, "The project to mark the Great Western Cattle Trail from its origins in Matamoros, through the United States and all the way to Canada, is of special historical importance for us as Mexicans. Given the time to reminisce, we must not forget that we are literally connected by geography that forever joins us, creating bonds of brotherhood as much from our location as from our cultures."[3] She added that having Tamaulipas recognized for its contributions of longhorns and cowboy skills helped foster the spirit of the GWT in their community and unify it with other communities along the trail.

June 2, 2006, Brownsville, Texas, Dedication in Cameron County

The dedication ceremonies are placed in the narrative sequentially to correspond to the path of the trail going north, not chronologically. This format was selected to help clarify the path of the trail. The dates of the dedication ceremonies are given to document the history of the marking of the GWT. Following the Matamoros dedication, Brownsville in Cameron County is next on the path going north although the dedication ceremony itself was held the day before the dedication in Mexico.

The Rio Grande separates the Texas city from Matamoros. The Nueces Strip, a disputed area bordered on the south by the Rio Grande and on the north by the next major river, the Nueces River, defined the shifting border during the Texas Revolution and the Mexican-American War. It was also an area that provided herds of longhorns and young men/drovers, and it helped shape the trail path and era, as well as its legend, with its violent, turbulent political history. Five of the six counties on the trail from Brownsville to San Antonio are located in the Nueces Strip.

The GWT era coincided with what was considered the most violent time in the Nueces Strip. The land between the two rivers became infamous for its infestation of bandits, murderers, and thieves. Domestic criminals such as King Fisher and international cattle thieves such as Juan N. Cortina complicated the conditions caused by Reconstruction after the Civil War. Interested readers can find many works about the violent period between 1874 and 1880 when the Texas Rangers did their greatest work in the area.

During that time, crossing the Nueces Strip in South Texas required keenly skilled drovers who were capable of protecting themselves and their herds. The drovers often resorted to aggressive acts, many times as violent as the criminals, to stop those who attacked them. The Special Force of Texas Rangers, created by the 1874 legislature for protection of the frontier and suppression of lawlessness, of about thirty men under the command of Captain L. H. McNelly was assigned to the Nueces Strip.[4] McNelly and the "Little McNellys" became infamous for the ruthless methods they used to bring some semblance of law and order to this violent area of Texas. In the foreword to a memoir recounted by George Durham, the youngest of the Mc-

Nelly Rangers, historian Walter Prescott Webb wrote of McNelly, "Equipped with an iron will and totally unacquainted with fear, he acquired the art of taking care of his minority in the presence of a majority."[5]

The Rangers' first year in the Nueces Strip, 1874, is the first year a herd went up the Great Western Trail from South Texas. However, that herd departed from an area southwest of San Antonio in Atascosa County, north of the Nueces Strip. A trail boss, recognizing the dangers of straying too far from a well-traveled passageway, such as the Matamoros Trail, moved his herd toward that point instead of moving across lesser-traveled areas. In addition, that trail boss, understanding the more cooperative habits of cattle following an established trail, committed his herd to the closest well-traveled trail. These points were traceable elements for the South Texas trail teams who were searching for the path of the GWT.

More than thirty years earlier, an infamous event in the Nueces Strip gives insight into the politics, cultures, and conditions that shaped the GWT era. In 1843, Captain Ewen Cameron, for whom Cameron County was named, was killed. During those days of the Republic of Texas, Capt. Cameron had journeyed with the ill-fated Mier Expedition on the last of the raiding expeditions south of the Nueces River. Ill-fated in that he and 176 Texans were captured. Antonio Lopez de Santa Anna ordered the execution of the Texans. Governor Francisco Mexía of the state of Coahuila and others were able to get the decree modified so that every tenth man was ordered to be executed. Later known as the Black Bean Episode, seventeen black beans were included in an earthen jar containing a total of 176 beans. The seventeen men who drew black beans were blindfolded and shot. Captain Cameron did not draw a black bean, but Santa Anna ordered his execution anyway for being the leader.[6]

Given these violent events, along with traumatic Civil War experiences, the likelihood of the iconic cowboy evolving from these circumstances seems remote. As the various war veterans and loose-end drifters went up the trail, they were somehow shaped into worldwide icons of heroism and admirable manhood. The cultures and heritage of the young men must have played a part. Roughly equal numbers of young men of Mexican and Anglo descent made up the majority of the northbound drovers. They were seasoned by the violence of political differences, revolutions, the Civil War, and long-term conflicts in South Texas among Mexicans, Texans, and Americans.

Some of the deeds they left behind and some of the responsibilities of their trail job shaped the drovers as they worked their way north. They were free from the constancy of border wars and from government oversight. They were "on their own," a liberating situation they had never experienced before. Yet they had responsibilities for the safety and care of the cattle, and they had to manage the tedium and daily dangers of life on the trail. Thus, they came to realize the implications of their freedom, which helped shape their new perspectives. Within their freedom of movement up the trail, they were bound by their word to deliver the cattle safely to buyers at the railheads or to markets farther north.

Cameron County was the southernmost county in Texas in the Nueces Strip and the first county the Great Western Trail crossed going north. Albert Perez and Bill Stirling led the Brownsville Sunrise Rotary research team that verified and marked the route. Perez devoted numerous hours to locating evidence of the trail. They found that the path went north from the border across the most accessible path on the near-level coastal plains in Cameron County. The route later became US Highway 281. After passing through creosote brush country to Escantada, the trail turned north-northwest to Santa Rosa where the ground started changing to tall bluestem grasses and continuing on to a mesquite grass region.[7] To place markers every six miles along that route, a person with a pickup and skills for mixing cement and digging postholes was required. However, the first task was for someone to drive from Cameron County 620 miles to Vernon in North Texas to pick up the six 225-pound posts. The man who met the challenge was Bill Stirling. He used a trailer from his business and supplied wraps to cushion the posts for the ten-hour drive.

On June 2, 2006, the Brownsville Sunrise Rotary Club dedicated the commemorative marker at Prax Orive Jr. (Sunrise Rotary) Park. A large crowd gathered at the popular park that featured a small lake and weeping willow trees. After the introduction of dignitaries and out-of-town visitors, Hector Hernandez, the club president, told of the research team's efforts in their county. He spoke of the heritage of members whose families had settled on Spanish land grants prior to the trail days. Proclamations and resolutions reaffirmed the history of the GWT and recognized the shared trail heritage from Mexico to Canada. Water from the two rivers that define the north and south borders of Texas, the Rio Grande and the Red River, flowed down the marker as audience members participated in the ritual of dedication unique to the marker celebrations.

Shan Rankin Accepts Map of the Route of the GWT across Texas

A map commissioned by the Red River Valley Museum and drawn by Gary Kraisinger indicates the route of the GWT across Texas. Mary Ann McCuistion, executive director of the Red River Valley Museum, and Mickey Sharp presented the map to Shan Rankin, executive director of the Museum of South Texas History in Edinburg.

June 2, 2006, Edinburg, Texas, Dedication in Hidalgo County

The next dedication on the path of the GWT as it carried cattle northwest was in Hidalgo County at Edinburg, the county seat. The trail passed north on the eastern side of Hidalgo County; however, the markers were placed in the county seats. Three dedication ceremonies were held on June 2, 2006, at Edinburg, Donna, and Brownsville, and a fourth was held on June 3 in Matamoros, which is the reverse order to the path of the trail. (The fourth dedication during those two days, at Donna, Texas, is described in Chapter 1.)

The trail left Cameron County going northwest into Hidalgo County for a short distance. Then it crossed the tip of the southwest corner of Willacy County, re-entered Hidalgo County, and went toward Brooks County, bypassing Edinburg. From there the path went almost due north to San Antonio.[8] The next four dedications occurred on that route toward the next supply point at San Antonio.

GWT Marker Dedication, Museum of South Texas History, Edinburg, Texas
On June 2, 2006, in Hidalgo County at the Museum of South Texas History in Edinburg, Mark Peña, Rotary president (left), introduced County Judge Ramon Garcia, Commissioner Oscar Garza, and keynote speaker Texas Representative Aaron Peña. Others present included Rotary leaders Dr. David Fridie, Jorge Verduzco, Sylvia Mahoney, Dave Mason, Bill Huskinson, and museum director Shan Rankin (not pictured).

At Edinburg, a new museum was selected to be the site for the marker dedication. Fortunately for the local trail researchers, the Museum of South Texas History, with panoramic exhibits of area history, included information on the Great Western Trail. During the ceremony, Executive Manager Shan Rankin explained the exhibits and the symbolism of the design details of the recent $5 million expansion.

Due to rain, the ceremony was held inside the museum. Mark Peña and Tamara Sanchez, leaders of the Edinburg Rotary research team, organized the dedication ceremony. Along with State Representative Aaron Peña and other elected officials speaking at the dedication, the trail teams asked for support for a Congressional bill to designate the GWT and the Chisholm Trail as National Historic Trails. The trail teams, especially Rotary district leaders Jorge Verduzco of Laredo and Jim Aneff and David Mason of Abilene, continued this request at each dedication. Within three years, a Congressional bill was passed (see Chapter 10 for additional information).

From Hidalgo County, the herds continued across the east side of Brooks County, traveling north through bluestem grasses that provided forage for the cattle and horses. During the cattle-trail days, this area was sparsely populated because of its location within the Nueces Strip. Twenty-five Spanish and Mexican land grants had been awarded in the area that would become Brooks County. Despite this legal fiat, most of the land grantees avoided this violent area during the time between the Texas Revolution and the Mexican-American War.[9] Although these wars occurred prior to the GWT days, the violence in this area continued, exposing drovers and their herds to constant risk.

March 17, 2006, Falfurrias, Texas, Dedication in Brooks County

On March 17, 2006, the next dedication took place in Brooks County at Falfurrias. The commemorative marker was set on the front lawn of the Heritage Museum. A crowd of dignitaries attended the dedication. Lisa Ann Molina-Montalvo, museum president, gave an oral history of the area as visitors toured the museum prior to the dedication.

Robert Scott, Rotary trail-team leader, was an unexpected and welcomed primary resource. He traced his roots to the cattle-trail days. His great-great-grandfather Darius Rachal, a trail driver and rancher at White Point on Nueces Bay, became known for moving his herds at a fast pace to Kansas, then fattening them after they arrived. The standard practice was to move the herd slowly, letting them graze and fatten on the way to the railhead. Rachal's name became a term used by trail bosses when they wanted the drovers to move cattle faster. They would say, "Rachal 'em, boys, rachal 'em." In other words, move the herd faster.[10]

Fifteen Falfurrias High School students/historians attended the dedication. They had written an award-winning history project about the open-range ranching era in South Texas. It was titled "The Open Range, Cattle, and a Mission: Our Ranching Heritage" and was written by Ethan Shane Wilson, Christopher Andrew Morales, and Marlene Renée Morales. By virtue of its placing twelfth in a national history competition, the project was displayed by the National Museum of American History in Washington, DC. At the GWT dedication, each of the students, one-by-one, stepped up and dedicated the GWT post with Red River water poured from a Mason

High School Students with Award-Winning Project, Falfurrias, Texas
On March 17, 2006, award-winning student historians at Falfurrias High School attended the first GWT marker dedication in Brooks County at the Heritage Museum. Afterward, at the school, history teacher Sharon Wilson, Ethan Shane Wilson, Christopher Andrew Morales, and Marlene Renée Morales displayed their Smithsonian-award-winning research project titled "The Open Range, Cattle and a Mission: Our Ranching Heritage."

jar. One student said when I passed the jar to her, "Oh, I am so nervous." When she looked at me, I knew this action had connected her to the trail era. However, credit for her understanding the historical moment should be given to her teacher Sharon Wilson, who had guided the students through their award-winning project.

The trail team's visit to the high school to review the students' project supported both of our history research efforts. Among their resources, they mentioned major libraries, documents at Spanish missions, and the historical remnant of Rancho De Las Cabras, the only known mission ranch headquarters today. One student said that at the Dolph Brisco Center for American History at the University of Texas, "We were able to hold and read Don Bernardo Galvez's 1779 letter [in Spanish] about cattle for troops fighting in the American Revolution." This cattle-for-troops information gave the trail team a common point for discourse about the delivery of contracted cattle with the well-read students. In addition, we noted the students' research skills were enhanced by being bilingual.

March 17, 2006, Alice, Texas, Dedication in Jim Wells County

Leaving Brooks County, the trail progressed along the eastern side of Jim Wells County, crossing the northwest corner of Kleberg County for a few miles. The area served as a dividing point between brush country to the west and coastal plains to the east. The South Texas strip of land between the Nueces River and the Rio Grande is now known as the Llanos Mestenos, the Wild Horse Plains. The county seat of Jim Wells County, Alice, Texas, was named for the daughter of rancher Richard King. Alice married Robert Justus Kleberg, the legal adviser and ranch manager of the King Ranch, located southeast of the town.[11] The county was named for developer J. B. Wells Jr., a longtime Democratic boss for South Texas. Wells, an attorney and resident of Brownsville, specialized in settling land titles and disputed areas in the Nueces Strip; his cases accommodated land acquisition, especially for Anglos. After his partner Kleberg's death, Wells succeeded him as attorney for the King Ranch and Mifflin Kenedy.[12]

The GWT researchers' first contact with Jim Wells County citizens was at a meeting at the Alice Country Club on May 25, 2005. Homer Anderson, Jim Doughty, and other members of the Rotary club responded quickly to the project proposal. Doughty and the Hoffman brothers, George and Roger, ages ninety and eighty-six, had ties to the trail. George said the trail had crossed his ranch. George's son Charlie Hoffman corroborated in an email on June 28, 2005, that the trail crossed their ranch: "In the old days, the ranch was situated in a long east-west continuous piece of land that ran from today's Hwy 281 south of Alice, westward to just south of Freer, some 250,000 acres. It is not so today, but still relevant historically." Through communication with people owning land the trail crossed and others native to the area, verification for the trail was secured. A marker dedication was scheduled.

With the assistance of Jim Doughty, the project quickly moved forward. He called me to say that he would fly to Vernon to pick up the post. His plans changed, however, when he decided to pick up and deliver posts to Jim Wells County and four other South Texas county seats. Doughty drove his heavy-duty pickup with a trailer from South Texas to Vernon to collect the five 225-pound posts. He carefully cushioned the posts for the nine-hour

GWT Marker Dedication, Jim Wells County Courthouse, Alice, Texas
Participants at the dedication of the GWT marker, located on the Jim Wells County Courthouse lawn, were ranchers George and Roger Hoffman, ages ninety and eighty-six, who own ranches the trail crossed, and Jim Doughty, club president and project leader (wearing a necktie), who picked up posts in North Texas and distributed them to several of the South Texas counties.

trip back to Alice. Doughty, a constable born in South Texas in Hebbron-ville, knew people at all the county courthouses—he was able to secure help to unload a post at each courthouse. The South Texas Rotary trail teams were pleased, even relieved, to have Doughty provide this service.

The next spring on March 17, 2006, the Vernon Rotary trail team returned to Alice to dedicate a marker on the lawn at the Jim Wells County Courthouse. Doughty, local Rotary president and trail-team leader, and the Hoffman brothers recalled county and ranch histories.

Two nationally known large ranches, the King Ranch and Los Laureles, had brought recognition to this area of South Texas. The owners kept records that verified the number and destination for the cattle they sent north. In 1860, Mifflin Kenedy partnered with Captain Richard King in the steamboat industry on the Rio Grande during the Civil War and bought an interest in the King Ranch. Today, the 825,000-acre King Ranch spreads into Nueces, Kenedy, Kleberg, and Willacy Counties. In the 1880s, King crossbred Brahma bulls and shorthorns to produce the famous Santa Gertrudis cattle, which was officially recognized as a breed in 1940. Although the longhorn had been the foundation cattle for the King Ranch, the ranch owners added the new breed to continue efforts to expand their production of marketable cattle adapted to the South Texas ecosystem.[13] Eventually, King and Kenedy ended their ranch partnership, and Kenedy purchased and developed Los Laureles.

Unpublished, long-forgotten letters written by Mifflin Kenedy, who owned Los Laureles Ranch with his wife Petra, provided new verification for cattle that trailed north. The letters, published in 2007, gave specific numbers of cattle that went to Kansas using the two trails: the GWT to Dodge City and (earlier) the Chisholm Trail to Abilene. Richard King started sending cattle north before Kenedy did because Kenedy was busy with business in Brownsville. The letters document the years between 1869 and 1885 when Capt. King sent 70,000 head up the trail. In 1875, he made a net profit of $50,000 on a single herd of 4,737.[14]

From 1876 to 1878, Kenedy wrote about his herds that went to Dodge City, Kansas, and Ogallala, Nebraska. In 1876, he sent ten thousand head. On July 4, 1877, Kenedy arrived in Dodge City with eighteen thousand head of cattle and four hundred mules. In September 1877, he delivered 2,500 to Ogallala, Nebraska. The record of a murder in Dodge City provided documentation that the Kenedys were there in 1878. On one trip, Petra and Mifflin Kenedy's twenty-three-year-old son James "Spike" Kenedy stayed in Kansas to winter the cattle. On August 17, 1878, he accidentally killed Dora Hand, a popular honky-tonk singer, while trying to kill someone else. He was pursued by Ford County Sheriff Bat Masterson, Deputy Sheriff William Tilghman, Marshal Charley Bassett, and Assistant Marshall Wyatt Earp. The Kenedys went to Dodge, cleared Spike (through some political connections), and took him back to Texas. Capt. Kenedy's stories and unpublished letters re-created the Spike Kenedy and Dora Hand tragedy.[15]

The trail continued north for a short distance in Jim Wells County and crossed the northwest corner of Kleberg County. From there, it entered Jim Wells County again. Then the trail turned almost due north into Live Oak County, passing west of the town of George West. Some ten miles north of George West, drovers reached the confluence of the Atascosa, Frio, and

J. Frank Dobie Historical Marker, Live Oak County Courthouse, George West, Texas
Near the GWT marker in Live Oak County, two native sons are honored with a glass display case and a historical marker on the courthouse lawn. Drover George West's lead steer, Geronimo, is displayed in a glass case. The marker honors J. Frank Dobie, an author noted for his books about longhorns and cowboys.

Nueces Rivers. This site was important to the drovers because they had reached the northern boundary of the infamous Nueces Strip.

Live Oak County claims two native sons who brought national recognition to the trail era. J. Frank Dobie gained recognition for influencing the acceptability of longhorns and cowboys as subjects for literature. George W. West influenced the business of making money on trail drives north, investing in ranch land, and helping to colonize the area. They are honored on the George West County Courthouse lawn: Dobie with a historical plaque, and George W. West with a full-size glass display case for his longhorn, named Geronimo. The town was named for George W. West.

One possible reason that the GWT's history has rarely been considered for academic study could be akin to the problems that faced J. Frank Dobie while he was a faculty member at the University of Texas. For sixteen years, Dobie lived on the ranch where he was born in Live Oak County. His first-hand knowledge of ranch life equipped him to write about the cowboy, the longhorn, and their effect on the culture of the Southwest and America. Despite his real-life, grassroots experience, the academic world viewed those topics as unworthy subjects for a professor's scholarly study. Nonetheless, Dobie's works brought credibility and recognition for the trail era to the academic community and his promotion to University of Texas professor.

Dobie persisted in his endeavor to elevate the subject of the cowboy and the longhorn to their rightful place in the academic world. In 1922 Dobie became secretary of the Texas Folklore Society, and he began a publication program that supported his efforts to recognize the trail era. Dobie resigned his university position to manage his uncle Jim Dobie's ranch, Rancho de Los Olmos.[16] His fortitude resulted in success. His book *The Longhorns* and fifteen other works continue to be sought after by readers. His literary success led to his return as a professor to the University of Texas. Dobie said, "The Texas Longhorn made more history than any other breed of cattle the civilized world has known."[17]

The other favorite son, George W. West, made history with his many trips up both the Chisholm Trail and the Great Western Trail. West's childhood was brief. By age ten, he became a cowboy, doing a man's job. In 1867–1868, at age sixteen, he was one of the first to drive longhorns to the Kansas railheads. Through 1882, West drove cattle to Kansas, Colorado, South Dakota, Wyoming, and Montana. Although the youngest on the drive, he was the trail boss for a government contract to deliver 14,000 head to the Rosebud Indian Reservation in Montana. (The South Dakota reservation once extended into Montana.) Later, he divided his ranch to build a town with a courthouse, school, water works, light plant, and hotel. He donated $100,000 and free right-of-way through his ranch to secure a railroad line for George West.[18] Dobie admired West and used his anecdotes and tales in *Cow People* and *Voice of the Coyote*.

June 2006, George West, Texas, Dedication in Live Oak County

In June 2006, the Three Rivers Rotarians dedicated a GWT post near the Live Oak County Courthouse in George West on land set aside to honor the pioneers who settled the area and the events that led to their success. Jorge and Olga Verduzco traveled hours across South Texas from Laredo to present the post to the towns of Three Rivers and George West. Businesspeople from both towns belonged to the same Rotary club, and they gathered to commemorate their shared trail history.

Leaving Live Oak County, the trail crossed the three rivers and entered

Atascosa County where the drovers watered their cattle in the Atascosa River. With the river channeling through the grassy prairie, cattle traders and ranchers recognized it as good ranch land. A settlement, named Pleasanton, provided supplies for the area. It later billed itself as the "Birthplace of the Cowboy." That name could be justified if a list were made of area cowboys who were trail bosses, respected ranchers, cattlemen, and business leaders. To name a few, the list would include John T. Lytle; George W. West and his brothers, Solomon and Isaac; and John Blocker.

John T. Lytle was the first to claim a priority place in GWT history. In 1874, Lytle forged a new trail following a western route. He recognized that the Eastern/Chisholm Trail would no longer be viable for delivering cattle to Kansas with new state quarantine laws restricting the passage of trail cattle through the eastern counties. So, he moved his herd of 3,500 cattle west to an unrestricted passage going north. He trailed them up the edge of the frontier and delivered them to Red Cloud Indian Agency at Fort Robinson, Nebraska. Lytle had gathered the cattle near what is now Lytle, Texas, in Atascosa County. Earlier, in 1871, John Lytle and his cousin Thomas M. McDaniel had formed a partnership to herd cattle to Kansas. After several successful trips north using the Eastern Trail, Charles A. Schreiner of Kerrville and John W. Light of Kimble County joined Lytle and McDaniel. Their corporation was credited with a half-million head being trailed north up both trails.[19]

Lytle's business career highlights aspects of emerging cattle-related businesses during the trail era. Lytle, George W. Saunders, and Jesse Presnall established the Union Stock Yards in San Antonio. Lytle and partners bought the half-million-acre Piedras Blanca Ranch in Coahuila, Mexico. He was a founder of the Southwest Livestock Commission Company at Fort Worth. In 1904, he was named secretary for the Texas Cattle Raisers Association and served until his death in 1907.[20] The success of these cattle-related enterprises and organizations attest to the strong characters of the men who risked investing in emerging cattle-trail businesses.

June 2005, Pleasanton, Texas, Marker Delivered to Atascosa County

Pleasanton's cattle trail history made it a fitting place to locate a Great Western Trail post. It was the last stop on the old Matamoros Trail before it reached San Antonio. In June 2005, the Vernon trail team co-chair Jeff Bearden delivered a marker to Rotarians Odis White and Gene Clements. In 2011, Paul Noack, president of the Texas chapter of the Great Western Cattle

Trail Association, took photos of each GWT marker from Brownsville to Ogallala, Nebraska. When he asked about the marker in Pleasanton, he was directed to the future location in front of City Hall where he took a GPS reading for his records.[21] Although he didn't know when or whether the post had been placed in its permanent location, he included the GPS coordinate on his list of trail post locations.

The path of the Great Western Trail has been verified as following the same path as the Matamoros Trail from that city to San Antonio. To create recognition for the GWT, citizens from the six counties on the Matamoros Trail have marked its path with white GWT markers. Recognition for the two cattle trails west of Brownsville along the Rio Grande from Laredo and Eagle Pass have yet to be attained through formal trail research and verification. The project provides an opportunity for academicians to further research the path of the trail and document its continuing influence on the economy, the culture, and the ethics of the region. Without longhorns and cowboys/drovers from South Texas going up the trail after the Civil War, Texas and the Great Plains would have been vastly different than they are today.

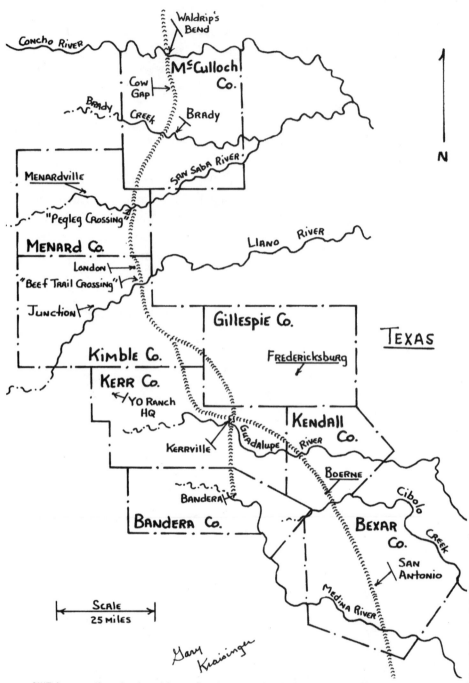

GWT from southern border of Bexar County across Kendall, Kerr, Kimble, Menard, and McCulloch Counties

CHAPTER 4
San Antonio to the Heart of Texas

When the drovers from Matamoros arrived at San Antonio in Bexar County, the first major cattle-trail hub, they had been on the trail approximately three weeks. Trail bosses would take on new supplies, prepare for the trip to the next major supply stop, Fort Griffin, and visit places for entertainment. From San Antonio, the trail veered to the northwest and then moved almost due north, traveling to the area known as the heart of Texas. Trail teams in Bexar County and the next six counties verified the route for this part of the trail and scheduled dedications to promote trail history.

San Antonio, a crossroad of cultures, became a hub for entrepreneurs to invest their trail-earned wealth in new cattle-related businesses. San Antonio's size and being a major supply town for the Chisholm Trail and later the Great Western Trail supported a growing cattle economy. The names of the trails were never a concern for the business leaders in San Antonio—their concern was the number and flow of the herds going to northern markets and promoting their cattle-related businesses.

Although the Great Western and Chisholm Trails carried cattle north, one took a path to the east and later, the other took a path farther west. Two things did not change when the trail moved west; the Matamoros Trail continued to be the common name for the trail to San Antonio from the south, and drovers called the next segment of the western trail Fort Griffin.

In modern metropolitan San Antonio, the name GWT prompted questions from Rotary clubs, who initially had less interest than the rural citizens in marking the path. The city's vast, diverse historical sites, such as the Alamo and the more recognizable Chisholm Trail, made the recognition of the GWT seem inconsequential. Many San Antonio cattle-related businesses had branch offices up the Chisholm Trail in Fort Worth, thus linking the two major cities to that trail. The GWT went west instead, toward Fort Griffin. The path through a less populated area benefited the drovers, but it compromised the GWT's chance for publicity. Fort Worth's famous cowtown image and Chisholm Trail roots far overshadowed in the minds of San Antonio citizens their connection to the GWT.

Competition for cattle during the transition period between the two trails created a rivalry for dominance between Fort Worth and Fort Griffin. Some trail bosses left Fort Worth and connected with the GWT at Fort Griffin. That fort, which once catered to buffalo hunters, offered supplies and entertainment to trail herders. Both Fort Griffin and Fort Worth businesspeople encouraged cattlemen and trail bosses to move their herds to their town. ". . . *The Democrat* in Fort Worth berated the merchants there for letting this business slip out of their hands. This through drive is worth thousands of dollars to any city."[1] For a brief time, the Chisholm Trail and the GWT overlapped in origin and destination to Dodge City. Drovers, finding the route of the new trail west to be shorter, soon made it the primary trail. This brief overlapping of paths created problems for the GWT researchers as well as for previous researchers who misconstrued it to be the Chisholm Trail only. Drovers could not disprove this assumption, nor did they know to disprove it, as trail stories faded with the passing of time.

The importance of San Antonio to cattle-trail history cannot be discounted. Its location positioned it as a crossroad for cattle trails and cultures for decades as drovers moved herds across the Southwest to the Gulf and California. But the lack of a consistent and profitable market destination kept the cattle-trail entrepreneurs searching for new markets in California, New Orleans, and Missouri.

In 1857, Frederick Law Olmsted wrote in *A Journey Through Texas or, A Saddle-Trip on the Southwestern Frontier* that on his horseback tour with his brother, he observed a herd of cattle headed for California. Olmsted discovered that only a few people were paid wages: the old frontier men and experienced drovers. "The remainders were young men who wished to emigrate to California, and who were glad to have their expenses paid for their services."[2] Later, after the Civil War, drovers going north were hired to deliver a herd, and they often repeated the paid journey many times. Some of these cowboys eventually established successful businesses related to the

Gutzon Borglum, Bronze, Old Time Trail Drivers Museum, San Antonio
On September 3, 2007, a GWT marker was dedicated near the Gutzon Borglum bronze in front of the Old Time Trail Drivers Museum and adjacent to the Witte Museum. San Antonio Rotary leaders Bruce Flohr and Cliff Borofsky, Old Time Trail Drivers' Association President Pat Halprin, and Witte Museum President/CEO Marise McDermott directed the dedication of the GWT marker.

cattle industry. Others carved out ranches that are still operated today by their descendants.

Three major cattlemen, who eventually called San Antonio home, influenced the GWT in different ways. The first two, John T. Lytle and John R. Blocker, are chronicled in the Atascosa County section of Chapter 3. Lytle and Blocker are credited with being the first and last drovers to move large herds up the GWT. In 1874, Lytle made the initial trip, and in 1893, Blocker and his brothers made the final trip. In 1915, Blocker and George W. Saunders helped organize the Trail Drivers of Texas. Blocker was the first president, and Saunders was vice president and later president. They promoted the collection of oral interviews about life on the trail. In 1925, the interviews were published as a book: *The Trail Drivers of Texas* by J. Marvin Hunter. This collection of trail history, some thirty years after the trail days, provides one of the most significant sources of firsthand information on the cattlemen and trail drives.[3]

Saunders envisioned and started new businesses to meet the needs of the burgeoning cattle industry. In 1871, he went up the Chisholm Trail for the first time, three years prior to the opening of the GWT. A year later, he and a partner purchased a livestock commission in San Antonio. After selling the company, he drove horses to northern markets. In 1886, he joined two others in the livestock-commission business. In 1889, he helped direct the construction of the Union Station Stock Yards. By 1910, the George W. Saunders Livestock Commission Company had offices in San Antonio, Fort Worth, Kansas City, and St. Louis.[4]

Saunders, an example of trail-era ingenuity, saw opportunities practically everywhere. He introduced roping at the 1892 San Antonio Fair. He participated in the Southwestern Cattle Raisers' Association and the Texas Cattle Raisers' Association (now, Texas and Southwestern Cattle Raisers Association), powerful forces then and now in the cattle industry. He also promoted art to help preserve cattle-trail history: Saunders led efforts to bring sculptor John Gutzon de la Mothe Borglum (who sculpted the presidential heads at Mount Rushmore) to San Antonio to create a bronze sculpture as part of a trail drivers' memorial. It stands today in front of the Old Time Trail Drivers Museum near the Witte Museum.[5]

September 3, 2007, San Antonio, Texas, Dedication in Bexar County

On Labor Day, September 3, 2007, a large group gathered at the Old Time Trail Drivers Museum (OTTDM) in San Antonio for the dedication ceremony. The museum is a repository for cattle-trail memorabilia and historical documents. The white marker now stands near the Borglum sculpture. Approximately eighty people filled chairs set on the green lawn between the OTTDM and the Witte Museum. TV-news cameras arrived to publicize an event that was original news to many in San Antonio: the GWT went through their town. Witte Museum President/CEO Marise McDermott and the Old Time Trail Drivers' Association President Pat Halpin explained the significance of the GWT to San Antonio. Bruce Flohr and Cliff Borofsky, district and Alamo Heights Rotary leaders, recognized four trail descendants: Jason Fritz, Michael Austin, and Jack and Evelyn Kingsbery. Marco A. Barros of the San Antonio Area Tourism Council, forwarded DVD copies of the TV coverage to me, and wrote, ". . . so that you can see the great coverage for Rotary and your community project."[6]

September 2, 2007, Boerne, Texas, Dedication in Kendall County

After leaving Bexar County and the coastal plains, the herds entered Kendall County. This area, known as Texas Hill Country, is noted today for its profusion of bluebonnets and grazing longhorns. The path advanced northwest to Beckman and trailed along the east bank of Leon Creek to Leon Springs, a good watering spot. (Later, the trail route from Leon Springs became Highway 87.) From there, the trail crossed two creeks, Balcones Creek and Cibolo Creek, where it veered west of Boerne.[7] The mesquite-shrub and short-grass area offered a route for the herds to circumvent the Balcones Escarpment, a fault line that forms the eastern boundary of the Hill Country and the western boundary of the coastal plains. The Edwards Plateau, which defines the Great Plains on the south, lacked deep soil for farming, so it became an outstanding area to graze cattle, where they fatten well.[8] The Guadalupe River with spring-fed streams flowing into it goes from west to east through picturesque hills north of Boerne.

GWT Marker Dedication, Agricultural Heritage Museum, Boerne, Texas
The first GWT marker in Kendall County was dedicated on September 2, 2007, in Boerne, Texas, at the Agricultural Heritage Museum. Ron Cisneros, Rotary president (shown speaking), organized the event with the help of Robert Cisneros, John Krause, and other community leaders.

When we visited Boerne, the structure of buildings and the choices for restaurants reflected its mix of Spanish and German cultures. During the dedication, Ron Cisneros, Rotarian and historical commission member, explained the selection of historical sites for their three markers. One was placed at the main plaza in downtown Boerne. Another was set along Boerne Stage Road, once a part of the Old Spanish Trail highway system. The third one was placed at the Agricultural Heritage Museum, the dedication site.

On September 2, 2007, about eighty people gathered on the front lawn of the Agricultural Heritage Museum where Cisneros and Boerne Sunrise Rotary members staged the dedication of the trail marker. A reception and luncheon at the museum afforded the group time to exchange ideas about documenting, preserving, and promoting trail history. After the luncheon, the group toured the extensive collection of antique farm and ranch equipment, an exhibit of an earlier time.

From Boerne, the trail went northwest into Kerr County. After crossing the Guadalupe River at Comfort, the herds moved along the north bank of Cypress Creek to Kerrville. At this point, thousands of cattle converged to continue their trip north. By the time the herds reached Kerrville, the South Texas cattle and horses had traveled some 350 miles up the Matamoros Trail. The two trails from Laredo and Eagle Pass converged at Castroville, then followed the winding Medina River to Bandera; near Kerrville they finally joined forces with cattle from the Matamoros Trail.

In Kerrville, Sue Whinnery, a Rotarian, took the leadership role in the planning and production of GWT marker dedications in Kerr County. She organized three dedications and coordinated agreements for the location of four markers in the county. The four-stop tour included, as the first stop, a photo opportunity at a marker in front of the Kerrville Convention and Visitors Bureau, and then continued with dedication ceremonies at the Museum of Western Art in Kerrville, the Y.O. Ranch, and Old Ingram Loop, all historical trail sites.

January 12, 2007, Kerrville, Texas, Dedication in Kerr County, at Museum of Western Art

The Museum of Western Art proved to be an appropriate location for the first dedication ceremony in Kerr County. Jack Steele, executive director, pointed out Western art inspired by the trail days and the cowboy culture. On the tour of the art gallery, Steele noted the importance of art to the preservation of trail history. The tour called to mind Southwestern historian C. L. Sonnichsen's statement about history and poetry being necessary companions: "History without poetry is dead, or is at least in a state of suspended animation. Call no man historian unless he makes you feel."[9] Instead of *poetry*, *art* would work equally well in that statement.

After the art tour, approximately sixty people gathered for the ceremony in a room framed by Western art. Many came to the ceremony at the invitation of the Kerrville and the Kerrville-Morning Rotary clubs. Judge Pat Tinley and Mayor Gene Smith emphasized the importance of art, the GWT, and the longevity of the Y.O. Ranch to heritage tourism in the area. The GWT marker was placed in front of the museum.

January 13, 2007, Historic Y.O. Ranch, Dedication in Kerr County

The next morning, January 13, 2007, the Vernon trail team left the Y.O. Ranch Hotel, which is decorated with Texas Hill Country stone, carved wood, polished brass, branding irons, brown-leather furnishing, and Western bronze sculptures and art. The historic name marketed the hotel while promoting the history of the cattle-trail era. The Y.O. Ranch is thirty-one miles west of Kerrville near the small town of Mountain Home. The ranch, established on the GWT in 1880, is like other major Texas ranches along the GWT that are still owned and managed by the same family that established it from funds earned trailing cattle to northern markets.

The large-monogrammed gate at the entrance of the ranch displays the famous YO brand. The first stop on dedication day was for lunch at the Chuck Wagon Lodge. Afterward, we gathered in the main lodge. On the cold January day, the logs in the man-tall fireplace crackled with warmth and welcome. The large room, made of native stone and furnished with leather and Western art, silently served to remind us of the ranch's deep roots in the cattle industry and the trail days.

Owners Gus and Lori Schreiner and their two small daughters welcomed us warmly. Somehow, the respect the Schreiner family had for their own family heritage was conveyed with the gentleness and warmth of their welcome. Their heritage was perpetuated in the names of the girls: Audry was named for her grandmother; Gasele's initials spell GUS, her father's name. Having seen the picture of Lori Schreiner and her two daughters on the cover of *Country Woman* magazine, I recognized them as I walked into the large, warm room.

GWT Marker Dedication, Y.O. Ranch Lodge with the Gus Schreiner Family
On January 13, 2007, Y.O. Ranch owners Gus and Lori Schreiner and their two daughters welcomed everyone to the GWT dedication ceremony at the ranch lodge. Afterward, the group toured the ranch to see the exotic animals and longhorns.

The teams' research revealed much information about business relationships, especially in counties around San Antonio, that helped promote success for the new trail-related enterprises. Several early powerbrokers in the cattle industry found success by forming partnerships. Captain Charles Schreiner and John T. Lytle, the cattleman who initiated the GWT, organized a partnership that included two other cattlemen, John W. Light and T. M. McDaniel. In 1880, Schreiner purchased the Y.O. Ranch with money earned on the cattle trail. Capt. Schreiner drove some 300,000 longhorns up the GWT to Dodge City. On the ranch, he developed a herd of longhorns marked with the YO brand. Youngs O. Coleman had first used the brand in 1840s on the Gulf Coast. In 1880 Captain Schreiner purchased the land, the cattle, and the YO brand used on the animals. That brand has identified the ranch since then.[10]

Generations of Schreiners have worked to keep the ranch profitable and respected. Charles Schreiner III, a grandson of the founder, understood the longhorns as representing more than just beef in the late 1800s.

Schreiner and others, in 1964, recognized the American icon was disappearing through interbreeding, so they established the Texas Longhorn Breeders Association of America (TLBAA). During Schreiner's three-year tenure as president, the organization started a Longhorn Registry.[11] To perpetuate the breed, the Y.O. Ranch partnered with Red McCombs Ranches and Dickinson Cattle Co. on a bull named Super Bowl, with seventy-two-inch horns T2T (tip-to-tip).[12]

A more recent and innovative use of the Y.O. Ranch land caters to hunters of native and exotic animals. On a tour of the ranch, the North Texas trail team, with the help of a guide, spotted some of the fifty species of native game, such as deer and turkey, that are on the property. The ranch also includes exotics, such as Red deer, Axis deer, and Nilgai antelope, and super exotics, such as Blesbok antelope, Gemsbok antelope, and Pere David deer.

After the ranch tour, approximately forty people helped dedicate the GWT marker in front of the historic lodge. Gus Schreiner said, "This ranch was born from cattle, banking, and mercantile." When he was a young boy, he recalled, the ranch had held a commemorative cattle drive. In 1965, the drive included one hundred head of longhorn cattle that were driven from San Antonio, forded the Red River at Doan's Crossing, and crossed Oklahoma to Dodge City, Kansas, where they were sold.[13]

January 13, 2007, Ingram, Texas, Dedication in Kerr County

After the Y.O. Ranch dedication, the group circled back to Old Ingram to dedicate another GWT marker. The trail to Old Ingram, located at the mouth of Johnson Creek, progressed northward from Kerrville along the south bank of the Guadalupe River. Near Old Ingram, the trail crossed the river and went up Johnson Creek to Mountain Home, near the Y.O. Ranch. At Old Ingram, near a State Historical Marker, the white GWT marker stands in front of an art center and galleries on the property of Harold and Judy Wunsch.

August 4, 2006, London, Texas, Dedication in Kimble County

From the Y.O. Ranch, the trail turned north toward Kimble County. This was Frederica Wyatt country, a noted GWT historian, Rotarian, and moving force for the Kimble County Historical Commission. She documented the locations for the five posts in Kimble County. She explained where the trail entered the county between the Pedernales and Little Devil's Rivers on the

Frederica Wyatt Dedicates First GWT Marker in Kimble County

Frederica Wyatt, respected GWT historian and Rotary leader, directed the dedication for the GWT project in Kimble County. In honor of her contributions, on August 4, 2006, Frederica was the first to christen the marker in London, Texas, near where the trail passed.

Peril ranches. East of Harper on Highway 290, Jaydeen Young and other Peril family members placed a marker on their ranch adjacent to the roadside. From there, the trail went north to the east fork of the James River, a tributary of the Llano River. Just below Noxville, Frederica's cousins Gene and Gayle Ake placed a marker at their Salt Block home, the site of the first settlement at Noxville. From there, the path went west, crossing a small chain of hills that paralleled the James River. The intersection of Kimble County Road 430 and FM 385 became the permanent location of a trail marker. Gwen and Sammy Plumley placed a GWT marker on their ranch on FM 385 to commemorate its history as a trail ranch.[14]

Then turning north, the drovers prodded their herds toward the Llano River. The cattle forded that river at a place historically known as "Beef Trail Crossing," just below the present-day crossing at Yates. A Texas Historical Marker designated that site as the place where a majority of the herds crossed the Llano River. Nearby, a GWT marker was installed at the home of Aaron Alexander. Paralleling present-day FM 385, the trail went through the landmark Reichenau Gap and into London.[15]

On August 4, 2006, the Kimble County dedication took place at London, a small town on the GWT. Frederica Wyatt and Derrick Ard, Rotary leaders, had made the trip to Vernon to pick up the six markers for their county. County Judge/Rotarian Delbert Roberts directed the installation of the marker posts. A crowd gathered at the London Community Center for the ceremony. Frederica's oral review of trail history included introductions of trail descendants. Sixty-seven registered Rotarians, trail descendants, citizens from eleven communities, and two Rotary exchange students from Germany and Switzerland helped spread the history of the trail from Texas to Europe.

Frederica Wyatt, a repository for GWT history, prepared a list of thirty-three GWT descendants from Kimble County. The list of drovers included dates of birth and death as well as burial locations. To mention a few: George W. Hodges was killed on an 1883 cattle drive; on another cattle drive, Isaac W. Baker II was murdered in Oklahoma; George M. Pearl, first cousin of Frederica's father (Matt Burt) went up the GWT to Miles City, Montana. Renowned photographer Laton Alton Huffman took Pearl's photo while he was there, and Huffman's fame helped corroborate Pearl's time in Miles City. Photos like this helped trace the path of the trail. Pearl returned to Texas and was later buried in the Little Saline Cemetery near London.

August 3, 2006, Menard, Texas, Dedication in Menard County

West of London, the trail followed the left bank of the Saline Creek until it reached the head of MacDougal Creek in Menard County. From there, the cattle crossed the San Saba River at Pegleg Crossing, twelve miles east of the county seat of Menard. The trail continued east along the north bank of the San Saba for five or six miles. From there it advanced northeast until it entered McCulloch County and proceeded to Calf Creek.[16] Tina Hodge, Menard Chamber of Commerce manager, immediately saw the potential for heritage tourism and began promoting the GWT to attract tourists to Menard.

On August 3, 2006, during the GWT ceremony, a taste of the old West came running through the city park in Menard. As a crowd of more than one hundred sat in the park, shaded by the live oaks, Tina Hodge alerted the

Oreo and Cowboy Craig, Menard, Texas

In Menard, Texas, Cowboy Craig attracted a crowd when he took his longhorn, Oreo, to the car wash to spruce him up for the GWT marker dedication at the park.

crowd to watch for Tommy Crisp and some working cowboys as they herded longhorns down Main Street to the park. When the longhorns reached the park, they spotted its lush green grass. They stampeded! The crowd loved it. Cowboys chased the longhorns across the park while the audience clapped and cheered. After the cowboys rounded them up, the ceremony began, and Hodge's special moment for the day became a true trail tale. Next, Cowboy Craig Davies entered on his black and white longhorn, Oreo. With many clicks of their cameras, the audience captured the saddled longhorn carrying a cowboy. Earlier, tourists had spotted Cowboy Craig shining Oreo up at a local car wash.

With longhorns, horses, cowboys, and flags setting the background, Tina Hodge's twin rodeo-cowgirl granddaughters, Sierra and Sheridan Hodge, sang the national anthem. Tina's ninety-year-old mother, Lois Sikes Beirschwale, took a ride on Oreo; like the trail drovers, Tina's family incorporated cattle and horses in their businesses. Hodge knew how to promote Menard, and she filled the program with congressional, state, and local

Menard Marker Dedication with Four Generations of Cowgirls

On August 3, 2006, cowboys herded cattle into the Menard park, the location for the first GWT dedication in Menard County. An unexpected cattle stampede preceded the highlight of the day, four generations of ranch/rodeo cowgirls who dedicated the post. Tina Hodge, chamber manager and event organizer (left), her ninety-year-old mother, Lois Sike Beirschwale, who rode Cowboy Craig's longhorn, Oreo, and Kim Todd Hodge listen to Tina's twin granddaughters, Sierra and Sheridan Hodge, sing the national anthem.

elected officials. Many local and area businesspeople (listed in the appendix) were in the audience. Steve Self, a local businessman, donated one post and dug the holes for the other six placed every six miles across the county. Four area radio stations and a TV station from San Angelo recorded the exciting dedication ceremony.

Menard, a small town rich in local history, had somehow overlooked the history of the GWT. It had historical ties to the Spanish colonial period, to the Texas forts era, to Alamo defender Jim Bowie, and to Jake Spoon, whose name was used in the novel *Lonesome Dove*. After the project was presented to them, Hodge scheduled the first twenty-first-century GWT annual event, "Around the Campfire on the Great Western Cattle Trail." Held at Stock Pen Crossing Park on the banks of the San Saba River, the covered pavilion filled the first year with more than 230 people who experienced cowboy poetry, music, storytelling, a chuck-wagon meal, and Dutch-oven desserts and snacks.

November 16, 2006, Brady, Texas, Dedication in McCulloch County

From Menard County, the trail advanced northeast to the Calf Creek tributary of the San Saba River in McCulloch County, approximately where Farm Road 1311 is today. Several minor trails from Mason, San Saba, and Lampasas Counties joined it there. The trail ascended that stream to its source and forded Brady Creek, where the cattle were watered, about six miles above the town of Brady. At this point, the trail struck a due-north course to Cow Creek and followed the western bank of that stream as it wound its way through Cow Gap, where the trail left the Hill Country. At Waldrip's Bend on the Coleman County line, near the mouth of Bull Creek, the cattle forded the Colorado River at Beef Crossing.[17]

Brady, the next dedication location, is in the Heart of Texas—the geographic center of Texas and the county seat for McCulloch County. Mark Day, an attorney and the lead trail-team volunteer for McCulloch County, personifies the spirit of both a Texas rancher and a drover. His roots run deep into Texas history and the Great Western Trail. His family history is analogous to the history of drovers who left Texas going up the trail. Mark Day had no club or association to support his efforts working on the project, but he said in an e-mail on September 11, 2006, that even if he didn't round up help, "I ain't quittin.'" Mark Day didn't quit; he did round up help to support his efforts.

On November 16, 2006, the GWT marker was dedicated on the grounds of the Heart of Texas Historical Museum, a Romanesque Revival–style three-story building that had once been the county jail. The museum president, Chris Leifeste, rancher Jim Ross, and others joined Mark in welcoming the Vernon trail team and in describing the trail's path across McCulloch County and their ranches.

Mark Day set a standard for finding and verifying primary sources for the trail. Mark said in an e-mail, "Oh, be forewarned, I am not much on shindigs. I will do whatever I can on getting the trail marked, but I don't do ceremonies, other than maybe describe the route of the trail in this county and offer thanks to folks." Day authenticated the path of the trail and marked it across McCulloch County with the help of other ranchers on the trail and with additional funding by local business people. Mark said, "We have 12 markers, all obtained from the Vernon Rotary Club and all located on privately owned land, with the exception of the one at the old jail (HOT Historical Museum), in addition to the State Marker at Cow Gap." Mark drew a location map and recorded GPS coordinates for each marker.[18]

Mark Day's passion for the project, in part, stemmed from his family's deep Texas roots. Like many drovers, Day's family members had served in three wars on American soil: Republic of Texas, Mexican-American War, and Civil War. The fact that family members served in three wars, wars that were fought to determine who would govern, was a heritage that many drovers' families had experienced. With the blood of their ancestors mixed in the Texas soil, the effect on the drovers as well as on Day cannot be discounted.

Mark Day's family history contains evidence of the power and passion inspired by memories of sacrifices, especially those of family members who gave their all to preserve their way of life. Mark said, "My GGGGrandfather, Andrew Kent, was killed in the Alamo. Kent County, Texas, is named for him. He was one of the Immortal 32, a member of the Gonzales Ranging Company of Mounted Volunteers, whose commanding officer was George Kimble for whom Kimble County is named." Mark's great-great-grandfather Bosman Clifton Kent was in Ben McCulloch's Company in the Mexican-American War. Kent served in the 2nd Texas Infantry Regiment in the War of Northern Aggression and as a Texas Ranger in Neal Coldwell's Company in 1874. Mark said, "I have the original letter from Bosman to his wife in 1864 from old Caney on the Texas coast after he and his unit had been paroled as Prisoners of War from the fall of Vicksburg."[19] This historical information about Mark Day's family roots is important to trail history. As the project progressed, it became evident that others along the trail with links to the land exhibited the same strength of character and passion for the land and for its history.

April 23, 2010, Bluff Pens, GWT Natural Holding Area, Rancher Murray Jordan

From the front porch of their ranch home, Mark said that he and his wife, Betzy, could see their neighbor's ranch where the Bluff Pens were located. The pens were a natural formation used as a holding area for bedding down cattle going up the trail.[20] Physical evidence of the GWT, such as Bluff Pens, is rare. Near where Brady Creek and Bowie Creek converge, Brady Creek

Murray Jordan and Mark Day, Aerial View of Bluff Pens, Near Brady, Texas
Brady ranchers Murray Jordan (left) and Mark Day view an aerial map of Bluff Pens, a natural U-shaped bluff formation on Jordan's ranch. Cowboys used the three-sided area to contain their herds when they bedded them down.

had cut ten- to forty-foot bluffs in the limestone that made a natural "U" with the open end to the west, near the location of Brady Lake Dam. The three-sided space became a natural holding pen. Springs fed the creeks even during drought times, and large trees gave shade along the creek banks.

Mark Day spoke with his friend V. Murray Jordan to arrange a visit to Murray's ranch, which now incorporates the Bluff Pens. We drove west of Brady to Murray's ranch headquarters to see an aerial map of the hundred-acre Bluff Pens area. From there, Murray took us in his Jeep to the "cabin with a view" on the bluffs that overlooked the valley.

The drovers herded the cattle into the natural pen and set up camp with the chuck wagon in the open end to the west. In places, they built stone fences to close off small areas where the creek moved on east. To build the fences, the men stacked large, flat limestone rocks without mortar. The natural pen with water and grass allowed the cattle and drovers to rest a day or two before moving north.[21]

Returning to town and to modern times, Murray took us to see his GWT marker, located about four miles northwest of Brady at the intersection of Highway 87 and Coleman Road. Murray agreed to a photo if Mark would stand with him by a special GWT marker with letters painted burnt orange, for the University of Texas Longhorns. Mark's marker had maroon letters, Texas A&M University colors. Here stood two men—football rivals—both attorneys who worked to uphold the law (Murray is a retired district judge), both had deep Texas roots, and both owned and operated ranches the trail crossed. Despite the obvious enjoyment of their football rivalry, their discussions implied that their friendship grew from their respect for the land and their understanding of the stewardship required to preserve it. They both recognized that others had their blood mixed into the soil to preserve their land and state as a place of opportunity for future generations. Although often subtle, others along the trail showed this same dedication to an earlier time of sacrifices, work, and responsibility related to making a living and a life on the frontier.

The economy in San Antonio, the largest city on the GWT, had boomed during the cattle-trail days. That boom continued with the establishment of cattle-related businesses. The GWT had been a presence through the years in most of the counties, and descendants had kept trail history alive. A rare physical rock formation used by the trail hands to secure their herds at night provides evidence of the trail days. As Walter Prescott Webb said in *The Great Frontier*, "It is hoped that this introductory study will open up a broad front of investigation, in the humanities and in the sciences, . . . and reveal just how important the opening and closing of the Great Frontier has been and will be in the history and destiny of mankind."[22] As we traveled the modern trail, it became apparent that the trail era united with earlier Texas history to produce people with a passion for that history, for their land, and for the values that are expressed by the legendary cowboy.

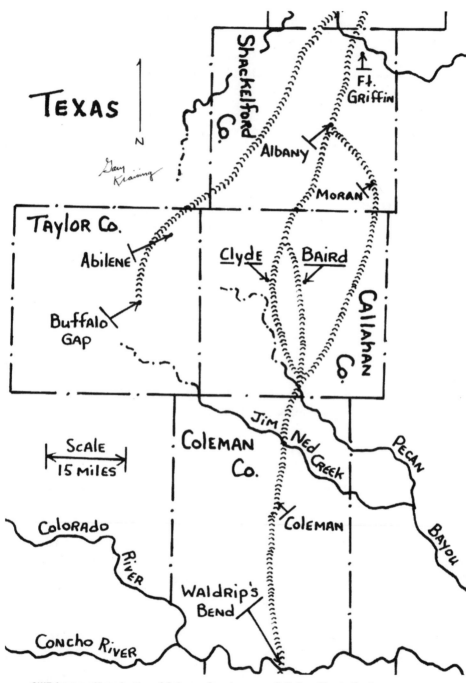

TEXAS

Shackelford Co.

Ft. Griffin

Albany

Moran

Taylor Co.

Abilene

Clyde   Baird

Callahan Co.

Buffalo Gap

Coleman Co.

Jim Ned Creek

Pecan

SCALE
15 MILES

Colorado River

Coleman

Bayou

Waldrip's Bend

Concho River

GWT from southern border of Coleman County across Callahan, Shackelford, and Taylor Counties

CHAPTER 5
Coleman, Callahan, Shackelford, Taylor Counties

At this point in Texas on the Great Western Trail, the drovers had been pushing their herds some four to five weeks. Getting to and crossing the Red River would take another three to four weeks. As the trail progressed slightly to the northwest, the terrain became more consistent as the route approached the border of Oklahoma [Indian Territory]. The herds traveled almost due north across grassy landscape with few obstructions. Coleman, Callahan, Shackelford, and Taylor Counties were prime country for drovers to establish ranches. Many of the ranches have been owned by the same families since the trail days, and their records added to the recovery of primary sources.

While visiting in these communities, some important aspects of trail history came into focus: positive changes in the roles for women and the conflict between homesteaders and open-range ranchers. In addition, the old nemesis of trail-name confusion resurfaced. But the modern ranch families were able to provide history for their drover ancestors that illustrated their legacy and documented the trail.

The small, rural towns on the trail in the next four Texas counties, some now struggling to survive, appeared from the road to be somewhat isolated from other parts of Texas. However, as we visited the towns, it became apparent that although people might be scarce, those few who remained made it clear that their past was powerfully tied to their present way of life. Personal memories, created from historical events and engagements in the cattle industry, had woven their way into a collective reminiscence. For the descendants, it was not academic history. It was family and ranch history tied to the land they still called home. The ties to the land, deep and resolute, influenced their families, businesses, historical societies, chambers of commerce, and communities.

From the last dedication in Brady, the trail continued almost due north, paralleling Highway 283 across the grassy, rolling plains into Coleman County. The peaceful countryside flourished with quail, deer, dove, and other wildlife—today, a hunter's paradise. The trail had once forded the treacherously deep Colorado River, which defines the county line between McCulloch County and Coleman County.

South of Coleman, according to drover Jasper (Bob) Lauderdale, cattle forded the Red Bank and Holmes Creeks. From there, the trail followed what is now Colorado Street in Coleman, through the center of town. Along the way, small feeder trails from the east and west enlarged the GWT with additional cattle and horses. In the northern part of the county, the herds watered at Jim Ned and Hords Creeks. The creeks there converged and flowed east as Pecan Bayou. The Southern Tom Green County–Concho River feeder trail merged with the GWT where the cattle forded Jim Ned Creek. Several small towns in the county, including Trickham and Santa Anna, once provided supplies for area ranches and feeder trails.[1] Today, they provide supplies for ranches and travelers.

October 31, 2005, Coleman, Texas, Dedication in Coleman County

The Coleman dedication on October 31, 2005, a cool rainy day, contrasted with the warm welcome the Coleman Rotarians offered the trail team at the Coleman County Courthouse. Judge Jimmy Hobbs, a Rotarian, offered the use of the courtroom to the group to escape the drizzling rain. Our easy access to this courtroom differed from the near absence of courtrooms, jails, and law enforcement on the trail during its heyday.

For this occasion, Joe Rose, Rotary president, welcomed the Vernon and Abilene Rotary trail teams. Some thirty-five people filled the courtroom. Heath Hemphill, a local rancher, explained the locations of the GWT markers in Coleman County. By the time the indoor ceremony ended, the rain had stopped. The post was placed in its permanent location on the courthouse lawn.

The local and visiting trail-team members discussed the perennial issue of the confusion between the name of the Chisholm Trail and the GWT, even in Coleman County. Knowing that the two trails parted ways at San Antonio, it seemed improbable that there would be confusion with two trails separated by some 140 miles. This time, the names of Chisum and Chisholm compounded the problem. Prior to the initial herd going up the GWT, cattleman John Chisum had maintained a ranch headquarters southeast of Coleman at Home Creek. He provided supplies for drovers at his store in Trickham, the first town in the county. In 1863, Chisum and other cowmen moved herds from the Denton area to Coleman County, where they soon had 18,000 head grazing along the Concho River near the junction with the Colorado River. In 1872 Chisum relocated to New Mexico near Roswell.[2] In 1958, Coleman County author Carolyn Rabon in the article "The Western Trail" said that tradition held that the man who gave his name to the Chisholm Trail once lived in Coleman County at Trickham. The same article said that the Chisholm Trail originated in the Brownsville–San Antonio area, ". . . and the Western Dodge Trail, began at San Antonio, and terminated at Dodge City, Kansas."[3] As early as 1958, the Chisholm Trail was credited with originating as far south as Brownsville, but the GWT, abbreviated, was limited to San Antonio.

The trail research project gained importance not only for discovering evidence of erroneous history but also for recovering primary sources of historical data. One ranch family member's personal collection was a rich resource. Heath Hemphill, Coleman Rotarian, attorney, and rancher, lives on a ranch that his great-great-grandfather established during the trail days. The lush, open-range grassland had caught the eye of his ancestor Dewitt County rancher J. P. Morris as he trailed cattle through Coleman County. Eventually, using his trail income, Morris returned with his wife Martha and established the largest ranch in the area. Morris was known for using a lead steer to help move his herds with ease. One year, in Nebraska on his way to Canada, he used his lead steer to help several other herds cross the swollen Platte River.[4] Records of incidents such as this one provide yet more trail primary sources and evidence of drovers giving a helping hand.

Another research method was the investigation of relationships among ranch families. These living connections identified names found in primary sources, ranch families' intermarriages, and the origins of herds delivered to northern markets. But they provided even more—they served as examples of trail culture, of the transitory workers, and of the permanent citizens. They served to provide links from the modern year to a yesteryear.

Heath Hemphill's extensive ranch roots began with marriages among two major ranch families in contiguous counties, Coleman and Callahan. Heath drew his family tree on a yellow legal pad for me. In 1913, Heath's great-grandfather Press D. Morris, son of a ranch founder in Coleman County, married Carrie McCoy, daughter of the founder of Belle Plain in Callahan County. In 1942, their daughter Josephine (Jo) Morris married her childhood sweetheart Zeno Hemphill.[5] Their son Joe Pat Hemphill and his wife had two sons: Heath and Brent. Heath said, "My wife, Danyelle, and I today live in their house (Jo and Zeno's) on the banks of the Jim Ned Creek."[6] Heath, the fifth generation to call the ranch home, talked about his respect for his family, the land, the water, the cattle, the horses, and the animals that were native to the land.[7] This vignette of a ranch-founder's descendants taking care of their families, the land, and the various animals for generations represents a common scenario discovered along the trail. This trail legacy is a strength that binds the people of like kind across the Great Plains.

In communities along the trail, historical evidence of societal changes became apparent. Family histories revealed the changing roles of ranch women. Their roles had evolved away from the stereotypical niches of cook, homemaker, and child bearer to cowgirl and even ranch manager. Rancher Carrie Morris was good with a gun, a rope, and a fishing pole. She helped her husband Press Morris "with the cattle work, and he helped her with the washing." Blending the two gender roles was a rarity during the early twentieth century. Heath said, "Both grandparents were very active in the management of the ranch. My grandmother Jo, Carrie's daughter, had survived two knee replacements and a quadruple bypass and continued to oversee all cattle work horseback on her gray mare."[8] Necessity, in part, freed ranch-raised women from societal restrictions against being owners/managers of ranches. Evidence showed the influences of place, time, and conditions on generational independence and self-actualization of women in these counties.

Another Coleman County cowgirl, Evelyn Bruce Kingsbery, raised on a ranch near Santa Anna, nine miles southeast of Coleman, had equally independent, self-sufficient women in her family. Kingsbery's grandfather John Banister went up the GWT in 1874, its inaugural year. He was elected Coleman County sheriff in 1914. Evelyn's mother, Leona Banister Bruce, at age sixteen, became his deputy because "she could drive a car and he couldn't." Sheriff Banister died in office, so his wife Emma Daugherty Banister was appointed sheriff on August 1, 1918, two years before women were enfranchised in the United States. She became "probably the first woman sheriff in the United States."[9] She instructed deputies, ran the office, managed prisoners, kept the records, oversaw the preparation of meals for her family and the prisoners, and did domestic duties for John's four children from a previous marriage and their five children.[10]

Leona Bruce grew up listening to the stories her mother told about the trail days, her grandfather, and her grandmother. She captured this history in a number of "well-known and well-reviewed books . . . a great leader and chair of the Coleman County Historical Survey Committee. . . ."[11] The characteristics of these strong but gentle women continued in Evelyn, who married a Santa Anna rancher's son, Jack Kingsbery. At college, Evelyn helped found a new college sport, college rodeo, governed by the National Intercollegiate Rodeo Association. She and other ranch-raised students aspired to compete in rodeo events on the collegiate level. She was the first woman elected to the national board. A review of female descendants of drovers indicates that possibly the lifestyle encouraged women to excel. Other examples were discovered while visiting one-on-one with trail teams.

Another aspect of the trail era was documented by the trail teams' research. The introduction of barbed wire affected Coleman and other counties along the trail. Resistance to fencing the open range engendered fence-cutting wars, not only in Coleman County, but across the Great Plains. In 1883, the Texas legislature changed the penalty for cutting fences from one year to five years imprisonment. The fence cutting came to an end soon after that.[12] However, the issue of open-range ranching versus homesteading captured national attention as a result of the level of violence, especially in Wyoming. This part of the history will be detailed when the trail project goes farther north.

On-site visits by the trail teams were compelling—each new location revealed new personal histories. The trail left Coleman going north, still following the route that would become US Highway 283. A short distance west of the present highway, the trail entered Callahan County. White seven-foot GWT markers are placed along the highway throughout the county: two at roadside parks located thirteen and sixteen miles south of Baird. The marker at mile number 13 joined a historical plaque that recognizes Heath Hemphill's great-great-grandfather Jasper McCoy, who established his ranch on Pecan Bayou in 1874. Two other markers were set at six and eight miles south of Baird. The final marker, the one dedicated, added a new dimension to the roadside park near Baird on Highway 283. It joined a railroad caboose, creating a setting symbolic of the trail days.

In Callahan County at Baird, Tommie Jones, chamber of commerce manager, offered her help in March 2005. She also enlisted Tom Ivey, a drover descendant. Ivey's advocacy for the project was immediate. After we met, he often sent copies of trail-history clippings to me from the *Callahan County Clarendon* archives and other sources. One primary source was a transcription of an interview with his father, Lee Ivey. Lee, born in 1888, helped his father, GWT drover Holley Ivey, drive cattle to town when he was eight. Later, Lee participated in cattle drives from Lubbock to Plains, Texas. Holley made two trips up the GWT, one to Montana and one to the Black Hills of the Dakotas. He worked for the Reynolds Cattle Co. and the Reynolds-Matthews Cattle Co. near Albany. Tom Ivey said that Lee went to the fourth grade, but "he had a whole head full of experiences about how to do things and could do them."[13] Again, a drover's history gave clues to the length of the trail when it mentioned the GWT going to Montana and the Black Hills of the Dakotas.

July 2, 2005, Baird, Texas, Dedication in Callahan County

On July 2, 2005, the Callahan County dedication ceremony took place, and it was a gala affair. The Callahan County Historical Society members and its president, Reggie Pillans, provided a ceremony replete with elements related to the historical moment. Ten members of the Vernon trail team and three Rotarians from nearby Abilene gathered at the Baird train caboose park at the intersection of Highway 283 and Business 20. To start the ceremony, the Callahan County Sheriff's Posse posted the US and Texas flags in front of the historic colorful railroad caboose. Drover descendant Tom Ivey told the crowd of approximately sixty people about the two trips his great-great-grandfather made. The Baird delegation invited the trail teams to a Texas-hearty lunch at the historic 1880 Baggage House Restaurant, originally used by the Texas & Pacific Railway.

Always in search of primary sources, a living resource presented himself when trail descendant Bill Hatchett, a lively eighty-something, invited us to his ranch east of Baird. He pointed to places where the cowboys bedded their herds near water holes. Along the way, he showed us a flat area where the cowboys held horse-race competitions. Bill also included a bit of history about the establishment of the county's management system. He directed the group's attention to a large tree with spreading branches that had shaded the first commissioner's court because it was too hot to meet indoors.

Drover Descendant Tom Ivey Speaks at GWT Marker Dedication, Baird, Texas
On July 3, 2005, the GWT marker dedication at the train caboose park in Baird in Callahan County started with the sheriff's posse presenting the flags. After the presentation of GWT resolutions and trail project history, drover descendant Tom Ivey recounted the life of his grandfather Holley Ivey who went up the trail twice.

On the way to the ranch headquarters, we stopped at Callahan City, once a supply point for drovers. All that remains is a small cemetery where 1888 is the most recent headstone date. At Bill's home, while we stood in the yard and looked across the valley toward the water holes, he recounted the stories of his drover ancestors. The cattle mooing in the distance created sounds reminiscent of the past. Again, as with the Bluff Pens near Brady, tangible evidence of the trail made its history a present reality.

Prior to entering Shackelford County, where the trail crossed Pecan Bayou south of Baird, it had split into three alternate routes for a distance across the grassy terrain. The most easterly trail went northeastward through Belle Plain, now a ghost town, and on to Moran in the eastern part of Shackelford County. The second alternate route, between the other two routes going north to Baird, was located almost in the center of the county. The third route took a northwest path to Clyde, a few miles west of Baird.

Drover Descendant Bill Hatchett on His Ranch, Near Baird, Texas

East of Baird, drover descendant rancher Bill Hatchett points to where cattle bedded down on his ranch on their trip north. (l-r) Mickey Sharp, Jeff Bearden, Hatchett, and Mary Ann McCuistion of Vernon, Texas.

The routes through Baird and Clyde, located today on Interstate 20, rejoined a few miles north of the two towns and continued as one trail into Shackelford County. It went to Albany, the county seat. The route through Moran rejoined the other trail at Albany. In 1883, a collateral branch of the GWT, first called the Potter-Bacon Cutoff, then, the Potter and Blocker Trail, went northwest from Albany across the Panhandle Plains and into Colorado. The infrequently used route, some twenty miles shorter than the main path of the GWT, proved risky because of the lack of water.[14]

In Callahan County, where the trail split into three paths, each path led to a supply town and had a grassy plains area on which to trail north. This might indicate that the trail bosses allowed their herds to spread across the plains to graze, since supplies were available on each route. However, a newspaper clipping from the *Callahan County Clarendon*, on May 14, 1881, stated that the blame for the diverging of the path of the trail was "laid at Baird's door . . . " The town of Baird denied that a man had been sent south to the "old beef trail" to turn the herds up the bayou to Baird and to Albany. The article opined that the stockmen did not like having cattle driven through their range. It said that the Texas Legislature had restricted the herds from grazing more than two miles from the road or trail. The Baird and Clyde routes were the most frequently used routes northward.[15] The truth about this controversy remains unresolved.

The history of the small town of Belle Plain illustrates the politics and competition for trail business, a problem common to the GWT and other trails. In the 1880s, trains frequently altered the geographical and social landscapes of towns by bypassing them, similar to the fates of towns today that are bypassed by interstate highways. The eastern alternate route had crossed Callahan County to Belle Plain, established in 1876. Belle Plain's broad streets had once been lined with stores, saloons, a jail, fraternal lodges, a newspaper, and Belle Plain College. This thriving community, located one mile east of Highway 283, eventually failed when the Texas Pacific Railroad bypassed it. This traversal enabled Baird, established in 1880, to become the county seat.[16] Previous to those times, supplies for drovers had been available at the first county seat, Callahan City, where Jasper McCoy and John Merchant operated a general store before moving to Belle Plain.[17] The small towns that failed to entice trail business and were later bypassed by the railroads became ghost towns.

October 27, 2007, Moran, Texas, Dedication in Shackelford County

From Belle Plain, the trail entered the southeast corner of Shackelford County and traveled along the eastern side to Moran. In 1882, the town was established when the Texas Central Railroad arrived. However, the railroad later closed its operations there. By 2000, the population of Moran was only 233.[18] Despite its limited population, Moran's residents are active in community events and knowledgeable about their trail history. In fact, one resident, rancher Bennie Parker called me and requested that she be allowed to join the research project and organize a dedication ceremony. The Vernon trail team readily accepted her request.

Bennie demonstrated talent for contacting ranchers and businesspeople in the area to support the research project. Since the eastern part of the GWT had split below Baird and traveled to Moran, Bennie ordered markers for that eastern route across Shackelford County. She brought her trailer and pickup truck to Vernon to get the markers. One was placed two miles south of Moran at the Joe and Bennie Parker ranch, which had been in the family since 1904. Another was placed north of Moran on FM 576 at the Bert Jones family ranch. A third one was located on Highway 180 at County Road 113. The fourth one was at the ranch of Morris D. and Cindy Snyder, located on the trail from Baird to Albany. The first settler in the county, C. B. Snyder, established the Snyder Ranch in the 1880s.[19] At Albany, the county seat, a marker was placed on the courthouse lawn. That location designated the town where two branches of the GWT rejoined as one trail on its way north.

The recognition of Moran's early-day participation in the GWT and the honoring of local school alumni at their annual Homecoming were combined to add local color to both events as well as to remind the attendees of their past history. Small towns such as Moran have large homecoming festivities built on high-school friendships that have been maintained over time by personal or social media networks. The Moran dedication included alumni such as James and Sara Shelton, from Bridgeport. Other area ranch owners, such as Fort Worth Rotarian/ranchers Ted and Nancy Paup, also attended. The Paups funded the marker for Moran.

Ted Paup is an example of the many ways trail history was inculcated into the lives of young people. As a youth, Ted spent time in a town that celebrated its trail history, Vernon, where his grandparents Mr. and Mrs. T. Edgar Johnson lived.[20] His family had owned a ranch near Albany, another town that had successfully marketed its early-day history. Ted's mother, Mary Frances "Chan" Driscoll, before her death in 2007, worked to preserve the Chimney Creek Ranch history with its ties to Fort Griffin, the Butterfield Overland Mail, the Reynolds-Matthews family, and the descendants of her grandfather, G. R. Davis.[21] To understand these connections is to understand the term *living history* of the trail. Early in life, trail history was ever-present for members of ranch families through local events and generational ownership of those ranches.

The eight-member Moran Amity Club, part of the Texas Federation of Women's Clubs, sponsored the dedication. The setting for the dedication, like a Hollywood Western, included cowboys, mules, steers, glamorous ladies, and cowboy brew. Rancher Morris D. Snyder and his cowboys drove fifty longhorns to the dedication. On their way to gather the cattle, Morris D., mounted on a mule, and his cowboys stopped to quench their thirst. It wasn't at a river, but at a "Party Barn" with drive-through service. The mounted cowboys rode right into the barn and placed their order. Morris D. dismounted, signed his credit card ticket, mounted, and they went south to gather the herd of cattle.

Cowboys in a Party Barn, Moran, Texas

On October 27, 2007, Shackelford County rancher Morris D. Snyder and his cowboys drove fifty steers to the GWT dedication at Moran, Texas. On their way to gather the cattle, Morris D., mounted on a mule, and his cowboys stopped to quench their thirst at a drive-through party barn. The mounted cowboys ordered; Morris D. dismounted, signed his credit card ticket, and remounted; and they moved on to herd the cattle.

With skills learned from many hours in the saddle, the Shackelford County cowboys eased the cattle down the bar ditch toward the dedication site and settled the fifty steers to graze behind the marker. One of the cowboys' ancestors was GWT drover Billy Wilson. Longhorns and cowboys made the perfect backdrop for Bennie Parker's marker dedication. She welcomed everyone. Her long, emerald-green taffeta gown with a bustle, matching picture hat, and black lace gloves created an ambiance of the past. The keynote speaker was Lester Galbreath, Shackelford County historian, retired director of the Fort Griffin State Park, and Longhorn manager. He wore a red bandana, suspenders, brown military boots, and brown pants. The crowd caught the spirit as they dedicated the marker with Red River water.

From Moran, the trail crossed lush, grassy, prairie ranch land to Albany, where the three branches became one trail again. The ranchers' conservation

Ted Paup and Bennie Parker Remove a Cowhide from the GWT Marker, Moran, Texas

On a fall afternoon in October 2007, at Moran, Texas, in Shackelford County, event organizer rancher Bennie Parker helped post donor Chimney Creek Ranch co-owner Ted Paup of Fort Worth remove a cowhide covering the GWT marker. Jeff Bearden, Vernon trail team co-chair, watches. In the background, fifty head of steers graze under the watchful eye of local cowboys.

practices provided cover and sustenance for indigenous animals, creating a hunter's paradise. Albany's annual outdoor musical drama, the *Fort Griffin Fandangle*, preserves and promotes the history and culture of the area. Held in northern Shackelford County along the Clear Fork of the Brazos River near Fort Griffin, the musical drama has kept the people close to their past. Dating back to 1937, the *Fort Griffin Fandangle* now boasts some four hundred cast and crew members, and members of the cast typically have ties to Shackelford County. Family members often referred to the year they were members of the cast, a much-sought-after honor—one similar to the annual crowning of the young queen and king at Doan's Picnic.[22]

This was Watkins Reynolds Matthews country, who brought fame to the ranch lifestyle and created popular interest in the area's history. The rancher (known as Watt), an unassuming old-time cowboy whose austere ways were coupled with a Princeton University education, is legendary in this part of the country. Watt, like a movie star, was often featured in the national media for his lifestyle and his ethics. He, like others from historical trail ranches, left an indelible imprint on the area, an imprint that captured the best of the past. The history associated with area ranches often defined the attitude and image of a town. Two books about Watt's family and ranch history kept the past alive in the Albany area. In 1936, Watt's mother, Sallie Reynolds Matthews, wrote *Interwoven: A Pioneer Chronicle*, and in 1982, a companion book, *Lambshead Before Interwoven: A Texas Range Chronicle 1848–1878*, written by Frances Mayhugh Holden, was published.

The draw for heritage tourism in Albany is interwoven in various ways with Watt Matthews, Lambshead Ranch, and the *Fort Griffin Fandangle*. Watt died at age ninety-eight in 1997. His funeral service typified the image he portrayed. The obituary article said, "His simple wooden casket, crafted by a local carpenter and furnished with patchwork quilt made by a friend, was placed atop bales of hay for viewing and surrounded by floral arrangements featuring barbed wire and cattle motifs. The casket was carried by a horse-drawn carriage to the ranch amphitheater where excerpts of the local extravaganza, the *Fandangle*, had been performed for more than 30 years." After the simple service, the mourners dined on the meal that Watt served each year at his annual *Fandangle* party: prime rib, green beans, and apple crisp.[23]

Fort Worth and Albany were two GWT towns that the Vernon trail team showed Dr. Frank Norris, the lead historian for the Congressional Feasibility Study, on August 5, 2009. Harold Hardcastle and Dr. Don Robinson showed Dr. Norris the route of the trail from Vernon to Seymour, Throckmorton, Fort Griffin, and Albany. At the Shackelford County Courthouse in Albany, Judge Ross Montgomery explained historical details about the courthouse dating back to 1883. He described the trail era, the first permanent jail built in 1878 (now a museum), and the restored downtown area. The preservation of the town's buildings added tangible evidence for visualizing and understanding the trail era.

The tour of Fort Griffin, led by site manager Mitch Baird and Longhorn herd manager Dr. Will Cradduck, included an observation of the official State of Texas Longhorn herd that peacefully grazed nearby. Dr. Cradduck knew the habits and temperament of each longhorn. Baird told the history of the fort and its twenty restored historic buildings, including the infamous

Frank Norris and Will Cradduck, Fort Griffin, Texas

The State of Texas has helped preserve a major player in the GWT days: the Texas Longhorn. On August 4, 2009, historian Dr. Frank Norris (working on a Congressional Feasibility Study) listened to Dr. Will Cradduck, the manager of the Longhorn herd at Fort Griffin, explain the history and merits of their herd.

Beehive Saloon. The fort, established in 1867 and overlooking a bend of the Clear Fork of the Brazos River fourteen miles northwest of Albany, provided protection for area settlers. Later, it became notorious for providing assorted entertainments to buffalo hunters, trail drivers, and those looking for a wild time.

In 1874, Albany replaced Fort Griffin as the county seat, which was also the first year cattle went up the Great Western Trail. It soon became a supply point for the two trail branches that joined south of Fort Griffin.[24] The part of Fort Griffin known as The Flat was a destination for a variety of folks. Located below the fort, the area provided supplies and entertainment for drovers and opportunists hanging around the town. It was also known as Hide Town, a carryover from the earlier brisk, lucrative buffalo-hide business. Its transitory residents included soldiers, buffalo hunters, drovers, gamblers, saloon girls, and outlaws who comingled lawfully, but as often lawlessly. This unruly frontier outpost attracted many who would become infamous. Loose women, referred to as "soiled doves," such as "Big Nose" Kate Elder, Lottie Deno, "The Poker Queen," and Millie McCabe spent time in The Flat. Joining them at Fort Griffin were notorious lawmen Pat F. Garrett, Doc Holliday, and Wyatt Earp, along with outlaw John Wesley Hardin. Adding to The Flat's reputation were others who vacillated between lawmen and outlaws, such as Shackelford County Sheriff John M. Larn and Deputy John Selman. The carriers for the Butterfield Overland Mail route, which passed north and west, and the GWT drovers added to the town's reputation.[25]

September 18, 2004, Dedication in Shackelford County at Fort Griffin

On September 18, 2004, a commemorative GWT marker was dedicated during a historical reenactment at Fort Griffin. The dedication scene reflected the trail era. Before the ceremony started, a steer hide covered the marker. Dressed in period clothing, Jeff Bearden drove his mule-drawn chuck wagon to a location behind the marker to create a background reminiscent of the era. The trail marker was placed near a Texas Historical Marker titled, "The Western Cattle Trail Crossings at Fort Griffin." It states, "By 1879, as rail lines extended across The Eastern Trail (Chisholm Trail) area, the Western Trail became the primary Texas cattle route and continued as such until the last drive, led by John Blocker in 1893."

The competition between Fort Griffin and Fort Worth for the cattle moving north is a rivalry often overlooked in trail history. When the Chisholm Trail's route to eastern Kansas railheads closed, trail bosses crossed the herds over to Fort Griffin. Being the shorter route, the Western Trail, in 1878, outnumbered the Chisholm Trail by about 50,000 cattle. In 1879 scathing editorials between the editors of the Fort Griffin and Fort Worth newspapers led to a monetary bet as to which trail was the dominant one. That year, the old Eastern Trail won by a narrow margin. After 1880, the Western Trail won outright through the end of the era.[26] This bet corroborated the transition from the Eastern Trail to the Western Trail, although South Texas people were unaware that the cattle drovers had shifted to the trail to the west.

April 29, 2006, Abilene, Texas, Dedication in Taylor County

The next dedication focused on an important feeder trail that passed through Buffalo Gap and Abilene in Taylor County. Cattle were trailed across that county thirty-five miles northeast to join the GWT at Albany. That pathway added thousands of longhorns to the main trail. Albany and Abilene, Texas, have much in common, except size. Both towns and Buffalo Gap have cap-

Crossing Catclaw Creek, **Bronze, by T. D. Kelsey, at Frontier Texas, Abilene, Texas**
On April 28, 2006, the first GWT marker in Taylor County was dedicated at the
Frontier Texas museum. The large bronze sculpture by T. D. Kelsey, *Crossing Catclaw
Creek*, depicted Anglo, Hispanic, and black cowboys driving eleven longhorn steers
across Catclaw Creek. The sculpture, according to the museum website, symbolizes the
importance of the GWT.

italized on their cow-town legacies. Abilene, while growing into a city with
three universities, continues to exhibit its Western roots with, among other
events, rodeos, cutting-horse events, and the interactive museum Frontier
Texas.

In the foyer at Frontier Texas, art and a longhorn steer head help visitors visualize the trail era. A large bronze sculpture by T. D. Kelsey, *Crossing
Catclaw Creek*, depicts Anglo, Hispanic, and black cowboys driving eleven
longhorn steers across Catclaw Creek. The sculpture, according to the museum website, symbolizes the importance of the Western, or Dodge City Trail,
and the influence of the longhorns on the area. The Texas Longhorn steer
head in the foyer, raised by Fayette Yates of Abilene, has a horn spread, tip
to tip, of six-and-a-half feet. Fayette's grandfather, Ira "Cap" Yates, was one
of the seven families that saved the Longhorn breed from extinction. A few

miles south of Abilene, Buffalo Gap Historic Village, located in a gap in the Callahan Divide, offers a Western frontier-town setting where buffalo once roamed and cattle herds once grazed.[27]

In 2005, David Stubbeman, Abilene Rotary leader, invited two of the Vernon trail team to introduce the trail research project to one of the three Rotary clubs. Paul Hawkins, Vernon Rotary president, and I presented the program. Following that, Abilene Rotarians became major advocates for the trail project. Jim Aneff and David Mason, both during their tenure as district Rotary governors, embraced the GWT with enthusiasm and became trail partners, traveling from Mexico to Canada. They also provided connections to other Rotary leaders across the trail states, making possible the recovery of additional primary sources.

Both Jim Aneff and David Mason have ancestors connected to the trail and Texas ranches. Instead of gold earned on a trail trip, Jim's grandfather went to the Klondike Gold Rush in 1898, married his Texas girl in 1900, and later they returned to Abilene using their earnings from gold to purchase ranches, some that showed evidence of buffalo wallows and Indian camps. When Jim was young, his parents returned to the Abilene ranch, where they lived for several years. Jim has continued that ranching legacy with ownership of another ranch near his grandparents' place.

On April 29, 2006, Jim united the Abilene marker dedication with the Rotary district conference at Frontier Texas. The two events came together with élan: the marker was paired with an almost life-size buffalo covered with wine corks to reflect the theme: "Abilene, where the fashionable buffalo roam!" Jim presented the Governor's Award of Excellence for outstanding leadership to the fourteen-member Vernon Rotary trail team. Will Speight, Abilene Rotarian, was recognized for creating the gold-lettered parchment proclamations that were presented at each of the thirty-seven dedications.

State Representative Bob Hunter presented a proclamation from the State of Texas House of Representatives that "Abilene and Taylor County are proud to be 'marked' as official sites on the Great Western Trail." Peter Fox, Rotary club president, introduced Frontier Texas executive director Jeff Salmon, who invited everyone to see the exhibits, especially the depiction of a stampede with visuals, movement, and sound. The floor shook when the cattle scattered during a storm filled with lightning and rain. Rattlesnakes coiled by the trail enhanced the reality of the experience.

The goal for documenting the path of the trail had branched out. The trail teams recognized the sense of community in trail towns strengthened by their familial, historical, and cultural ties to the trail era and by a network provided by a service club, Rotary. The camaraderie among the volunteers across the nine trail states, connected by the common cause of finding and documenting the path of the Great Western Trail, refuted the idea of a decline since 1950 of social capital in the United States. Social capital is defined as all forms of interpersonal social intercourse that Americans use to educate and enrich the fabric of their communal lives and strengthen democracy. Social capital grows from ". . . social clubs, like Rotary or Lions, [that] mobilize local energies to raise scholarships or fight disease at the same time that they provide members with friendships and business connections that pay off personally." As the project to find the path of the GWT progressed, it connected volunteers with their friends and neighbors and with strangers, who became friends.[28] Trail research teams discovered civil engagement, also called social capital, working with volunteers in the towns on the trail.

Throughout the trail research, especially notable in these four counties, evidence of cultural modification appeared—the independence of ranch women was striking. Another shift, the growing conflict between small and large landowners was reflected in the documentation of the GWT. The trail-project research was expanding into areas beyond the project's mission. On-site visits with ranch families and community leaders indicated a bond with place and traditions. A sense of community united the volunteers along the trail, a unity commonly in place in the small towns. The influence of the trail culture itself was becoming evident in the modern trail communities.

When the drovers left Shackelford County, north of Fort Griffin, they had been on the trail for almost six weeks. After traveling more than five hundred miles, they had yet to exit Texas. They slept on the ground at night, stayed in the saddle all day, crossed treacherous rivers, chased strays, overcame stampedes, and watched for rattlesnakes. The men became brothers through bonds crafted mainly by the need for survival and their responsibility to deliver the herd. Three more Texas counties lay ahead of the drovers before they forded the perilous Red River and entered Indian Territory. In the twenty-first century, when the Texas trail team reached the Red River, they planned a Texas-sized celebration for meeting Oklahoma's challenge to mark the trail across the state.

The research teams noted that the continuous family ownership of trail ranches, with their cattle and horse businesses, had unified cowboys and cattlemen across the state. Major ranches from South Texas to North Texas, established in the late 1800s with cattle-trail profits, had continued to contribute to Texas's economic stability. Many of the ranches had evolved into large family-owned corporations that required many types of employees to work the ranches, run the businesses, produce the oil discovered underground, and oversee the investments. In addition, evidence showed range conflicts that had flared often during the trail days were eventually resolved with the help of legislation, law enforcement, and newspapers.

An additional discovery was that long-term family ownership of ranches supported growth in breeding good cattle and prime horses, horseracing,

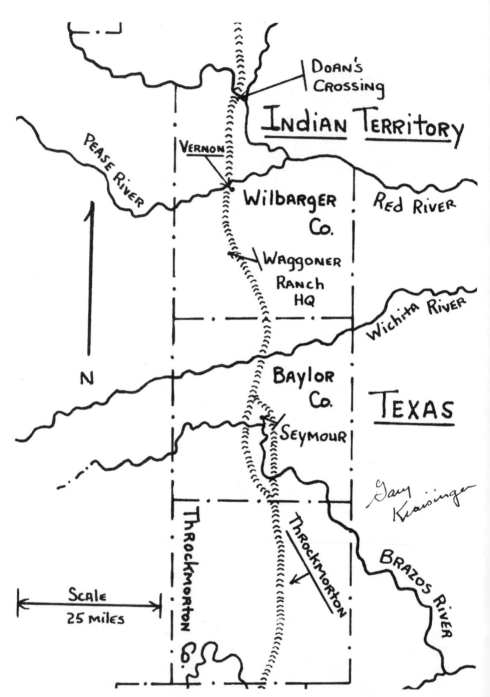

GWT from southern border of Throckmorton County across Baylor and Wilbarger Counties to Doan's Crossing on the Red River

rodeo, community projects, the arts, and philanthropy. Many of the heirs were trendsetters and flamboyant promoters of Texas. Historian Lawrence Clayton dedicated a booklet on Chimney Creek Ranch in Shackelford County: "To the ranching culture that has helped shape Texas and Texans."[1] Ranchers helped form and strengthen the culture and the economy through being good neighbors and responsible stewards of the land and water resources. They assisted in preserving the history of their Western heritage through actively supporting museum collections and other heritage endeavors. Concomitant to these attributes was the discovery that ownership of land required work and guardianship of domestic and indigenous wild animals. These common responsibilities served to create a set of core values among landowners that unified them with other landowners who followed the same practices.

For five generations in Throckmorton County, the R.A. Brown Ranch, established in 1895, has continued to be a leader in the stewardship of the land and in raising top-quality registered Quarter Horses and cattle. Wildlife preservation is often a priority for the ranches as they provide hunting opportunities to complement the ranching enterprises. In 2013, Rob and Peggy Brown chose to pass the ranch on to their four children as a way to keep it in the family, and to keep the family on the ranch. In October 2013, Rob and Peggy were honored for their life's work at the ranch's seed-stock sale. More than 118 years of superior genetic seed stock was made available to the public. Buyers from forty states, Canada, and Mexico purchased animals for breeding stock.[2] This event typifies the economic impact and the generational family ownership necessary to attain it.

The big business of ranching is different from big businesses on Wall Street and other so-called white-collar professions that are focused on inanimate objects. The owners of land, horses, and cattle must monitor them, often daily. The responsibility for cattle, horses, and indigenous wildlife seems to inculcate and perpetuate a love in the owners for the land and its wild and domesticated inhabitants, creating a desire to conserve and preserve these animate resources. Much has been written about this idea, especially in memoirs of ranch owners. From the GWT study, it became apparent that ownership of land, especially generational ownership of ranches, perpetuates the range of values so common to the legendary cowboy.

As the trail continued north from Fort Griffin into Throckmorton County, persistent but unfounded rumors about danger kept the drovers on constant alert. The drovers would have heard about Indians abducting white hostages as late as 1869; one incident occurred at the Elm Creek crossing, a scant twenty miles from Fort Griffin. From 1854 to 1859, Throckmorton County was the site of a Comanche Reservation. In 1859, the Comanche population was relocated to Indian Territory. During that period, for protection of the sparse inhabitants of the area, Camp Cooper was established south of the reservation site.[3]

Prior to fording the Clear Fork of the Brazos River near the old Butter-field-Military Road, the drovers welcomed the shade and rare comfort of groves of pecan, elm, and mesquite trees. Their comfort was usually short-lived, however, as the Northern Tom Green County–Buffalo Gap feeder trail joined the GWT near this point. The addition of other herds in close proximity presented problems. To keep the herds of cattle from mixing as they sought water and forage, they had to be separated by a distance of several miles—not an easy task for the cowboys. Teamwork among the trail bosses and drovers was essential for the herds' safety and survival. This teamwork, in turn, affected the potential prosperity of the cattlemen.

September 25, 2004, Throckmorton, Texas, Dedication in Throckmorton County

At the time of the GWT marker dedication, Throckmorton was a small ranching community of fewer than one thousand inhabitants, but it had faithfully maintained its cattle-trail heritage. When the trail researchers visited, cowboys wearing boots (some with spurs still attached), jeans, and classic hats could have walked off a Western movie set, but instead they were just going about their daily lives. They drove pickup trucks, pulling horse or cattle trailers, as a regular part of business. And the pickup beds were usually full, too.

So it was no surprise that the town's celebrations included events that were spinoffs from the cattle culture. Two citizens, Jack Faultleroy and Mack Pirtle, while "having an adult beverage at the local watering hole," decided that a calf fry cook-off would be the perfect festival for Throckmorton.[4]

From the trail days through today's ranch operations, branding time has included the castration of young bulls, thus creating the opportunity to dine on calf fries (deep-fried testicles). Castrating bulls was extra work, but it added to the drovers' safety going up the trail and to the profits at the end. A steer had a better temperament and a propensity for gaining weight on the trail, resulting in better steaks. Because of this improved temperament, drovers signed on to herd steers, whenever possible, rather than bulls or cows. They told tales about the dangers of herding bulls, usually including a narrative about one South Texas longhorn bull that dispatched an entire cavalry troop, and about the complications of herding cows, especially when they calved on the trail.

The two Throckmorton citizens' plans resulted in a trail-inspired event: the World Championship Rocky Mountain Oyster Festival. This tribute to the drovers and their method of overcoming problems on the trail almost doubled the size of the town, at least for the day of festivity.

Jack Faultleroy selected the rodeo grounds north of the town as the site for another GWT marker (the first one was located in Throckmorton), thus featuring the historically significant area. Chimney Creek Ranch co-owner Ted Paup had purchased markers for both Throckmorton and Shackelford Counties. Ted's association, through his intercounty ranch, cattle, and other businesses, identified a subtle part of community life along the trail: generational ownership of ranches and related businesses in contiguous counties promoted interconnected county citizens who bonded over their respect for the trail days, for the land, and for the cattle enterprises.

Ted represented another commonality among citizens in counties along the trail—he is a Rotarian and a Texas A&M University graduate. Underlying the deep-seated respect for trail history and stewardship of the land are two other bonding elements: community service and education. Much has been written about the importance of these aspects of life for the growth of the economy and the happiness of its citizens. Visiting towns on the trail brought forth evidence of these business and cultural solidifiers: respect for history, stewardship of the land, community service, and education.

On September 25, 2004, the citizens of Throckmorton were treated to two events linked to the GWT. The Bandera Trail Riders, headed for Dodge City, Kansas, arrived in town on the same day as the dedication ceremony. Throckmorton newspaper editor Terry Armstrong spearheaded the dedication arrangements, and Judge Trey Carrington and Harrell Keeter, chamber of commerce president, welcomed everyone. The first GWT marker was dedicated in a small park across the street from the courthouse. At the end of the ceremony, the Bandera Riders passed through town going north. Despite the fact that fifty wagons and approximately one hundred out-riders had been on the trail for nineteen days, they entered Throckmorton as if timed to be the finale of the dedication ceremony. They traveled through the center of Throckmorton along the highway, a road once defined by the hooves of longhorns, and then continued north to the rodeo arena to set up camp for the evening.

Memories of trail days were revisited that evening. The rodeo area had been a site where the longhorns were bedded down before trailing on north. The aroma of barbecue and hot bread and the sound of cowboys strumming guitars and singing trail songs such as "Home on the Range" created a mellow mood for the trail-weary riders. With the horses making faint noises while eating hay, the setting in the small ranch community captured a bit of the romanticism of the trail era. Trail history was being made while trail history was being preserved. This on-location visit to an old trail site complemented by trail reminders such as food, music, horses, wagons, and cowboys linked memory to reality.

September 27, 2004, Seymour, Texas, Dedication in Baylor County

After leaving the Throckmorton rodeo grounds, the wagons and riders went north to the next gathering and dedication at Seymour. We made plans to meet again when they entered Seymour in two days on September 27, 2004.

The original trail north had crossed both the north and south forks of Boggy Creek, three or four miles west of their confluence. A few miles beyond, the drovers took advantage of nearly level country as the trail entered Baylor County along what is now Highway 183/283. At that point, the cattle fanned out across tall, bluestem grassland. Some of the herds trailed up the west bank of the Brazos and others forded Millers Creek, going up the east bank to Seymour Creek on the Salt Fork tributary of the Brazos River. The cattle then continued up the trail north through what would become the center of Seymour. The northbound trails often defined the main streets of trail towns.[5]

The idyllic images of herds moving north while peacefully grazing are just that—idyllic. An experienced drover, who understood cattle well, worked constantly to manage a herd so that the cattle would graze peacefully and gain weight going up the trail. Many interruptions, such as storms, rivers, and other animals, often dispelled the tranquil atmosphere. In Baylor County, however, the disruption was often man-made. The county was plagued by violence and contention while the trail was in use. Ranchers and farmers fought over the vast, unpopulated grasslands during the open-range ranching era. The first herd up the GWT through this area was in 1874. In 1876, Colonel J. R. McClain brought settlers from Oregon to the county, but they were driven off by cowboys running cattle over the farmers' corn. Baylor County's first two county attorneys were forced to resign over the conflict. In June 1879, County Judge E. R. Morris was shot and killed by saloon keeper Will Taylor because of the cattle versus land quarrels.[6]

In 1879, ranchers from Guadalupe County in South Texas, Millett brothers Eugene C., Alonzo, and Hiram, began ranching in Baylor County. Sources say, "They ran a tough outfit and used their armed cowhands to intimidate would-be settlers and the citizens of newly founded Seymour."[7] The Hashknife outfit soon bought the Millett ranch, and in 1882, the Hashknife ranching enterprise in Baylor County became the center of a vast cattle empire. Hashknife ranches spread south into Taylor County, west along the Pecos River, and into Arizona. Partner John Simpson influenced the laying of the Texas and Pacific rail line into Taylor County, resulting in Abilene's development. The site of the Taylor County Hashknife headquarters is a part of the Abilene Christian University campus.[8] The Hashknife Ranch located south of Seymour now has a GWT marker at the gate to the headquarters. The once-contentious farmers and ranchers now live peacefully side-by-side in Baylor County.

The Seymour Chamber of Commerce manager, Myra Busby, used her ideas and leadership skills to recover evidence for the path of the trail. On the chamber website, she added an interactive GWT map, making each Texas trail town just a click away. When the National Great Western Cattle Trail Association (GWCTA-N) was organized, everyone pointed to Myra to lead the new organization as the first president. She often attended meetings in other GWT states to help establish chapters.

Myra designed a romanticized Great Western Trail dedication ceremony. At the city park on the east side of Seymour Creek, the marker was placed near a trail campsite and bedding grounds for herds. Again, timing was perfect for the arrival of the Bandera wagons and trail riders to be the finale for the marker dedication. Seymour school superintendent Dr. John Baker gave the students a reality history lesson that day. The students lined the streets to watch history being made as the horse-drawn wagons and riders passed by on their way to Dodge City. Not surprisingly, there was yet another rodeo space for the riders to use as camp for the evening. That night, after a hearty meal around the campfire, they once again played guitars and sang songs such as "Don't Fence Me In." The 1934 song could have been a memoir of a warning to those who did not respect the open range and a cowboy's freedom. It could have also been a warning to settlers and those who installed barbed-wire fences.

John Gaither Welcomes Trail Boss Suzie Heywood, GWT Marker Dedication,
Seymour, Texas

On September 27, 2004, the first GWT marker in Baylor County was dedicated at Seymour. Myra Busby, Chamber of Commerce manager, organized the ceremony to coincide with the arrival of the Bandera Trail Riders on their way to Dodge City, Kansas. Schoolchildren lined the streets, and ninety-year-old working cowboy John Gaither welcomed the trail boss, Suzie Heywood.

At the dedication, key elected officials acknowledged the importance of the trail project, including Judge Butch Colthorp. Texas Representative Rick Hardcastle, the keynote speaker, spoke of the importance of the small towns he represented, of the cattle industry, and of the pride in ownership of the land, including pride in ecological and wildlife preservation. Judge Colthorp emphasized a strategy they used to keep their small town viable: Seymour citizens worked to entice their educated young people to return to serve in leadership positions, such as school superintendents, businesses entrepreneurs, ranch managers, and community service organizers. Two of those who returned were Dr. John Baker and Myra Busby. The ceremony also honored locals with deep ranch roots. John Gaither, a ninety-year-old working cowboy, was a vision of the past with his leathery, sun-stressed face and hands, cowboy boots, and hat.

After the ceremony, it was time to chart the trail going north to Vernon. For a distance in Baylor County, the trail followed the same path as Highway 183/283. Then it turned west across lush, grassy, rolling hills, where the cattle forded the Wichita River. The trail dropped down into the breaks that eventually became Lake Kemp, a body of water created from the Wichita River. This water source now serves as a getaway destination for day fishermen or for longer stays in shoreline lake houses. This large lake in Baylor County is along the southern pastures of the vast W. T. Waggoner Ranch.

The 535,000 contiguous acres, some 836 sections, are spread into six counties: Baylor, Wilbarger, Archer, Wichita, Foard, and Knox. Ranch heirs live in two homes on the ranch, located approximately thirteen miles south of Vernon. The offices for the W. T. Waggoner Estate, the trust established to manage the ranch's assets of oil, cattle, horses, farming, and hunting preserves, are headquartered in Vernon.[9] The ranch is important to the economy of the area and is a link to the past—every day the modern working cowboys practice cattle- and horse-related skills developed on the trail.

Originally called the Waggoner Ranch, the property was expanded and enhanced from the sale of a herd trailed to Kansas. The ranch has remained in the same family since it was organized. Ranch patriarch Dan Waggoner, born in Tennessee in 1828, came to Texas as a young boy and took advantage of the opportunity to trail longhorns north. Dan based near Decatur in 1850 and started amassing cattle and enlarging his pastures. In 1870 Dan took his son W. T. (Tom) and trailed a herd from the Little Wichita to Kansas. He came home with $55,000 in his saddlebags (equivalent today to about $1,010,000).[10] He and Tom invested in more longhorns and added pastures in six counties, creating the largest Texas ranch under one fence.[11]

The larger-than-life members of the Waggoner family enriched the legends of Texas cattle barons, giving the media a constant flow of articles. This publicity contributed to the public's interest in the GWT and the lifestyle of cowboys and ranchers. In 1923, the Waggoner Cattle Empire became the W. T. Waggoner Estate. Members of the Waggoner family lived in Fort Worth as well as on the ranch. Tom and Ella's three children, Electra, Guy, and E. Paul, were Texas ranching celebrities. Tom built Electra a mansion in Fort Worth called Thistle Hill to encourage her and her husband to return to Texas. Tom and his two sons built Arlington Downs in 1929, which lasted the four years (1933–1937) that Texas allowed pari-mutuel betting.[12] Thistle Hill, a historic landmark in Fort Worth, has been prominent in encouraging the interest of twenty-first-century visitors in Waggoner Ranch and trail-era history. The publicity garnered by pari-mutuel betting in Texas continues in current times to include trail history in its retelling.

Another media favorite, E. Paul, the youngest of Tom's three, was a

Doan's May Picnic, King and Queen, 2008

The King and Queen of the 2008 Doan's May Picnic represent the seventh generation of the families that established the W. T. Waggoner Ranch and the White family farms. Helen Biggs Willingham (and husband, Gene, not pictured) helps her grandson Philip Williamson, son of Jennifer and Philip Williamson, prepare for the Crowning of Royalty ceremony. Queen Emma Parmer, daughter of Rochelle and Roger Beam and Kenneth Parmer and granddaughter of Sheila and Dan White, proudly displayed the train of her gown.

breeder of Quarter Horses, helped build Arlington Downs racetrack, and started the annual Santa Rosa Roundup Rodeo in Vernon. E. Paul's flamboyant lifestyle worked like a magnet, bringing top professional rodeo cowboys and cowgirls to the rodeo. In 1945, his purchase of Poco Bueno brought fame to the Waggoner Ranch. The stallion won all the major cutting-horse awards. E. Paul even left burial instructions in his will for the famous horse: on Highway 283, at a gravesite across from the ranch headquarters entrance, Poco Bueno was to be buried in a standing position. Two years after E. Paul's death, Poco Bueno died in November 1969. He was buried as instructed. The memorial granite marker reads: "Champion and Sire of Champions."[13] E. Paul's love for well-bred, fast horses and rodeo kept the media writing about his pursuits, the ranch, and its origin.

Sculpture, as noted previously, can crystallize a time in history, such as the trail era. Internationally recognized sculptor Electra Waggoner Biggs, named for her aunt and the only child of E. Paul and Helen Buck Waggoner, was acclaimed for her ability to sculpt precise images of famous people. At the center of Texas Tech University stands her sculpture of Will Rogers astride his horse Soapsuds. The sculpture typifies the bygone era of the cowboy and presents the legend to new generations of college students.[14] In Vernon, Will Rogers is remembered for his attempt to correct erroneous information about the name of the GWT. His letter in the Red River Valley Museum in Vernon is a palpable tribute to efforts to set the record of Great Western Trail history straight.

Because of this long and influential history, Vernon citizens reacted with shock, dismay, and sadness when a judge announced in 2014 that the W. T. Waggoner Estate ranch was required to be placed on the market for sale. The courts became involved in 1967 when Judge Tom Davis of the 46th District Court in Vernon ruled that one-half the ranch belonged to A. B. Wharton III. The other half belonged to the two daughters of Electra Waggoner Biggs. As of this writing, the heirs have been unable to reach a decision about the division of the vast holdings, and the ranch has been left on the market. The community's reaction to the sale notice added a new dimension to the research project: What happens to a community when its claim to fame, a noted Texas ranch, is sold to a non-resident or to a corporation that might divide and sell it again? What happens when a family that has influenced the community for generations moves away?

May 5, 2007, Vernon in Wilbarger County, Last GWT Marker Dedication in Texas

The trail continued north from Baylor County into Wilbarger County across more pastures of the sprawling W. T. Waggoner Ranch. The herds grazed on the grassy rolling hills and watered at Beaver Creek, south of Vernon. Due east of Beaver Creek, the southernmost GWT marker in Wilbarger County was placed on the east side of the intersection of Highway 283 and Coffee Creek Road. The next marker south of Vernon was placed at the point of a day's cattle drive from the Baylor-Wilbarger county line.[15]

The herd would have watered next on Paradise Creek before traveling through the area that would become the town of Vernon. Old-timers point to an area in southeast Vernon that once looked like a buffalo wallow where herds were often bedded down. The booming cattle industry eventually required the registry of brands in each county. Without brands, local cattle and trail cattle could easily become mixed, especially during the 1880s when thousands were being herded north. The first cattle brand registered in Wilbarger County was on October 31, 1881, by W. A. McKinney.[16]

From Vernon, once called Eagle Flat, cattle hooves marked the route of future Highway 283 north toward the Wilbarger Airport. At an earlier time, a wagon supply road cut northwest from this location toward the present site of the almost nonexistent town of Fargo. As in other places along the trail, settlers arrived as early as 1878 to claim land, four years after the first herd passed through the area. Sometimes the weather misled the new residents. When the settlers arrived to farm during a rainy year, it gave them false hope. In the dry years, they had to resort to other ways of earning enough to survive. Some poisoned coyotes for their hides and/or gathered the plentiful buffalo bones. These enterprising settlers would sell the hides when they hauled the bones to Gainesville, where the bones could be sold at twenty to twenty-two dollars per ton to eastern fertilizer plants.[17]

The settlers also supplemented their larders with wild plums, grapes, currants, persimmons, and pecans. In the good years, the drovers and settlers would see an abundance of antelope, deer, buffalo, wild turkey, and prairie chickens. This sounds like an ideal arrangement, but the herds of 2,500 to 3,000 trailing through each summer caused continuous disruption to the people's lives. The settlers, especially the wives, made note of the problems they faced, some as seemingly innocuous as having to roll down burlap over their open windows to keep out the large flies that came with the cattle.[18] It was yet another of the daily hardships the homemakers faced as they tried to survive prairie privation.

In Wilbarger County, as well as in other rural areas along the trail across the Great Plains, news was passed by word of mouth, letters, and newspapers. Formally organized in 1881, Wilbarger County attracted businesspeople, who established the town of Vernon south of Doan's Crossing.[19] As the town grew and business increased, the Vernon *Guard*, edited by B. Wilson Edgell, published its first issue on January 18, 1883.[20]

While searching for primary sources, I recovered evidence that Asa Shinn Mercer had established the Vernon *Guard* in 1883, which surprised the *Vernon Daily Record* publisher and the editor. Mercer's ownership of the paper lasted only a few months in 1883, so his name was lost to local history. Mercer had also established five other area newspapers: the Bowie *Cross Timbers*, Henrietta *Shield*, Sherman *Courier*, Wichita *Herald*, and the *Texas Panhandle* (Mobeetie).[21] Cattlemen from Henrietta and Fort Worth had collaborated with Mercer to start the paper as "an organ to fight rustlers in Wilbarger County," but editor Benjamin Wilson Edgell's office was shot "full of holes" by nightriders carrying Winchesters. Despite the ambitious start, Mercer sold all his Texas newspapers except the Mobeetie paper during the first year and moved to Wyoming in the fall of 1883.[22]

Mercer followed the GWT to Wyoming, where the conflict between ranchers and homesteaders often led to violence. To help stop the feud, Mercer tried to help correct rumors that encouraged the violence by publicizing events with names to identify the perpetrators. He became a larger-than-life figure, a man whose accomplishments, at first glance, seem improbable. He was the first president of the University of Washington, relocated young women from the East to provide brides for men in Washington, started newspapers in Oregon and Texas, and became a firebrand for truth in Wyoming's Johnson County Range War.[23] More about Mercer's involvement in that conflict is included in Chapter 9.

Range wars complicated the already hazardous lives of drovers. Two 1879 federal land laws incited the conflicts. These laws encouraged the sale of public lands, which threatened the cattle-trail business as well as open-range ranching. One law priced "school lands" at one dollar per acre, with a four-section limit to each buyer. The second law offered the rest of the public domain at 50 cents per acre, with no limit. Land dealers filed on large tracts secured with contracts requiring payment in ninety days. The dealers became promoters, working hard to sell the land prior to the ninety-day contract deadline. This increased opportunity for smaller buyers to purchase land, and the recent invention of barbed wire created a volatile situation. Fencing soon appeared on (newly) private land, some on public lands, and occasionally even crossing county roads. Access to water also became a target for fencing.[24] These changes became good copy for newspaperman Mercer, who had experienced conflict resolution in 1883 as chairman of a meeting of seventy-eight ranchers in Henrietta, Texas. The ranchers met to find ways to solve the epidemic of cattle rustlers, who crossed into Indian Territory for sanctuary.[25]

The Vernon *Guard* brought to light additional problems that trail bosses and drovers faced. Rustling was rampant in the area and continued in Vernon after Mercer sold the newspaper. In the spring of 1885, during the height of trail days, the *Guard's* editor Edgell promoted a vigilante effort to rid Wilbarger County of "cow thieves, horse thieves and incendiaries, etc." According to the Dallas *Herald*, three men were killed during the vigilante action, and the Texas Rangers arrested twenty-three men, including the *Guard's* editor, the county sheriff, and the "best men in Wilbarger County." While in jail, the editor wrote that it was difficult to write surrounded by a gang of lawless characters whom he had for the past two years used his best endeavors to rid the county of, and whom he knew would pay a high price for his blood."[26] To counter the volatility, the paper's editor used the

Guard newspaper to solicit help from outside law enforcement who eventually quelled the violence.

Coming back to modern days, the publisher and editor of the Vernon newspaper, now called the *Vernon Daily Record*, used the paper in a similar way as his predecessor to promote Saturday, May 5, 2007, as "Celebrate the Great Western Trail," the event that would commemorate marking the trail across Texas. It had taken three years. Dedications had been held in eighteen of the twenty Texas trail counties. Only San Antonio and Boerne had to schedule their dedications a few months after the Vernon celebration.

When the first marker in Texas was dedicated on May 1, 2004, the idea was fresh, and the anticipation was running high for marking the trail across Texas. Having experienced the Texas dedications and others in the northern states, the last Texas celebration (which included everyone who had participated in some way) brought a deeper, more profound sense of unity and purpose to the twenty-first-century trail drivers. The project had taken on a life of its own, bigger than any one group or person. A diversity of people gathered on May 4–6, 2007, to dedicate the final Texas marker. The volunteers who contributed to the success of the project included Rotarians and local historians from many states, the Red River Valley Museum employees and members, descendants of the GWT and Chisholm Trail, Old Time Trail Drivers' Association members, the Oklahoma trail team, elected officials, academic historians, retirees, and friends who had been gathered along the way.

As trail bosses usually did when the cattle were delivered, they paid the cowboys, celebrated, and made plans for the return trip home. The loss of lives on the trail was a constant consideration. The loss of a trail partner was woven into the 2007 celebration. The goal had three parts: dedicate the final GWT marker in Texas, honor descendants of the GWT and Chisholm Trail drovers, and pay tribute to the originators of the project. The centerpiece of part three would be honoring three Oklahomans and one Texan. The finale would be a tribute to the memory of Oklahoma Senator Robert Kerr.

The celebration started with a Red River Valley Museum event on Friday night. The invitation to "The Tastes and Tales of the Western Trail" went to friends from Mexico to Canada. They were invited to "Shine up your boots and join us for a boot scootin', lip smackin', good time." The evening started with the viewing of an international juried art show in the museum galleries followed by sampling gourmet delicacies related to the trail. Guests selected trail food from tables laden with quail with cherry barbeque sauce, wild boar on biscuits, elk on sourdough, salmon (no one could connect this treat to the trail, but it disappeared quickly), cowboy venison stew, deep-fried rattlesnake, and buffalo meatballs, to name a few. Mary Ann McCuistion, museum executive director and artist, among other talents, produced the international juried art show that many artists entered, hoping to win one of the premier awards. She also organized the museum activities for the evening.

Lonely trail songs and toe-tappin' music inspired by cowboys set the mood for the evening at the museum. The guests saw the past come alive with a presentation of *Mr. & Mrs. Charles Goodnight*, a performance based on the trail boss and his wife. Dressed as the couple in period clothing, cowboy poet Lanny Joe Burnett and Cindy Baker of Bonham, Texas, sat in rocking chairs and discussed the hardships and pleasures of their isolated life living in Palo Duro Canyon, a lonely, long gorge located in the Texas Panhandle.

The next morning, a breakfast at Doan's Adobe, north of Vernon, kicked off an event to honor trail descendants. Jeff Bearden and many volunteers helped prepare and serve breakfast from Jeff's chuck wagon. Guests were picked up in a horse-drawn carriage from the pasture parking area and delivered to the breakfast area. After the cowboy breakfast, the crowd of some two hundred people watched the ceremony honoring old-time-trail drivers and their descendants.

The Santa Rosa Palomino Club held Texas flags and formed an honor guard for the laying of an Old Time Trail Drivers memorial wreath at the base of a ten-foot marble monument on which sixty-two trail drivers' brands had been inscribed. The green wreath had red flowers, centered with a longhorn skull, and a blue bow with the Rotary logo and silver letters, "In Memory of All the Old Time Trail Drivers." Many of the brands on the memorial are still used today for large Texas ranches. Descendants of drovers were recognized, honoring their drover ancestors.

Two drover descendants were available to represent the two dominant Texas trails: Tip Igou of Vernon represented Corwin Doan's family, whose home was Doan's Adobe. Tom B. Saunders IV, a fifth-generation rancher from Weatherford, Texas, represented his great-great-uncle George W. Saunders and the Chisholm Trail. George W. Saunders had worked "to keep the record straight" when P. P. Ackley attempted to change the name of the GWT. Other Vernon drover descendants recognized were Gary Chapman and Ken and Bobbie White. Out-of-town descendants recognized were Bobby and Mary Bynum, Colonel George Hahn, Gail and Jerry Sales, and other family members.

The next event, Doan's May Day Picnic, started in 1884 by drovers' wives, would include the annual crowning of a young queen and king selected from county families, usually descendants of drovers or settlers. The Doan's Picnic Man and Woman of the Year would also be presented, to honor older county citizens for nurturing trail memories, values, and generational ties to ownership and stewardship of the land. Following the picnic, the next GWT event was the commemorative ceremony held at the Red River Valley Museum. Many people participating in the ceremony were from other states that had held dedications prior to the completion of the marking of the trail in Texas.

Gary Chapman, descendant and local Rotary president, started the ceremony. The Vernon Ambassadors on Horseback formed an honor guard for the presentation of the flags. Rotary leaders and other research volunteers presented nine state flags and the flags of three nations. Some volunteers had traveled almost two thousand miles to carry their state flag in the ceremony. Each of the approximately two hundred attendees had contributed to the project's success. The district attorney, the mayor, the county judge, and other local officials paid tribute to those who had helped and to the camaraderie among the project's volunteers. National Cowboy Symposium and Celebration President Alvin G. Davis applauded the research project and its resultant success in determining the length of the GWT. He noted that the project had grown from an initial meeting at the Symposium in Lubbock, Texas, in 2003.

Jeff Bearden's chuck wagon, along with Rotarians holding the twelve flags, set the stage for the honor ceremony. Bob Klemme, eighty-two-year-old Chisholm Trail historian, of Enid, Oklahoma, was honored for originating the project idea. Two Oklahomans, Dennis Vernon and John Barton, were recognized for challenging Vernon Rotarians to mark the trail in Texas. Texas Representative Rick Hardcastle was honored for providing state-level recognition and support for the project. Jim Aneff of Abilene saluted the honorees with framed Rotary Proclamations.

Sadness permeated the crowd when the last Oklahoman was honored posthumously. Senator Robert Kerr, like Gus in *Lonesome Dove*, had showed great determination to survive, to win his battle with cancer. During this portion of the ceremony, Dennis Vernon carried a Oklahoma flag and Larry

Honoring "GWT Marking Founder" Bob Klemme,
GWT Marker Dedication, Vernon, Texas
On May 5, 2007, Gary Chapman, Vernon Rotary president, presented an appreciation award to Robert "Bob" Klemme, who initiated the idea to mark the Great Western Trail with seven-foot white posts with red letters. Bob's son Mike Klemme (right) attended with him.

Crabtree carried a Texas flag. Following them, John Barton led the traditional riderless horse with the boots turned backward in the stirrups. The senator's wife Robbie and their children joined in the eulogies that featured the vast influence Bob had on the project and on those who knew him.

Following the marker dedication, several other activities were held at the museum. That afternoon, four authors signed books; that evening, a Texas-size trail driver's ball was held. Two-stepping followed a dinner of cowboy-size steaks with all the trimmings. During an interlude, Alan Smith, manager of the Vernon United Supermarkets, announced that United Supermarkets had pledged a $1 million challenge grant that would go toward a Western Trail Heritage Center adjacent to the Red River Valley Museum.

With the last official Texas dedication finished, it was time to cross the Red River into Indian Territory. But before leaving Texas, a bit of folklore (a regular influence on trail history) must be added. Typical of old, historical

Honoring Texas Rep. Rick Hardcastle and Oklahoma Sen. Robert Kerr, GWT Marker Dedication, Vernon, Texas

At Vernon, Texas, the weekend of May 4–6, 2007, in recognition of their efforts, Texas Representative Rick Hardcastle and Oklahoma Senator Robert Kerr, recognized posthumously, were given plaques and Rotary proclamations during the dedication ceremonies. In 2007, three years after the first Texas dedication, the same six gathered again: Texas co-chairs Sylvia Mahoney and Jeff Bearden, Rep. Hardcastle, Robbie Kerr standing in for Robert, and Oklahoma co-chairs Dennis Vernon and John Yudell Barton.

houses, Doan's Adobe has a ghost story. In 1999, Paul Combest, an eighty-four-year-old man from Knoxville, Tennessee, told Vernon newspaper editor Jimmy Carr that he had seen a ghost at Doan's Adobe. In the late 1940s, while Combest was working in Vernon at George Backus's monument company, he went to Doan's Adobe to see the ten-foot trail monument. While there, Combest saw a man who "looked to be 100 years old. He had a very long beard, white as snow, and all the store shelves were empty, except for cobwebs." He said he talked to an old lady who delivered the mail in an old open Model-T car that was boiling over from the Texas heat. The steam clouds obscured his view of her. She beckoned him over, but she disappeared when he approached her.[27]

Other evidence of the effects of the past was shared when the Bandera wagons and riders crossed the Red River. Larry Holmes, Vernon College history professor, said as he watched the trail riders and wagons cross the Red River Bridge in 2004, "You could feel the spirits in the air. Thanks for y'all's commitment to the ghosts of the past."[28] Folklore cannot be discounted as a way to preserve and promote memories of the trail; not history, but a type of memory common to a culture.

❦

The miles and the experiences across Texas had changed the trail cowboys. The trail-team members had also changed. The influence of the trail era continued to show in the generational ownership and stewardship of ranches. The ranchers, many with vast holdings, remained close to the range of values attributed to the legendary trail days, including hard work and responsibility. They emphasized education and community service. Ranches along the trail had a powerful influence on the economies and cultures of small, rural communities along the trail. Citizens from the sparsely populated counties readily joined the research project. Newspaper editors in the communities continued to use the voice of their papers: once to combat violence, and later to promote the preservation of history and heritage tourism. The recovery of evidence to document the path of the trail had led to the discovery of the continuing influence of the trail on the culture.

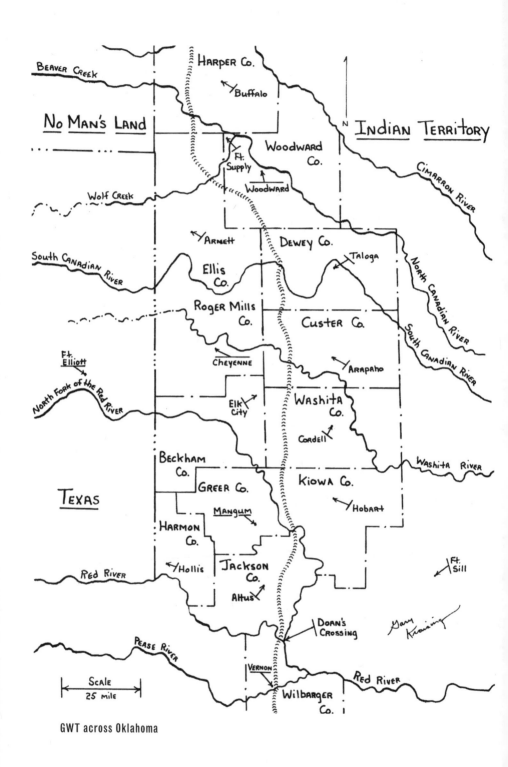

GWT across Oklahoma

CHAPTER 7

Oklahoma and Kansas

When the drovers crossed the Red River into Indian Territory—Oklahoma—they had become trail worthy while on their approximately 650-mile trip from Mexico. In the territory, the drovers were trailing through country that was home for some fifty Native American tribes that had been relocated from other states. So that the drovers would not stray from the trail to Kansas, they used the distinctive Wichita Mountains north of Altus for a landmark. The grasslands between Altus and Frederick, known as the Big Pasture, later attracted Texas ranchers with political ties to Washington, DC. They enticed President Theodore Roosevelt to visit the area. The Oklahoma trail team used a primary source, the 1876 pocket journal of trail driver Lewis Warren Neatherlin, to mark the trail across Oklahoma to Kansas. While marking the trail, the team also stopped to pay respect to a member who lost his life.

On January 30, 2006, the Vernon trail team crossed the Red River to pay tribute to the memory of a prominent trail partner, one whose life was cut short too soon. Senator Robert M. Kerr had fought a good fight on the trail with another treacherous obstacle, cancer. His services were held in Altus, Oklahoma, his home. Without showing evidence of his internal fight except for a stylishly shaved head, Bob traveled many miles to participate in dedications. Epitomizing the iconic cowboy, Bob showed no remorse or complaint when life dealt him a bad hand. His wife, Robbie Tinney Kerr, of some fifty years exuded the strength that comes from mutual sharing and shoring up through the years with a mate of equal strength and integrity. The overflow crowd at the Altus High School Auditorium reflected the esteem and respect the citizens had for Senator Bob Kerr.

The GWT project greatly benefited from Senator Kerr's support. He sponsored Oklahoma Concurrent Resolution #61 that designated May 1, 2004, as "Great Western Trail Appreciation Day" in the state. It honored the day that Oklahomans gave "a special gift of its first marker to enable the citizens of Texas to begin marking the trail." In turn, Sen. Bob and Robbie Kerr were honored in the Texas House and Senate on May 16, 2005. The House Resolution presented by Texas State Representative Rick Hardcastle and Rep. Carter Casteel stated in part, "Citizens of the State of Oklahoma began the process of marking the Western Trail through their state to commemorate the rich history of the cattle drives and the importance of this trail." In the Texas Senate, Resolution No. 417, initiated by Senator Frank Madla, stated in part, "Whereas, The importance of the Great Western Trail to the development and history of Texas cannot be overestimated, . . . Resolved, That the Senate of the State of Texas, 79th Legislature, hereby commemorate the Great Western Trail and extend sincere best wishes to all those associated with the modern project of marking its path through the Lone Star State." More than fifty trail friends from Oklahoma, Vernon, Seymour, and Bandera gathered at the Texas State Capitol to raise awareness of GWT history for the legislators. Mary Ann McCuistion, Red River Valley Museum executive director, set up a GWT exhibit in the lower level of the Capitol Rotunda.

The end of life for two more trail friends gave the trail project a poignant significance. Texas Senator Frank Madla died in a house fire the day after Thanksgiving, on November 24, 2006.[1] The senator entered our lives at the Bandera marker dedication and again at the State Capitol trail recognition. The trail team lost another member, Dr. Lewis Edwin Clark, on November 26, 2007. He had helped initiate the trail-marking project and kept Rotarians apprised of its progress in its newsletter. In addition, he and his wife, Jean, had attended the State Legislators' recognition for the project.

After the interlude to pay respect to our trail partners, it was time to continue across the land that would become the state of Oklahoma. The drovers entered Indian Territory at a fifty-yard-wide low-water crossing on the Prairie Dog Fork of the Red River. The crossing into the territory, lacking sharp embankments, allowed the chuck wagon, drovers, horses, and cattle to navigate the water and the quicksand successfully. From there, the drovers moved their herds toward the Wichita Mountains. All the while, they watched for roaming bands of Indians. Often, Indians confronted the drovers with requests for compensation for crossing their land, perhaps the first instance of a toll road in the Southwest. Trail bosses tried to negotiate an unobstructed passage by donating one or two steers or horses to entrepreneurial Native Americans. The herd bosses, who understood the history of the tribes and their cultural differences, were usually able to navigate safe passage through the territory. Nonetheless, during the forging of the Great Western Trail, this part of the journey became a notable challenge for the trail bosses and drovers to pass their herds through potentially hostile and dangerous territory.

Even though the drovers had rifles and pistols to help them forge their way north, the Indians, if they chose to do so, had their impressive set of warriors to impede this migration. The drovers worked with the Indians for safe passage across the Kiowa-Comanche Reservation. The path crossed the southwest boundary between present-day Altus and Frederick, Oklahoma. The trail ascended the east bank of the North Fork to Comanche Springs where it then entered the central section of the Cheyenne-Arapaho Reservation, called "No Man's Land." The North Fork of the Red River had been regarded by Mexico and later the Republic of Texas as the northern boundary of Texas. This area had originally been organized by Texas as Greer County, named for Texas Lieutenant Governor John Greer.[2]

Although the following event occurred after the trail era, it demonstrates the influence and political relationships that cattle barons along the GWT had and continue to have with Washington, DC. After the turn of the century, Texas ranchers Burk Burnett and W. T. Waggoner leased the vast grasslands where the trail once crossed between Altus and Frederick from Chief Quanah Parker. In April 1905, several famous men held a meeting at that location: President Theodore "Teddy" Roosevelt, Chief Quanah Parker, Texas ranchers Burk Burnett and W. T. "Tom" Waggoner, wolf hunter Jack Abernathy, Texas Ranger Bill McDonald, and others. The president arrived in Fort Worth to the cheers of thousands, where he was hosted by Waggoner and Burnett. Then they took Roosevelt on a wolf hunt in Comanche country in Indian Territory, accessing the lands they had leased.[3]

The six-day wolf hunt was not only a publicity jaunt for the president, it was also an information-gathering business trip to Indian Territory. All parties had their own self-interests in mind: Chief Quanah knew President Roosevelt, as Parker had ridden in the presidential inaugural parade in Washington. Tom and Burk wanted to extend their rights to graze cattle in that area, known as the Big Pasture. The chief wanted to extend his tribe's leases as a source of income and to keep the approximately half-million acres intact. Homesteaders wanted the president to open the land for settling.[4] Much political maneuvering was happening at this gathering. The business deal that was sealed among the ranchers, the Native Americans, and the government indicated that occasionally a land-usage contract could be satisfactory for all three parties.

The presidential party left Fort Worth by train. The first stop was Vernon. According to newspaper reports, "Thousands flocked into town just to catch a glimpse of the President of the United States."[5] After the president spoke at Vernon from the cotton platform on the Frisco Railway, the party boarded a special train for Frederick, Oklahoma. The wolf hunt was held between the Red River and the Wichita Mountains. The president joined the famous Oklahoma wolf hunter Jack Abernathy in the action. Roosevelt and the mounted hunting entourage raced behind greyhounds until a wolf was found. Jack would leap from his horse on top of the wolf's back, thrust his gloved hand into the wolf's mouth, grasp his lower jaw, and bend it down to keep the wolf from biting him.[6] He caught fifteen wolves on that trip. (Legend says the animals were wolves; other sources say they were large coyotes.)

The Texas governor had sent the famous Texas Ranger Bill McDonald on the historical trip to protect the president.[7] McDonald, who is buried at Quanah, Texas, is known for the statement used for his epitaph, "No man in the wrong can stand up against a fellow that's in the right and keeps on a-comin.'" The governor recognized McDonald as a lawman who lived by his code of ethics.

Although the following anecdote does not relate directly to the trail, it is a snapshot of the bravery, even foolhardiness, of those who called that grassland area home. It also reveals their business acumen in their dealings with President Roosevelt. In 1910, Jack Abernathy's two sons—Bud, age ten, and Temple, age six—rode their horses alone from Oklahoma to New York City to meet Teddy Roosevelt when his ship docked on his return from an African hunting trip. Jack joined them later in New York and negotiated a deal with Brush Motor Car Company to acquire a car. Bud and Temple drove the automobile 2,500 miles back to Oklahoma.[8] The town of Frederick honored these remarkable boys with a bronze statue placed on the courthouse lawn.

The prominent, adventurous, even reckless men who frequented the area created a rich history, memories of which persist into current times in Oklahoma, especially in Altus. The citizens work continuously to collect

THEODORE ROOSEVELT AND GROUP OF NOTED WEST TEXANS ON FAMOUS WOLF HUNT, MAY, 1905

A Wolf Hunt along the GWT with Theodore Roosevelt, Tom Waggoner, Burk Burnett, and Jack Abernathy, Near Frederick, Oklahoma
President Theodore Roosevelt and ranchers Tom Waggoner and Burk Burnett traveled to the Big Pasture, a location along the GWT between Altus and Frederick, Oklahoma, to join the famous hunter Jack Abernathy. He caught fifteen animals bare-handed on this hunt. Also participating was Chief Quanah Parker, shown kneeling by Jack Abernathy with a wolf in his hand. To Abernathy's left is Burnett, Roosevelt is next. Texas Ranger Bill McDonald is standing second from left. Guy Waggoner is seated fourth from the left. Image courtesy of Valarie Platz, Vernon, Texas.

and preserve their area's colorful history. On the Jackson County Courthouse lawn, the Altus Rotary Club sponsored an eleven-foot bronze sculpture, *Crossing the Red*, by Harold T. Holden. The artwork depicts a drover attempting to drive two longhorn steers across the Red River.

In the spring of 2003, the Western Trail Historical Society (WTHS) of Altus voted to sponsor the GWT marker project. Chris Jefferies, director of the Chisholm Trail Heritage Center in Duncan, Oklahoma, had spoken to the WTHS in 2002 to encourage them to mark the trail. The action plan began. Dennis Vernon and John Yudell Barton agreed to be co-chairs. Bob Klemme, who had marked the Chisholm Trail in Oklahoma from 1990 to 1997, made a GWT mold for the new markers. Joe Harkins consented to collect the global positioning system (GPS) placements. Maurice King started speaking to community organizations. Senator Bob Kerr provided the initial donation to launch the project. The group selected the north bank of the Red River in Oklahoma for the location of the first GWT marker on July 12, 2003. The marker, a seven-foot white obelisk with red letters, would be located every six miles at intersections of township lines where the trail crossed, according to a 1933 state engineering map.

Oklahoma cattle-trail history benefited when the Choctaw and Chickasaw lands in what would become south-central Oklahoma were approved to be subdivided. Surveyors Ehud N. Darling and Theodore H. Barrett, who had surveyed Indian land in the Dakotas, designated the Initial Point and subdivided the lands using the US Public Land Survey System that had been conceived by Thomas Jefferson. From the Initial Point, the land was divided into townships, north and south, and ranges, east and west, each six miles long. They plotted the location of rivers, streams, mountain ranges, wagon roads, and trails. In 1931, Oklahoma House Bill 149 was enacted, "providing locating, tracing, mapping and plats of the lines of the old established cattle trails across the state of Oklahoma, and providing for the expenses of such work . . ."[9] In 1933, the map was completed by the Engineering Department of the Oklahoma State Highway Commission. This state map documented the route of the GWT across Oklahoma.

Since the Oklahomans had the official path of the trail available, they progressed more easily with their marking project. John Yudell Barton, retired pharmacist, personally made the markers in his back yard. Even after the Texas trail project had officially been completed, Yudell continued to make posts for Texas ranchers who wanted to commemorate the path of the trail across their land. The trail across Oklahoma required fifty-six markers to achieve their standard of a marker every six miles.

July 12, 2003, Altus, First GWT Marker Dedicated in Oklahoma

Oklahomans dedicated the first GWT marker on July 12, 2003. In a grove of cottonwood trees on a pleasant summer morning, some two hundred people gathered on the north bank of the Red River. On land where the trail crossed, people sat on bales of hay waiting to enjoy a chuck-wagon breakfast and witness the history-making dedication of the first marker. Cowboy-humorist Kent Rollins, cook for the Red River Ranch Wagon, which is the official chuck wagon of the state of Oklahoma, demonstrated his skills with

· **First GWT Marker Dedication, Near Altus, Oklahoma**
Some two hundred people gathered on July 12, 2003, in Oklahoma to enjoy a chuck-wagon breakfast and to witness the first-ever Great Western Trail marker dedication. Near the north bank of the Red River in a grove of trees, people sat under shade trees to listen to music and trail history. Altus co-chairs Dennis Vernon and John Yudell Barton told about the process for marking the trail, and Illinois historian Dr. Walter "Chick" Bishop reviewed GWT history.

the bacon, eggs, biscuits, gravy, and cowboy coffee. Dr. Walter "Chick" Bishop, historian, spoke about the past trail history and the new trail history. Maurice King, master of ceremonies, invited Dennis Vernon and John Barton to explain the project and the purpose of the trail. They thanked Bob Klemme for originating the idea.

At section lines along the trail, fifty-six markers were cemented into place. Dedications, held at historically significant places along the trail, were located at trail ranches and places for annual trail commemorative events. On an icy-cold day in late April 2004, approximately 150 trail fans gathered to dedicate the second GWT marker at the historic LeVick Ranch. The marker is located at an area where millions of cattle and horses had traversed going north. The ranch is on the south bank of the North Fork of the Red River between Jackson and Kiowa Counties, formerly the Kiowa-Comanche-Apache reserve.

Approximately one hundred miles north of Altus, another post marked the trail at the small town of Vici. Rancher Jim Peck held the annual three-day Great Western Cattle Trail Drive there. At the event, many tourists experienced herding longhorns across the prairies, creeks, and canyons. Then they paraded down Vici's Broadway Street, driving the longhorns. Afterward, they socialized at a fish- and calf-fry dinner, a ranch rodeo, and a "real boot scootin' dance."[10] Two more markers were located at Elk City, one at the National Route 66 Museum and the other at the Farm and Ranch Museum.

On June 12, 2010, a GWT marker was dedicated near Altus, but for a special reason: possible national recognition for the trail. The marker was placed in a roadside park along with several red-granite monuments etched with trail history and a map. This marker recognized the Congressional Feasibility Study that, if approved, would designate the Great Western and Chisholm Trails as National Historic Trails. The study was led by two National Park Service employees at the National Trails System Office in Santa Fe, New Mexico. Embedded in this marker are the names Dr. Aaron Mahr and Dr. Frank Norris. A group of almost one hundred people in attendance at a Feasibility Study Town Hall meeting reconvened afterward for the dedication.

Marking the GWT across Oklahoma was a project that fit naturally with other local efforts in Altus to preserve trail history. The town of Altus had also preserved trail history with collections and exhibits of trail and Indian history at the Museum of the Western Prairie, an Oklahoma Historical Society facility. The museum society funded the reprinting of a pocket journal written by GWT drover Lewis Warren Neatherlin in 1876 as he rode up the trail.[11] Bart McClenny, museum curator, also created a calendar with daily entries from Neatherlin's journal, twenty-first-century GWT dedication dates, and other trail events. Oklahoma was preserving and promoting GWT history very effectively for their state.

Oklahoman musicians, artists, and videographers also perpetuated trail experiences through their media. Oklahoman cowboy poet and musician LeRoy Jones, a Mountain View farmer and rancher, wrote and recorded "The Great Western Trail." At the National Cowboy and Western Heritage Museum, his song won the 2009 Wrangler Award for best original composition. Jim Carothers of Perry, Oklahoma, designed a GWT branding iron with a four-plait braided-steel handle and two other design choices. His designer boards with a longhorn logo and GWT brand were often used for awards. All the trail groups supported Oklahoma videographer J. L. Courtney's suggestion that Bob Klemme be awarded the first one for his leadership in marking both trails. On October 23, 2009, in Fort Worth at a gathering of the Great Western Cattle Trail Association and Chisholm Trail Association, Bob received the award. J. L. stood quietly behind the lens of the camera, recording yet another historical trail event. Copies of his collection of videos have been donated to several museums, university archives, and the GWT Special Collection at the Texas Tech Southwest Collection/ Special Collections Library.

The Oklahoma group followed drover Neatherlin's journal entries to place the markers across that state. Neatherlin had signed on to help his cousin John H. Slaughter, who had been a Confederate soldier, Texas Ranger, and sheriff at Tombstone, Arizona. Slaughter appointed Neatherlin as trail boss for the nine thousand head of cattle he was sending north. The longhorns were separated into three herds. On March 12, 1876, Neatherlin joined the herds six miles west of San Antonio. He delivered some of the cattle to Slaughter at Dodge City but took others on to Nebraska. After a ten-day train trip, Neatherlin returned to Texas on July 17, four months and five days after he left.[12] His journal also included his earlier experiences going up the Chisholm Trial to Kansas.

On May 18, 1876, two months and six days after joining the herds near San Antonio, Neatherlin crossed his herds into Oklahoma. He set up camp southwest of the Wichita Mountains. He said "It was a very fine valley of rich productive land. . . ." That night it rained and two of the herds comingled, so they had to be separated. The next day Wichita Indians asked for two cows, which Neatherlin gave to them. They asked for sugar, coffee, flour, and soap, but they were appeased with only coffee and soap. The next five days were rainy as they traveled over smooth prairie, finally arriving on May 25 at the Washita River (near present-day Hammon on Highway 34). Six other herds that Neatherlin thought had crossed over from the Chisholm Trail were waiting to cross the river. On May 28 (near the present-day Camargo on Highway 34), they crossed the Canadian River after having to splice the wagon tongue with rawhide. On May 29, 1876, Neatherlin hunted for Camp Supply as their chuck wagon had been without flour since May 27, but the Neatherlin herds passed approximately twenty-six miles west of what would become Fort Supply in 1878.[13]

The command at Fort Supply, to preserve the grass for the troops' animals, required all herds to go at least ten miles west of the fort. Camp Supply, established on November 18, 1868, in the valley between Beaver River and Wolf Creek, was directed to provide supplies for the winter campaigns against the Southern Plains Indians. From there, Lieutenant Colonel George A. Custer had led the seventh US Cavalry south to the Washita River and destroyed the village overseen by Cheyenne Chief Black Kettle. The Camp also served as a supply point for the Red River War of 1874–1875, which marked the final efforts to constrain the Southern Plains Indians. For the next twenty-five years, the post provided supplies, and the troops performed peace-keeping duties. One of their duties was to escort cattle herds across Indian Territory to Dodge City, Kansas. Today, five restored buildings serve to help visitors interpret the fort's history.[14]

On June 2, 1876, Neatherlin's herds forded the North Fork of the Canadian River. With no wood to build fires, they used buffalo chips. On June 9, the herds crossed the Cimarron River, also known as the Red Fork of the Arkansas. The crossing, called Deep Hole, offered a respite for the drovers and a chance to buy supplies. Neatherlin had ridden ahead to Dodge City on June 4 to meet Slaughter. He spent several days cutting some 1,500 cattle from the herds. Six cowhands quit; he settled with them and hired four more and started the herds toward Ogallala, Nebraska.[15] The path of the trail had been established two years before Neatherlin's longhorns trailed to Ogallala. This documented source is evidence that thousands of cattle were moving beyond Dodge City to accommodate markets in states north of the Kansas railhead.

October 23, 2004, First Kansas GWT Dedicated at Dodge City

Neatherlin crossed his herds into Kansas destined for the first supply point, Dodge City. Some 128 years later, the Bandera Trail Riders also crossed into Kansas. They arrived in Dodge City 48 days after traveling 655 miles from Bandera, Texas. At thirteen to fourteen miles per day, the Trail Riders made their historic entrance to Dodge City on October 23, 2004. The Oklahoma and Texas trail teams entered Dodge City along with the Bandera Trail Riders.

Prior to the cattle-trail days, Dodge City, located in western Kansas, had provided supplies and entertainment for Santa Fe Trail travelers and soldiers at Fort Dodge. Homesteaders bypassed the vast grassy prairie with its dry climate, preserving an unrestricted land for Comanche, Kiowa, and Kiowa-Apache Indians. This was significant for the homesteaders as the dry years compelled them to move on to land with sufficient water for farming. Buffalo hunters, however, came in to harvest the millions of buffalo for their

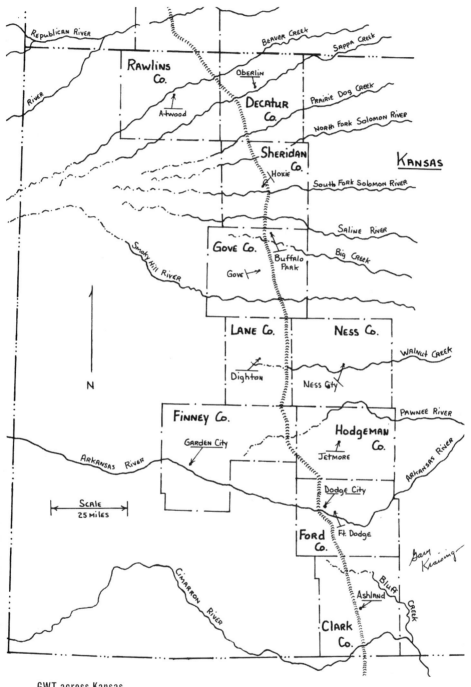

GWT across Kansas

lucrative hides. Dodge City filled with buffalo hunters, soldiers, prostitutes, saloonkeepers, gamblers, and others seeking fun and fortune.[16]

The arrival of the Santa Fe Railroad in September 1872 changed Dodge City into a railhead for shipping cattle brought up from South Texas. Only two years later, drovers arrived from the south to collect a paycheck and wash away the trail dust. At about this time, history and fiction began to run together like mountain streams. Legends and lore grew from the escapades of town residents such as Bat Masterson, Wyatt Earp, Luke Short, Clay Allison, J. H. "Doc" Holliday, Big Nose Kate Elder, Squirrel Tooth Alice, and Dora Hand. Dodge City, the Queen of the Cow Towns, welcomed cowboys who often involuntarily "migrated" from Front Street's Long Branch Saloon to the infamous Boot Hill Cemetery. Later, the trail town achieved immortality on the silver screen when it was portrayed as the "Bibulous Babylon of the Plains."[17]

Understanding the era of cattle trails requires a comprehensive look at a trail town. Dodge City is a good model for this analysis. The contrasting side to Dodge City's infamy shows that it had a literary society, churches, volunteer fire companies, benevolence groups, and a band. Indeed, in 1878 a fundraiser provided money to purchase instruments for the band, which eventually came to be called the Dodge City Cowboy Band. A stagecoach driver from Colorado, Chalkley Beeson, who played violin, helped organize it. Beeson and his partner William H. Harris built and ran the famous Long Branch Saloon, "one of the best establishments in Dodge." Beeson and four other musicians provided background music. No dancing or prostitutes were allowed, however. One room provided a bar, a billiard table, and space for the band. The second was for private gambling, but *professional* gamblers were banned. The third room contained cots for drunks to sleep it off. In 1883, Beeson sold his share of the business to Luke Short, a dapper gambler skilled with a pistol, who eliminated the restrictions that Beeson had enforced.[18]

To understand the politics that affected cattle businesses during the trail era, a look at Dodge City beyond the oft-told tales of gamblers and prostitutes on Front Street is important. The Dodge City Cowboy Band's fame spread. In 1884, the nineteen performers played at the First National Cattle Grower's Convention held in St. Louis, Missouri. With some ten thousand cattlemen attending, the Cowboy Band, dressed in white felt hats, blue shirts, leather leggings, boots, spurs, and belts with ivory-handled pistols, played and escorted delegations into the Exposition Hall. The drum major carried a five-foot tip-to-tip set of longhorns with a banner, "Cowboy Band, Dodge City, Kansas, $20,000,000." The figure indicated "the amount of hard cash represented in the band."[19] The band members included the owners of the lucrative Long Branch saloon and other businessmen. This information, printed in the program for the convention, whether it is accurate or not, indicated the affluence of businesspeople and cattlemen and the potential political power of the new organization.

One of the goals of the new organization of cattle growers was to unify ranchers and cattlemen. As the strength of the unification grew, the organization proved to be a source of power for cattlemen, ranchers, and cattle-related businesses. Inevitably, the political force that the cattle industry was developing on the Great Plains would affect the business of trailing and selling herds from the south. The cattle and the cattle trails were major issues at the first convention. Three issues created spirited discussion: Texas pressed for Congress to establish a National Trail, a corridor that would be designated for trailing cattle to circumvent areas that had been closed to cattle trails. The trail would allow the flow of cattle to continue moving north. Kansas opposed it. The North would not oppose it but would prefer that it failed. Wyoming pressed for governmental approval to lease large blocks of land by districts so that associations of cattlemen could prevent the fencing off of water sources. All the delegates agreed that Congress would be asked to pass rigid quarantine laws. According to the convention delegates, it was pleura-pneumonia from the East they feared, rather than tick fever. This contradicted later findings about tick fever, which was identified as a main perpetrator of death for domestic livestock.[20]

The vast area represented by delegates to the cattlemen's convention reflected the length of the GWT itself. The convention delegates came from twelve states and Mexico. The first elected president was Colonel Robert D. Hunter, a native of Scotland and a resident of St. Louis. Hunter's business acumen was exceeded only by the respect people had for him. Words used to describe Col. Hunter included sterling honesty, inflexible integrity, kind heart, and chivalrous deportment. "The great Convention of cattlemen, when it had resolved itself into a permanent Association, honored itself more than Col. Hunter, by choosing him its permanent President for the first year."[21]

The cattle industry was starting to show its power and influence as its members branched out into commerce and politics. Ethics and integrity continued to be touted as the criteria for selection of leaders and the conduct

GWT Co-Chair Jeff Bearden Delivers a GWT Post, Dodge City, Kansas
Texas GWT co-chair Jeff Bearden, with Rick Jouett riding shotgun, delivered a GWT marker in Jeff's mule-drawn chuck wagon. The seven-foot white post was carried down Wyatt Earp Boulevard to its location on Front Street in Dodge City, Kansas.

of the cattle business. For a brief time, the cattle-trail era created wealth and provided opportunities for people in the trail business to buy enough land to ranch or establish cattle-related business. The cattle-trail business seemed to invent itself even as it was emerging.

The political power of the cattle-growers organization was soon tested by the effects of the Homestead Act of 1862. The new government-ordained land ownership plan for homesteaders from the East caused a major conflict with ranchers on the open-range country on the plains. This act also had inherent flaws. Homesteaders' survival on their new land was complicated by a limit of 160 acres as well as their being strangers to the plains. They tried to work with unfamiliar terrain in very harsh weather. The opportunity for ownership brought the inexperienced to a land usable for open-range ranching but not adaptable for farming. After using their meager savings to leave the East, the homesteaders had no choice but to try to survive on their insufficient homesteads. Ranchers and farmers were doomed to the violence that sprung up between them given the adverse conditions and legislative flaws.

October 24, 2004, Dodge City, Kansas, Welcomes Trail Riders and Oklahoma and Texas GWT Partners

The inevitable violence between open-range ranchers and homesteaders is covered in more detail when it reaches a climax farther up the trail (see Chapter 9). For now, the first dedication in Kansas was celebrated in Dodge City on October 24, 2004. The Texas trail team made a grand entrance into Dodge City to deliver the GWT marker to its permanent location. On historic Front Street, the white marker would stand adjacent to a twelve-foot bronze longhorn lead steer named El Capitan. Texan Jeff Bearden drove his mule-pulled chuck wagon with partner Rick Jouett riding shotgun down Wyatt Earp Boulevard to deliver the marker. Rick obliged a lady's request: Kansas State Representative Jan Scoggins-Waite, Rotary president, requested to ride between the men on their drive down the car-filled streets to the marker location. The trail team was happy to oblige, as Rep. Scoggins-Waite had cut through quite a bit of red tape to make the trip through downtown possible. The clicking of the metal wheels on the pavement attracted local citizens' attention, giving Jan a chance to wave from the chuck wagon.

At the dedication ceremony, Rep. Scoggins-Waite welcomed the Rotarians and thanked the Oklahoma group for donating the marker. Bob Klemme, mastermind of the project, was recognized. Oklahoma Senator Bob Kerr presented the Kansas folks with an Oklahoma flag that had flown over the state capitol. Ford County Commissioner Kim Goodnight provided leadership for the outstanding dedication ceremony.

Afterward, Goodnight gave the trail teams a personal tour of Front Street, the Long Branch Saloon, the museum, and other stores representing the "Queen of the Cow Town" days. Commissioner Goodnight, a descendant of trail boss/rancher Charles Goodnight, had also attended the first Texas marker dedication at Doan's Adobe.

The legends surrounding Dodge City had complicated documenting the length of the GWT. Movies and fiction about the trail town often indicated that the cattle trails ended at Dodge City. With more than its share of notorious characters, Dodge often became the location for the climax of a novel or movie plot. Movies embedded cattle trails into the general public's memories along with the erroneous information about the terminus of the trail in Dodge City. Separating fact from fiction about the trail was difficult going north from Dodge City. The Great Western Cattle Trail-Kansas chapter worked to correct that misconception. With their books and maps,

First GWT Marker Dedicated in Kansas, Dodge City, 2004
On October 23, 2004, the first GWT marker in Kansas was dedicated at Dodge City and was witnessed by a large gathering of volunteers from many states. The post was placed near the bronze Longhorn steer on Front Street. State Representative Jan Scoggins-Waite, Rotary president (near the post), and Kim Goodnight (kneeling by the post) organized the dedication to coincide with the entry of the Bandera Trail Riders following their forty-eight-day trail drive from Texas.

Kansas GWT authorities Gary and Margaret Kraisinger helped to winnow the truth from the fiction about the length and location of the trail.

Even trail boss Neatherlin, who wrote his journal in 1876 (two years after the first herd went up the GWT), continued north beyond Dodge City. Thousands of longhorns left Dodge going north to Ogallala, Nebraska, typically an eighteen-day trip for herds. On June 10, 1876, Neatherlin took John Slaughter's herds north of Dodge City to Saw Log Creek, where they stayed until June 18. At this point, six men had quit, four new ones were hired in Dodge, and Neatherlin lost his pocketbook with $98.55 in it. He picked up twenty-five horses south of Dodge and hunted stray cows. A cold north wind was blowing; grass was short and dry—an indication that homesteaders would find farming the land difficult.[22]

On June 2, 1876, Neatherlin's herds crossed Walnut Creek, where two trails went north from Dodge City. One went almost directly north and the other went on the Hays City–Ellis Trail, more easterly to the Kansas-Pacific Railroad. That trail was closed the next year because of the 1877

Kansas Quarantine Law. The conflict between homesteaders, towns, and herds continued to be volatile in Kansas.[23] After the 1877 Kansas quarantine, the GWT moved ten or twelve miles farther west. Crossing Kansas, the trail split into four different routes for various reasons: grass, water, restrictions for cattle, citizens who protested the movement of cattle, and sometimes just preference of drovers. The major reason was the volume of cattle trailing across Kansas was unequaled by any other trail because the demand for cattle was at its highest.

The drover's journal continued to provide day-to-day trail details. On June 23, 1876, Neatherlin's herds crossed Smoky Hill River. On June 24, he took one man farther west to Buffalo Station, on the Kansas Pacific Railroad, to have a pain in his jaw and teeth checked by a rare dentist found in those parts. On June 25, after a twenty-six-mile drive without water, Neatherlin's drovers found water at Saline Creek, which was thankfully fresh in spite of its name. Unknown to them, Lieutenant Colonel George A. Custer had died in Montana that day. After several cold, rainy days while still in Kansas, they forded the South and North Forks of the Solomon River, Prairie Dog Creek, Sappa Creek, and Beaver Creek. On July 1, they crossed the Nebraska state line.[24] Thousands of cattle followed Neatherlin's route to Ogallala, Nebraska, where many of the cattle were shipped to eastern markets. However, the demand by open-range ranchers for cattle encouraged more than half of the drovers to bypass Ogallala and continue north to the Dakotas, Wyoming, Montana, and Canada. The trail north of Ogallala was called the Texas Trail, which has been documented as a long segment of the GWT.

🐂

A drover's journal and a land survey were able to provide trail documentation as the historic drovers moved across Oklahoma and Kansas. Along the southern part of the trail in Indian Territory, satisfactory land-leasing arrangements among ranchers, Native Americans, and the government were identified by the GWT researchers and others. The lifestyle of some of the area residents, with their risk-filled adventures and growing affluence, captured the attention of national leaders and typified many people who started ranches and business along the trail. The political power of the ranchers was demonstrated in Kansas and other states during the trail era. Dodge City, so often defined by its notorious residents, was determined to have a more balanced history than is typically rendered in trail books. Oklahoma and Kansas have shared the legacy of the cattle trails—and the legend of the cowboy—with Texas.

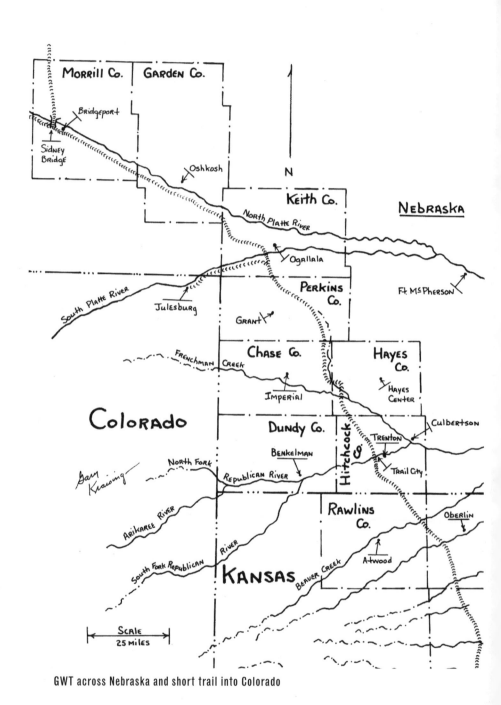

GWT across Nebraska and short trail into Colorado

CHAPTER 8
Nebraska, Colorado, the Dakotas

The trail project had expanded from Oklahoma and Texas into Kansas and Mexico when Rotarians meeting in Corpus Christi, Texas, were introduced to it. Nebraska became the pivotal state for the expansion into the northern areas. Nebraska was also where the GWT branched, with one part going to the Dakotas and the other to Wyoming, Montana, and Canada. After two dedications in Nebraska, Colorado was followed by North Dakota and South Dakota. When trail teams visited the communities, they noticed evidence of the various aspects of the trail era embedded in the activities of major ranches, exhibits at museums, the art, and reasons given for visits of famous Americans.

October 21–24, 2005, Corpus Christi, Texas, Rotary Zone Institute

Success for spreading the message about the GWT project started with a basic business practice. Rather than making a cold call to a person, the teams focused on being introduced by one respected colleague to another one, providing an opportunity to discuss the project. Jim Aneff, district Rotary leader, provided one opportunity at the 2005 Rotary Institute, Zones 25 & 26, in Corpus Christi, Texas. Jim invited the Texas trail team to set up a GWT exhibit for October 21 through 24. Zone Institutes are gatherings of elected Rotary leaders who represent large districts. The Great Plains states' leaders represented districts the trail crossed. It was a ten-hour trip to set up the exhibit, but this was the key to success in the northern states. With no one else available to go, I volunteered.

Rotary International President-Elect Bill Boyd and RI Director Ron Burton View GWT Display at the Rotary Zone Institute
At the Rotary Zone Institute in Corpus Christi, Texas, October 21–24, 2005, William "Bill" Boyd, Rotary International president-elect of New Zealand, and Ron Burton, RI director of Oklahoma (later, RI president), showed an interest in the Great Western Trail exhibit. Jim Aneff, Texas Rotary leader, and Sylvia Mahoney, GWT research project co-chair, explained the merits of the Vernon Rotary Centennial project. With the two Rotary leaders showing interest, other members visited the booth, and the project grew.

At the Zone Institute, Jim Aneff called attention to the trail exhibit. Rotarians viewed the cowhide that is often used to wrap a post prior to it being displayed for its dedication and saw photos of chuck wagons, mules, and the white posts at dedications where Rotarians wore jeans, boots, hats, and denim shirts bearing a GWT and longhorn logo. The Rotary International president-elect, William B. Boyd from New Zealand, and board member Ron Burton of Norman, Oklahoma, also stopped to look. Their presence and interest drew attention to the display. Zone leaders asked questions. William (Bill) E. Ballou of Kearney, Nebraska, made a proposal while standing in front of the display: "Nebraska needs to be marked. We will do this." His invitation to come to Ogallala furthered our project beyond anything we had imagined. Other district governors who joined the project were Jorge

Verduzco of Laredo, Texas; Doug Whinnery of Kerrville, Texas; and Cloyd Clark of McCook, Nebraska.

The Ogallala dedication would be held on May 6, 2006, two years after the decision to mark the trail was made. The Vernon trail team, after hearing Bill Ballou's invitation, started making plans immediately. A major problem centered on the post-makers themselves. For the 620 miles across Texas, Phil McCuistion, Rick Jouett, and Paul Hawkins had made and painted more than one hundred cement posts. To make posts for twelve hundred more miles stopped the post-makers and all of us in our tracks, but only briefly.

The solution was born from an aphorism: "Don't give them a post. Teach them how to make a post." The Texas trail team members did both: they gave each trail state a post and a metal mold to make additional posts. Rotarians from the other states were invited to the Ogallala dedication. The Texas trail team agreed to attend each state's first dedication. What an excellent plan to develop, but what a complicated plan to execute.

The Texas and Oklahoma trail partners started preparing for the Ogallala trip. Six metal molds had to be made. The six molds and six posts, each seven feet long, had to be transported 525 miles to Ogallala. When invitations went to other trail-state Rotarians for the Ogallala dedication, they were advised that their gifts included a metal mold and 225-pound post to transport back to their home states.

Bob Klemme, the creator of the first molds, offered to provide foundry-made letters for the new molds. Vernon College's welding instructor Gene Nessel volunteered to weld the six metal molds during his Christmas holidays. Vernon Rotary bought the metal. Gene invested thirty-six hours in cutting and welding the molds for Nebraska, South Dakota, North Dakota, Wyoming, Montana, and Saskatchewan. Julesburg, Colorado, Rotarian Jim Fender agreed to share a mold with Nebraska. The railhead at Julesburg, which ran only twenty-eight miles southwest of Ogallala, required just a few posts.

The Nebraska trail team in Ogallala prepared for an international gathering of volunteers from nine states and Canada. Bill Ballou's offer was as good as the gold that trail bosses carried home in their saddle bags. He contacted district leaders Tom and Janet Kraus of Ogallala. What a powerhouse couple they proved to be, addressing every detail for the dedication and a weekend of entertainment.

The process included a steady stream of emails that kept Rotary leaders in the other states and Regina, Saskatchewan, apprised of the plans for the Ogallala ceremony. Jim Aneff and David Mason, Texas Rotary leaders, signed on for another trip. Texas State Representative Rick Hardcastle sponsored House Resolution 270, which captured the importance of the dedication: "The Great Western Trail serves as a bridge between our states, and by celebrating this enduring landmark, we recognize the importance of our shared heritage and history."

Lewis Warren Neatherlin's 1876 GWT Journal

Drover Lewis Warren Neatherlin kept a record of his 1876 trip to Ogallala in a journal. On July 1, Neatherlin's herds entered Nebraska on the southern border into what is now Hitchcock County. On July 3, near Trail City, Trenton, and Culbertson, the herds crossed the Republican River, which converged with French Creek as it flowed from the northwest. The almost-level terrain of Kansas had already changed. The herds would soon experience a long, waterless expanse of land.[1]

After Neatherlin crossed the Republican River near Culbertson, the drovers faced Frenchman Creek and Stinking Water Creek, the last water crossings before the South Platte near Ogallala. Instead of celebrating the US Centennial on July 4, Neatherlin and the drovers experienced their "hardest day's work." The four trails through Kansas had merged into one again in Nebraska because of the rough terrain in southwest Hayes County, northwest of Culbertson. The herds would have to be pushed across a waterless strip of land before they reached the Platte River.[2]

The terrain changed when the drovers crossed the next two creeks. After crossing the brushy, rough Frenchman Creek, the drovers found deep canyons and steep hills. The ears of their horses were almost hidden by the dust. On July 5, they herded the cattle along Stinking Water Creek until time to cross a plain to the Platte River, some thirty miles distant, the driest portion of the trip. With the typical trail day for cattle being ten to twelve miles followed by reaching a waterhole or river, this was a difficult three-day trek without water. Expert drovers were needed to set a safe pace to keep the longhorns from dying on the trail. On July 8, they finally reached the river valley and moved on to their destination at Ogallala. Some of the herds would go directly to the Union Pacific Railroad, where cattle were loaded onto boxcars. Other herds followed the South Platte River southwest approximately thirty miles to another railhead at Julesburg, Colorado.[3]

Marla Makin Sings at GWT Marker Dedication, Culbertson, Nebraska
At the GWT dedication in Culbertson, Nebraska, Marla Makin of Hill City, Kansas, sashayed out in her dark-green taffeta dress with feathers and a bustle to present "Cattle Towns and Soiled Doves." The ceremony continued with Nebraska State Representative Mark Christensen and Rotary leaders Cloyd Clark, Bob Setter, and Jeanette Miller explaining the purpose of the trail project. Photograph courtesy of Cloyd Clark.

November 4, 2007, Culbertson, Nebraska, Dedication

Neatherlin's herds had passed near Culbertson, Nebraska, where a dedication ceremony would be held 131 years later on November 4, 2007. Nebraska Rotary leaders Cloyd Clark of McCook, Bob Setter of Valentine, and Tom Kraus of Madrid gathered in Culbertson. Clark, county judge and a Nebraska Historical Society Foundation trustee, knew the county and its trail history. Since Judge Clark lived only eleven miles east of Culbertson, he had promoted the dedication. At the dedication, Nebraska State Representative Mark Christensen focused on the cattle industry, preserving trail history, and promoting heritage tourism. Marla Matkin of Hill City, Kansas, sashayed out in her dark-green-taffeta period dress with feathers and a bustle to present a dramatic reading, "Cattle Towns and Soiled Doves." Some ninety trail fans attended the ceremony.

June 23, 2007, Julesburg, First Dedication in Colorado

The next dedication stop, Julesburg, Colorado, had a connection to Buffalo Bill. The Pony Express had passed through Julesburg, and legend says that William F. Cody, at age fourteen, had a brief career as a Pony Express rider. Although the Pony Express was a financial failure and the fact that Buffalo Bill was a rider has been disputed, Buffalo Bill used it in his shows to romanticize the West. His presentations contributed to the Pony Express becoming a part of the legendary American West. Whether it was Buffalo Bill's route or not, the Pony Express extended from the North Platte River seventy-six miles to Julesburg, the Colorado railhead used for the overflow of cattle coming up the GWT.[4]

Back to the Past with Buffalo Bill

Along the way, project teams recovered evidence that publicity for the West (garnered by showmen such as Buffalo Bill) helped elevate the trail and the drover into a well-known, romanticized lifestyle. That lifestyle contributed to defining the legendary cowboy. William F. Cody, who made his home at Scout's Rest, east of Ogallala on the North Platte River, capitalized on Americans' appetite for experiences about the romanticized West. They had imagined it from reading biographies, dime novels, dramas, and newspaper articles. Cody added his live-action renditions of America's Western frontier to this fanciful lore.

Using his entrepreneurial skills, Cody selected the stage name Buffalo Bill from a dime novel and created his Wild West persona. In 1883 he organized *Buffalo Bill's Wild West* to perform an American West reality show for Easterners. His cast included famous Native Americans, such as Sitting Bull and Geronimo, as well as Annie Oakley, Wild Bill Hickok, and many others. Cody's shows supported the growing myth about the American West. He also took *Buffalo Bill's Wild West* to European markets, exposing these newcomers to the unique cowboy era. Although considerably romanticized, Cody's influence on the establishment of the legend of the cowboy going up a cattle trail did lead to an almost universal admiration for this aspect of American culture.[5]

Cody also recognized the importance of using the media to fill the seats at his shows. While Cody traveled, Ned Buntline, pen name for Edward Z. C. Judson, created the Buffalo Bill legend. Cody's exploits set him as a hero in his shows and in novels.[6] Later, Colonel Prentiss Ingraham

First GWT Marker Dedicated in Colorado, Julesburg, 2007
On June 23, 2007, the site of the first GWT marker dedication in Colorado was the Welcome Center at Julesburg. Jim Fender, Rotary leader (seated at front table), organized the dedication. Colorado State Representative Jerry Sonneberg and Pony Express master historian Joseph R. Nardone gave highlights of the area's rich history. Sylvia Mahoney, GWT co-chair, reviewed the trail research project, followed by the dedication of the marker with Red River water.

added to the legend by writing many more Buffalo Bill dime novels.[7] His longevity in popular Americana helped establish his place in the history of the Old West and keep trail history alive.

In a more realistic vein, when drovers trailed herds to the railheads at Julesburg, Colorado, they found that it was a crossroad of cultures and a passage to the western states. Julesburg was relocated three times after it was burned by Indians in 1865 in retaliation for the Sand Creek Massacre. The small town was perfectly positioned in the path of the westward migration. Much of its history is tied to Plains Indians, the military, stagecoaches, railroads, and cattle trails. Fort Sedgwick, the Overland Stage route, the Pony Express, the Great Western Trail, and the Union Pacific all included Julesburg on their paths.

The Colorado Central Julesburg Branch, built by Union Pacific in 1882 as a cutoff for its Omaha-Denver traffic, connected its Nebraska mainline with the Denver Pacific line to Denver. The Julesburg line later became the first subdivision of Union Pacific's Wyoming Division, connecting La Salle on the old Denver Pacific with Julesburg on the Union Pacific mainline. Earlier, nearby Fort Sedgwick, made famous by Kevin Costner's movie *Dances with Wolves*, had protected the transcontinental telegraph in addition to travelers on the Overland Route.[8] The Union Pacific railhead at Julesburg absorbed the overflow of cattle from Ogallala, twenty-eight miles northeast. Julesburg rivaled Dodge and Ogallala for raucous saloons and gambling houses.[9]

The GWT marker dedication highlighted two parts of Julesburg's expansive history. The week prior to the GWT dedication, a larger-than-life bronze sculpture of a Pony Express rider had been dedicated at the Colorado Welcome Center. As mentioned, the Pony Express was short-lived. It existed from April 3, 1860, to November 20, 1861. The riders provided mail service between St. Joseph, Missouri, and Sacramento, California, until the completion of the transcontinental telegraph. After leaving St. Joseph, relays of riders went through Kansas to Great Platte River Road in Nebraska. The route dipped down along the South Platte River to Julesburg and back into Nebraska, then to Wyoming and to the West Coast.[10]

The GWT project benefited from the respect that citizens of Julesburg had for their town's history. The marker was set in the shadow of the Pony Express memorial. The dual dedications, spaced only a week apart, gave Joseph R. Nardone, national executive director of the Pony Express Trails Association, the opportunity to speak at the GWT dedication. He linked trail history and Pony Express history. From where he stood in front of the GWT marker, he was encircled by evidence of the diverse history of the area. The Colorado Visitors Center at the northeast corner of the state featured Julesburg's past with an Indian teepee, the Pony Express bronze, and the GWT marker. For dedication day, flags of nine US states, Mexico, and Canada were featured to represent the path of the trail.

Jim Fender, assisted by other members of the Rotary club, organized the dedication ceremony—no small feat. State Representative Jerry Sonnenberg reaffirmed the trail's place in Colorado's history. Representative Marilyn Musgrave had signed the Congressional bill proposing that the GWT be approved as a National Historic Trail. Although the trail dipped only twenty-eight miles into Colorado, Jim and others persisted in recognizing that history. Jim had attended the Ogallala dedication and the last Texas GWT dedication in Vernon. The Texas trip, a ten-hour drive, was indicative of the volunteers' support for other trail teams. The Julesburg citizens were joined by Rotary leaders from Jackson Hole, Wyoming, and Ogallala, Nebraska. Trail friends from Bandera, Texas, drove some sixteen hours to attend the dedication.

Also on display at the Colorado Welcome Center was an exceptional work of metal art: flying eagles made of minute metal pieces designed to create the illusion of feathers. Rotary president Terry Hinde, a welder by profession, had created the labor-intensive and intricate design. The same artistic presence continued on the main street of Julesburg. Their renovated old-time movie theater, the Hippodrome Theater, was being run by community volunteers. Local citizens sold tickets, made popcorn, and provided leadership for the youth who came to see the movies. These courtesies, given so generously, were necessary for all to enjoy a movie without interruptions. The theater itself brought back memories of Saturday afternoons spent at the movies, watching cowboys in white hats prevail over bad times and bad folks. The vitality of the town of approximately 1,450 people and their unified efforts to provide entertainment for their youth, display art, preserve buildings, and preserve their history, especially GWT history, showed their range of values. Without the door to the community being opened by the trail project, this intimate knowledge of the town and its leaders could have been undiscovered.

Photos of the dedications became records for the history-making twenty-first-century trail dedications. Heather Burell of Bandera, Texas, recorded Julesburg's new trail history with her camera, as she had at almost every dedication. She followed through with an often-neglected part of photo taking: she identified everyone in the shot and used her scrapbooking expertise to create a pictorial history of the trail events. Her record of current trail history has been included along with other trail documentation in the GWT Collection at the Texas Tech Southwest Collections/Special Collections Library.

After the dedication in Colorado, the next dedication was at Ogallala, Nebraska. On May 3, 2006, a convoy of Texas and Oklahoma trail drivers headed north to Ogallala. During the trail days, friends and strangers were often welcomed to share a fire and join a meal. On the way to Nebraska, the Texas trail team found this to be true when we stopped at Dodge City. Kim and Beth Goodnight asked us to share a meal, but it was not potluck. They treated our group of twenty-four travelers to cattle-country ribeye steaks at the historic Dodge Steak House. Their hospitality illustrated the friendship that united volunteers working on the project.

The project's magnitude and acceptance by so many were also evident at Ogallala when the large group of trail project volunteers reached their destination. Arriving first were Jeff Bearden and Rick Jouett in their heavy-duty pickups loaded with seven 225-pound posts and six metal molds. A convoy of travelers followed them to Ogallala's Front Street, where the posts and molds were leaned against stacked bales of hay in the center of the street made famous by celebrating drovers. On this street, the Livery Barn Café, the Cowboy's Rest, and the Crystal Palace Saloon provided a visual perspective of the trail days. The jail, a reminder of prairie justice, was only a few steps down the street. On Saturday, May 6, 2006, the posts and molds were officially presented to Rotary members from the other states, followed by the dedication of the first Nebraska marker at the foot of Boot Hill Cemetery.

At 4:30 that Friday afternoon, the Ogallala weekend celebration started. The trail teams went north seventeen miles to the internationally famous Haythorn Land and Cattle Co. ranch. The beef brisket dinner they provided set the tone for an evening of celebrating the storied ranch and trail's past. Some two hundred people assembled to hear descendants relate family trail histories. In turn, Texas trail team members noted that the project's success reflected the desire of the local citizens to keep the spirit of the trail alive.

What is now the Haythorn Land and Cattle Co. was founded by a drover and has been run by Haythorn descendants since that time. This large, famous ranch spreads across some 90,000 acres in the Nebraska Sandhills region. Beneath those sandy hills is the largest underground water source on the continent, the Ogallala Aquifer. With the continuity of ownership and good management, the ranch has become the largest breeder of Quarter Horses in the United States and third largest in the world. The history of the ranch is not surprising: In 1876, at age sixteen, ranch patriarch Harry Haythornthwaite left his home in Lancaster, England, as a stowaway on a ship going to Galveston. When he arrived, he hired on to help with cattle drives. He went north on four cattle drives from Texas. On the fourth trip in the early 1880s, he stayed in Nebraska. He opened a livery barn, shortened his name to Haythorn, and married a veterinarian's daughter, Emma Gilpin. Together, they worked, saved, and laid the foundation for their ranching dynasty. Today, their great-grandson Craig and his wife, Jody, their two sons Cord and Sage, and Sage's wife, Kelley, run the ranch.[11] The continuity of the ranch ownership helped provide documented trail history.

Important to the history of the GWT is the network among the people across the plains, especially the trail ranches linked through their cattle and horse enterprises. The Haythorn Ranch was no exception. In 1946, the Haythorn Ranch, recognized today for its Quarter Horses, bought a grand champion halter mare from the R.A. Brown Ranch at Throckmorton, Texas. The two ranches have continued a close relationship since then.[12] Along with the ranch network was the commonality of daily use of cowboy trail skills by ranch cowboys. These skills, such as roundups, brandings, and good horsemanship, have remained a usable part of the business of running ranches today.

As the ranchers expanded their horse and cattle enterprises, they connected with other ranchers and businesspeople in a variety of horse- and cattle-related businesses. What is more, during the trail days, drovers had become familiar with others traveling the same trail. The familiarity and trust served to pass information across the Great Plains. The network has persisted into modern times through horse, ranch, and rodeo competitions.

The network was usable for many purposes, but especially for marketing horses and cattle. When a cowboy was in the market for a well-bred horse, he let it be known. Someone might mention a specific Haythorn horse or a horse from another spread. The cowboy would ask other horsemen or rodeo competitors if they had watched the horse work. This type of intangible connection united individuals and communities along the trail and other places. It often contributed to other activities, as well. For example, rodeo competition promoted networks that helped Jody Haythorn's daughter Shaley choose a rodeo college in Texas—Vernon College. Rodeo competition also connected Craig Haythorn to Texas when he competed for Texas Tech University. He also made friends with college contestants from many states when he qualified for the College National Finals Rodeo. Through these contacts, ranchers always find friends and familiar faces at large gatherings along the path of the trail. The businesses of ranches has kept the skills and the spirit of the trail viable across the Great Plains.

At the Haythorn ranch that evening, the project volunteers added to their accumulation of primary sources. Many Nebraska trail descendants with ties to Texas were introduced. Harry Haythorn's granddaughter Beldora Haythorn and his great-granddaughter Sally Haythorn-Mayden joined in sharing trail stories. Douglas Parks, an Ogallala veterinarian, the grandson of Walter E. Baker, told of Baker's trailing cattle to Ogallala from 1878 to 1885. Baker, after working for several ranches, homesteaded in Scotts Bluff

County. Rita Shimmin of Ogallala, the granddaughter of George B. Melvin, recounted Melvin's two-year service as a Texas Ranger and his working for the King Ranch before heading north to Ogallala in 1881 and 1882. Melvin had delivered beef to the South Dakota Rosebud and Pine Ridge Indian agencies. Another Melvin descendant, Kendra Melvin Homola was also introduced.

As the descendants spoke about their ancestors, it was evident that memories of the trail for many people in Nebraska related to the drovers in their families. The great-granddaughter of Samuel David "Lep" Sanders, Mary Ellen Bacon of Longmont, Colorado, told about Lep Saunders's statue that stands in Boot Hill Cemetery. Lep had made eighteen trips up the Texas Trail (GWT). Brent Lewis of Minden, Nebraska, great-grandson of Thomas Dalton Lewis, reported that his ancestor trailed herds from central Texas from 1874 to 1886. Although drover Lewis had trailed cattle north, he had ranched in Texas. Terry P. Brown, with his daughter Peggy, and Jay Petersen of Harrisburg, related tales about the drover in their family, Christopher Streeks. He made at least two cattle drives and worked as a foreman for the Wyoming Stock Growers Association. At the conclusion of the descendants' oral trail memories, historian Jack Pollock said, "The sons of the trail drivers became leaders of the cattle industry in Nebraska."[13] These descendants and the oral histories they presented provided a wealth of primary source material for the trail research project.

Jack Pollock, Ogallala Rotarian and historian, recovered and distributed to the public a sizeable amount of GWT history collected from the descendants. His knowledge of trail days and descendants proved to be a valuable resource for the Ogallala occasion. Pollock and his wife, Beverly, who had bought the Ogallala-based Keith County News in 1966, were instrumental in collecting and publishing trail history in their newspaper through the years. One article, "Descendants of Trail Drivers to Be Recognized," provided biographies of the drovers.[14] In the "Lonesome Dove Edition," a special edition of the Keith County News, editor Beverly Pollock said, in "Lep Sanders Made 18 Trips up the Texas Trail," that Harry D. Lute of Ogallala in 1927 interviewed the real trail drivers, who settled in Ogallala. The Pollocks' newspaper, the many trail descendants, and the city's leaders (maintaining historic Front Street and Boot Hill Cemetery) supported Ogallala's strong sense of its trail heritage. On February 20, 2009, the search for trail history suffered a setback when Jack Pollock died. For his research and collection of history, especially GWT history, he was awarded, posthumously, the prestigious Wagonmaster

GWT Markers and Molds Given to Six Trail States and Canada
Finding the path of the GWT took a major step forward at the first marker dedication in Nebraska on May 6, 2006, in Ogallala. The Texas trail team presented Rotary leaders from Nebraska, Colorado, South Dakota, North Dakota, Wyoming, Montana, and Saskatchewan with their first GWT marker and a metal mold to make additional posts for their states.

Award from the Nebraskaland Foundation for his leadership in causes that benefit the state or nation.[15]

After the evening at the Haythorn Ranch, the next morning's ceremony took place on historic Front Street, and the transfer of the seven-foot cement Great Western Trail markers and the metal molds was completed. The Texas trail team presented a marker to start the trail project in their areas to each of the representatives from six states and Regina, Saskatchewan.

John and Jin Patton and their son Bill flew in from Wyoming. Eric Scalzo loaded the marker and mold to take back to Wyoming. Colorado Rotarians Jim Fender, Daphne Davis, and Ken Hodges took a marker; they would share a mold with Nebraska. Jim and Sonja Ozbun of Dickinson, North Dakota, stepped up to help the trail project by offering to deliver posts to other northern states. Jim loaded four posts and four molds into his pickup. One he delivered to South Dakota; he took the other three (for Montana,

First GWT Marker Dedication in Nebraska, at Boot Hill Cemetery, Ogallala, 2006
On May 6, 2006, at the foot of Boot Hill in Ogallala, the first GWT marker in Nebraska was dedicated. Boy Scouts and GWT trail teams from other states presented the flags on the steps that ascended to the cemetery. Nebraska Rotary leaders Bill Ballou, Tom and Janet Kraus, and Jack Pollock told about the research project and Nebraska trail history. Descendants and representatives from the Texas, Oklahoma, Kansas, Wyoming, and North Dakota trail teams attended.

Saskatchewan, and North Dakota) to his home in Dickinson. For delivering the posts, Jim asked one favor from the Texans. On May 1, 2008, at the Rotary district conference, he planned to feature the first North Dakota GWT marker dedication. To add to its significance, he asked the Texas trail team to participate in the ceremony. The team members gave their word to the native North Dakotan, who had returned from wide-ranging experiences to be president of the university where he had earned his first two degrees, North Dakota State University.[16]

On dedication day in Ogallala, one outstanding event followed another. At high noon at the Crystal Palace, everyone gathered for barbecue. During lunch, a songbird of the trail, Drew Blessing and the Front Street Crystal Palace Revue, entertained the crowd. After lunch, the crowd went north to Boot Hill Cemetery to dedicate the marker at the foot of the hill. At the site, the visitors walked up the rock stairs to the archway entrance to the cemetery. Mingled among the old graves were sculptures of cowboys. The wooden grave markers had simple messages: "Mrs. Mary Bieasdale, 1883"; "William Breedon, July 1, 1879, age 17"; "WM Coffman, Shot, 1875"; and more. With silence and reverence, the visitors passed through, sensing the spirit of those bygone times that seemed to permeate the area. From the hill, the group returned down the steps to the marker dedication.

The dedication ceremony had all the pomp and circumstance of an international history-making event. Don Andrews, Rotary president, started the ceremony with Ogallala Boy Scouts and trail teams positioning a flag on each step to the cemetery's archway entrance. After a trumpet rendition of "The Star-Spangled Banner" and the Pledge of Allegiance, William "Bill" Ballou read Nebraska Governor Dave Heineman's proclamation that declared May 5–6, 2006, as Great Western Trail Drive Days in Nebraska. Jeff Bearden presented Ballou a Texas flag, flown over the State Capitol on San Jacinto Day, the day that marked the final battle of the Texas Revolution. Jim Aneff and Dave Mason honored Rotary efforts with commendations from the Texas district. Nebraska descendants of drovers originally from Texas were introduced.

The GWT Crosses Nebraska, South Dakota, and on to North Dakota

After the ceremony, the trail team followed the path north across Nebraska to South Dakota and North Dakota. Like the volunteers, many herds, some sources say as many as percent of the Texas cattle, bypassed Ogallala and continued north. Gary Kraisinger's maps supported evidence that trail teams had also recovered.[17] From Ogallala, the herds went northwest along the North Platte River some eighty-five miles to Bridgeport, Nebraska, where the trail forked. One path went almost due north to Dakota Territory while the other angled west to Wyoming and then turned north to Montana. The one to the Dakotas used a toll bridge over the North Platte River called Sydney Bridge, officially named Camp Clark Bridge. The herds going to the Dakotas watered again on the Niobrara River, with the next watering hole at Fort Robinson on White River in the northwest corner of Nebraska, which was, in 1874, the destination for John T. Lytle's first herd up the GWT from South Texas.[18]

In South Dakota, the trail went a few miles west of Oelrichs. Texas drover John Wells told of his 1883 trip going past Crow Butte Mountain and crossing the Cheyenne River three miles below Hot Springs at the foot of the Black Hills. The drovers made a small bend in the trail to skirt the hills. They

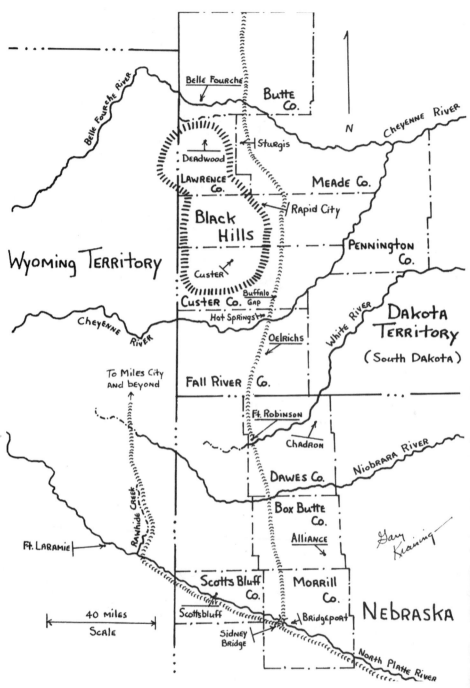

GWT across South Dakota

traveled a few miles east of Rapid City then turned northwest toward Belle Fourche on the Belle Fourche River. By that point in the trip, the drovers were ready to experience the town, which was established in 1884 as a way station, stage barn, and saloon, on the Deadwood-Medora stage line.[19] The Fremont, Elkhorn and Missouri Valley (FE & MV), an affiliate of the Chicago and North Western railroad, completed its line from Chadron, Nebraska, to Belle Fourche between 1880 and 1886. It became western Dakota Territory's first reliable, year-round transportation. Belle Fourche then became a shipping point for cattle.[20]

South Dakotans quickly joined the effort to mark the GWT across their state. The South Dakota Great Western Cattle Trail Association was organized. The group elected South Dakota Representative Betty Olson (now Senator) as president. They set a marker in Spearfish on September 5, 2012, and another one in Oelrichs on September 13, 2013. In 2014, the National Great Western Cattle Association and other state organizations met at the High Plains Western Heritage Center in Spearfish. Peggy Ables, executive director, said, "South Dakota is on fire promoting the trail—working with the highway department and legislature getting proposals passed to mark the trail on the roadways." A marker dedication during the national meeting brought local and area people to participate in the event on July 5, 2014.[21]

From Belle Fourche, the trail crossed what are now Butte and Harding Counties, going to a watering hole, Buffalo Springs, in Bowman County, North Dakota. From there to Medora, the GWT, also called the Texas Trail, passed between the Little Missouri River on the west and Cedar Creek, Cannonball River, and Heart River on the east. The drovers trailed the herds on a northward path to Fort Buford, their final destination. The fort was located on the confluence of the Yellowstone and Missouri Rivers in what is now North Dakota. At the fort, the longhorns provided meat for the soldiers, and government buyers purchased them for the reservations.[22]

P. P. Ackley Signs in North Dakota

One of the signs from the old nemesis of the trail, P. P. Ackley, was discovered in Scranton, North Dakota, near Buffalo Springs. His message on the sign, "Going Up the Texas Chisholm Trail 1867," was as questioned in that state as the signs were in Texas. A letter written by the collections manager of the Pioneer Trails Regional Museum in Bowman, North Dakota, stated, "Nobody in Scranton remembers when the signs appeared or when they put them up. We can find no documentation of the Chisholm Trail north

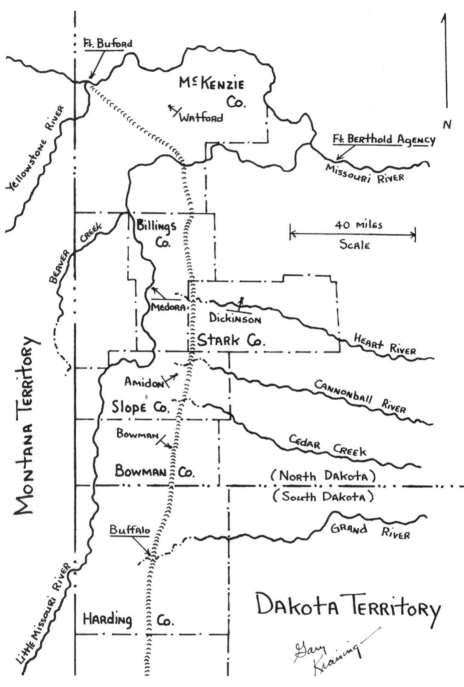

GWT across North Dakota

of Kansas."[23] Since Scranton was only thirteen miles east of Bowman, that community had checked sources to determine the validity of Ackley's signs.

June 13, 2009, Bowman, North Dakota, Dedication

On June 13, 2009, the Bowman dedication served more purposes than being a tangible reminder of the GWT herds that trailed through the town. It refuted the attempt by P. P. Ackley to change the trail's name to the Longhorn Chisholm Trail. It also became part of an international experience: David and Vonda Mason, Texas Rotary trail partners from Abilene, made a video of the dedication for their guest, Yulia Chrnova, a Russian Rotary Youth Exchange student. Along the trail from Texas to North Dakota, the Masons had filmed Yulia at historical sites and GWT markers. Yulia planned to show her video, *A Russian Student Rides the Great Western Cattle Trail in the U.S.A.*, to her high school classmates when she returned home. Bowman Rotary leaders Chris Peterson and Ron Petrowski planned and presented the dedication. They asked David Mason to relate some tales about his drover ancestor who trailed a herd close to Bowman.

Mason said that family research showed that the trail his grandfather took to establish a ranch in North Dakota passed near Bowman. In the spring of 1902, William Mason and his two sons, John William, age twenty-one, and Frederick (Fred) Arthur, age nineteen, drove a herd of several hundred cattle from Fairburn, South Dakota, to McKenzie County, North Dakota, where they stopped on Alkali Creek. The land had not been surveyed, so homesteading was not an option. They "squatted" there, spending the summer putting up hay and preparing a temporary shelter.

In the fall, Fred returned by horseback to Deadwood, South Dakota, where he spent the winter working for the Homestake gold mine. In the spring, Fred, William, and their stepmother, Anna, moved to North Dakota in covered wagons and trailed livestock. In 1906, they purchased the acreage where the spring was located. They built a ranch house, barns, cattle sheds, and corrals there.[24] The Mason family history is typical of many families that settled along the path of the trail.

May 1, 2008, Medora, North Dakota, Dedication

On May 1, 2008, the first dedication held in North Dakota was at the North Dakota Cowboy Hall of Fame in Medora. As Robert Frost, the New England poet, said, "I have promises to keep/And miles to go before I sleep." In 2006,

First GWT Marker Dedicated in North Dakota, Medora, 2008
On May 1, 2008, the first GWT marker in North Dakota was dedicated at the North Dakota Cowboy Hall of Fame in Medora. Jim Ozbun, Rotary district leader, introduced the keynote speaker, North Dakota Governor John Hoeven. (l-r) Ozbun, Jim Aneff, Gov. Hoeven, Texas co-chair Sylvia Mahoney, Dave Mason of Texas, Gene Griffith of Regina, Canada, and Medora Mayor Doug Walker. Not pictured, North Dakota State Representative C. G. "Buck" Haas.

the Texas trail team had promised Jim Ozbun, rancher and retired college president, of Dickinson, North Dakota, that they would participate in the ceremony. Ozbun's district leadership position in Rotary provided him an opportunity to give the GWT some much-needed publicity.

Jim worked out the details to set the marker at the Cowboy Hall of Fame, place a historical plaque by it, and feature the dedication at the Rotary district conference. The size of his district was vast: all of North Dakota and territory in Canada. However, the dedication date conflicted with the Doan's May Picnic and Celebration in Vernon, Texas. The promise to Jim would require a 1,200-mile trip to North Dakota from Texas. Only three members of the Texas trail team could make the trip—Jim Aneff, David Mason, and I volunteered to keep the promise.

My two Abilene partners came through Vernon on April 30, 2008, one day before the dedication was scheduled to start at 6:00 p.m. on May 1 in Medora, North Dakota. As we headed north on the three-day, 2,400-mile round trip, the weather was hot and dry. From a trail-drive perspective, what was now a three-day trip would have taken drovers some three months.

Our destination that evening was Rapid City, South Dakota. Dave, a retired Air Force pilot, had access to accommodations at Ellsworth Air Force Base, ten miles northeast of Rapid City. About an hour from Rapid City, Dave mentioned that the car thermometer indicated the temperature had dropped thirty degrees in the last hour. The weather forecast was predicting a possible thirteen inches of snow that night in the Black Hills, so we were happy to be sheltering in Rapid City.

The next morning, rather than a bit of snow, a true blizzard was blowing snow from the northwest almost parallel to the horizon. While we loaded the car, the gale force caught clothes bags and blew them down the street. The Air Force reported that the mountains had eight or ten inches and Rapid City had three or four, and the snow would continue all that day. The weather map showed that the snow line stopped about twenty miles north on the route to Medora. We had promised Jim Ozbun that we would be there that afternoon.

We headed north. Thinking of blizzards and drovers and longhorns, we welcomed the warm car and highway, although it was solid ice. We were the only ones on the road that day, and we needed all of it. Some twenty miles out, Dave navigated the car expertly closer to the center of the road after sliding toward a bridge abutment. A snowplow headed south stopped to give us welcome news. A few miles farther north, we would be able to see the white line on the road again. As we pushed on, the white line did become visible, occasionally, but mainly when the snow turned to a mix of blowing snow and rain. In spite of the conditions, we arrived in Medora safely, went directly to the museum, and were welcomed warmly by people accustomed to blizzards and sudden changes in weather. But even those who were used to it would not have expected the worst May 1 blizzard on record in the Dakotas to come through on this special day.

After experiencing the blizzard, the warm welcome by North Dakota Governor John Hoeven, now a US senator, and North Dakota Representative Buck Haas along with Mayor Doug Walker and North Dakota Cowboy Hall of Fame Executive Director Darrell Dorgan confirmed our decision to keep trying to make it to the dedication. Inside the beautifully designed building, exhibits displayed the horse culture developed by area Native Americans, champion cowboys from North Dakota, and re-creations of those who came West for adventure, rich land, and new business ventures. Jim Ozbun had displayed nine flags of the trail states and three flags of the countries the trail passed through—the U.S.A., Mexico, and Canada. Rain continued to fall lightly, so the ceremony was held in a large upper room that accommodated the approximately two hundred Rotarians, historians, and area friends.

Our Regina, Saskatchewan, friends, Bill Whelan and Gene Griffith, also Rotarians, drove to the Medora dedication to pick up their metal mold and post. The visitors spoke of their amazement regarding the scope of the project and their admiration for these who organized the dedication with the state leaders in attendance. Finally meeting the Canadians and the North Dakotans face-to-face after becoming e-mail friends (along with a few phone calls) was a part of the project that added unexpected new pleasures.

The rain abated briefly to permit photos with the governor, representatives, local dignitaries, and Rotarians from North Dakota and Canada to be taken at the GWT marker. A large marble plaque had been placed near the marker explaining the GWT history. After the dedication and a celebratory dinner, the three of us decided to attempt to outdistance the blizzard and head back to Texas. At 9:00 p.m. we drove east to Dickinson, some thirty-five miles. There, we turned south, hoping to leave the Dakotas before the roads were closed. We continued in the "almost white-out" conditions until reaching Pierre, South Dakota, at about 2:00 a.m. We asked for wake-up calls for an early start. We hoped to find the roads still open, but about an hour south, a flashing light and sign at an intersection said, "Road Closed." Our luck held; the closed road was to the west. We were going south.

We inched along thinking that we would soon find sunshine; however, another snowstorm caught us—one that had not been shown on the weather map. We kept going south. Finally, in Kansas, we made it to the end of the blizzard, but we were next confronted by blowing rain. With only brief stops as we drove on, we arrived in Texas to find sunshine in Vernon. We experienced one of the reasons that drovers, years later, felt that their trail partners were lifetime friends. The weather bonded us as it had once bonded drovers faced with many hazards along the trail, especially the weather. We could only marvel at the conditions those cowboys endured. Small wonder they have become icons of strength, vigor, and resolve for almost the entire world. Some foreigners may not care much for Americans, but they still care for the American cowboy.

Theodore Roosevelt's Effect on Promoting and Preserving the Legend of the Trail Cowboy

After traveling across nine states to North Dakota, it became apparent that larger-than-life people associated with the area had used their celebrity to give the cowboy and the trail national prominence. President Theodore Roosevelt was one of those people. The North Dakota Cowboy Hall of Fame property is adjacent to the Theodore Roosevelt National Park. This is significant because the twenty-sixth US president enhanced the legend of the cowboy. Young men of wealth and social status often took trips after graduation as the next step before seeking their place in politics or a career. Roosevelt, a prolific writer and an outdoorsman, came to the Dakotas when he graduated from Harvard in 1880. His years in the Dakota Territory contributed to his Rough Rider persona, desire to stay physically fit, and reputation as an adventurer.

The cowboy and cattle-trail drama on the Great Plains needed a national venue, a famous image-builder, and a public relations promoter. Roosevelt filled those roles easily—especially since he often traveled with journalists and photographers. They provided a constant flow of articles to satisfy Easterners' curiosity for a look at both the West and the dashing Teddy Roosevelt.

Roosevelt's first investment on the Great Plains was in the Teschmaker and Debillier Cattle Company, which had a herd on the open range north of Cheyenne, Wyoming.[25] He eventually returned to the Dakotas, purchased a ranch, and added to his image by using the term "Rough Rider," found in Buffalo Bill's "Wild West and Congress of Rough Riders of the World." Two of Roosevelt's "action packed, beautifully illustrated" books, *Hunting Trips of a Ranchman* and *Ranch Life and the Hunting Trail,* promoted the cowboy legend. He wrote that a cowboy ". . . must not only be shrewd, thrifty, patient and enterprising, but he must also possess qualities of personal bravery, hardihood and self-reliance to a degree not demanded in the least by a mercantile occupation in a community long settled."[26]

The status of women in the Great Plains states, especially in Wyoming, reinforced Theodore Roosevelt's attitude toward equality for women. In 1880 in his Harvard University senior thesis, "The Practicability of Equalizing Men and Women before the Law," he posited, "I think there can be no question that women should have equal rights with men." The West seemed to support his ideas about equality for women. The West, especially the Dakotas, also gave him solace when his wife, Alice Lee, and his mother both died on Valentine's Day in 1884.[27]

Roosevelt and two of his wealthy eastern friends made major contributions to fiction, to art, and to the creation of the American icon, the cowboy. They moved the cowboy from reality into the imagination. Harvard classmate, Owen Wister, author of *The Virginian: A Horseman of the Plains*, helped define the cowboy hero with traits such as bravery, integrity, self-reliance, independence, and respect for others. Frederick Remington, Roosevelt's friend, supported the ideal American cowboy through his romanticized bronze sculptures and oil paintings. Honoring his time as a colonel in the Spanish-American War, Remington presented *The Bronco Buster* bronze to Roosevelt as a gift from his men, the Rough Riders, to their commander. Today, it resides in the White House Oval Office. The influence of President Roosevelt, writer Owen Wister, and artist Frederick Remington cannot be overestimated in the creation of the larger-than-life cowboy image.

🐂

The GWT trail research project spread across the Great Plains states with the support of Rotary members. The project had grown so much that a change in the making and delivery of posts had to be made. Nebraska became the pivotal state for enlarging the project beyond the earlier efforts in Mexico, Texas, Oklahoma, and Kansas. A gathering of volunteers in Nebraska helped disperse posts and metal molds into the northern states and Canada. The trail-teams' experience at on-site visits revealed that romanticized versions of the cowboy by writers, artists, and national historic figures created viability for its history. The legend was a subtle moving force that maintained the vitality of the spirit of the trail and compelled the citizens to verify its path. In the twenty-first century, the nebulous history of the length of the Great Western Trail is coming into focus.

CHAPTER 9
Wyoming, Montana, Saskatchewan, Alberta

D rovers trailed longhorns along the western fork of the Great Western Trail into Wyoming, Montana, the southwestern corner of Saskatchewan, and the southeastern corner of Alberta. Evidence verified that the trail crossed the eastern plains of Wyoming and Montana, then crossed the border into Canada. Trail research was closely tied to the discovery of issues that pulled the drovers, ranchers, and homesteaders into the Johnson County range war. The violence erupted from a competition for open-range land between the ranchers and homesteaders. Novelists, artists, newspapers, nonfiction books, and family archives captured these times in a diversity of ways. These sources were sifted for evidence to substantiate the route of the trail.

Trail references were found in music, art, and literature. One trail song said, "Sing hooplio, get along my little doggies, for Wyoming shall be your new home."[1] This trail song is not specific, but even miniscule evidence gave direction. Strong evidence for the trail's existence was the thousands of South Texas longhorns located in the northern states. Since the source of the longhorns was South Texas and the longest, most consistently used trail from there was the GWT, logic says that this is solid evidence to verify it. Other evidence, however, corroborated the path of the trail. Canadian ranchers found that even in the twenty-first century, longhorns, identifiable as South Texas cattle, were found in Canada. Deciphering the connections between different names used for segments of the trail also validated the path. North of Ogallala, Nebraska, the Texas Trail was the most frequently used name for the GWT.

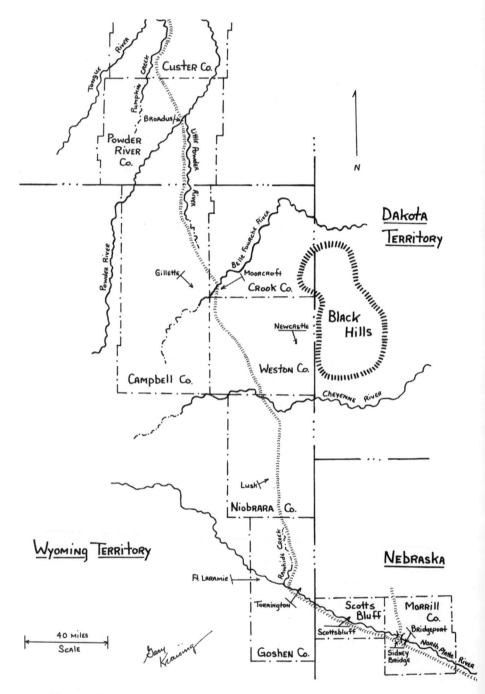

GWT across Wyoming

From Ogallala, the GWT followed the North Platte River some sixty miles northwest to where it forked near Bridgeport, Nebraska. The branch that went north to the Dakota Badlands was described in the previous chapter. The other branch went northwest along the North Platte River into Wyoming. There the Texas drovers continued across the eastern side of the states of Wyoming and Montana into Saskatchewan and Alberta.

In Wyoming, the trail, commonly called the Texas Trail, continued along the south side of the North Platte River to Rawhide Creek where the longhorns swam the river and turned north. The chuck wagons often had to travel sixteen more miles along the river to Fort Laramie, where they replenished their supplies and crossed the North Platte on a bridge. They then followed Rawhide Creek to Niobrara River, where the trail proceeded north across what is now Niobrara County. Texas Trail markers placed there at an earlier time stand on the east side of Lusk in Niobrara County and another one in Weston County. The trail crossed two branches of the Cheyenne River and went northwest across a dreaded long stretch of waterless terrain in Weston County to Moorcroft on the Belle Fourche River in Crook County. Many different routes were tried, but those routes, with even more long, waterless stretches, were discontinued. The drovers deferred to the route with the fewest stretches of waterless land. As a result, the GWT path became the main thoroughfare from Matamoros to Canada. Today, a collection of Texas Trail history can be found in Moorcroft, Wyoming, at the West Texas Trail Museum.[2]

From Moorcroft, the trail crossed another waterless expanse in Campbell County, where it then connected with the headwaters of the Little Powder River. The path went north another fifty miles along the valley into Montana, where it joined the Powder River.[3] With the historic importance of the trail to Wyoming's ranching history, details for the path of longhorns across that state present opportunities for further research. A GWT dedication has yet to be held in Wyoming, although volunteers there continue to work on the project.

The GWT was not just a cattle trail; it provided a blending and embedding of various cultures that evolved into one that is unique to America. An advanced American cultural change occurred in Wyoming during the trail era and into the early 1900s that was much slower to be accepted nationally. People in the sparsely populated state with few women promoted gender equality in state and local government. With a limited population and vast reaches of unsettled land, women had to learn to ride, to manage cattle ranches, and to be self-sufficient. Memoirs by women on the open range attest to these achievements. In 1868 Congress created the Territory of Wyoming. The next year, 1869, the Wyoming territorial legislature gave women the right to vote, hold elective office, and serve on juries. However, it was another fifty-one years before all US states enfranchised women. Wyoming had other trail-blazing examples for gender equality: In 1870, Esther Hobart Morris became the first female justice of the peace in the United States. In 1925 Nellie Tayloe Ross became the first female governor in the United States. In 1933 she became the first female director of the US Mint and served twenty years. Wyoming's motto "Equal Rights" has always included the belief in giving women equal rights.[4]

The state of Wyoming adopted a Cowboy Code of Ethics in 2010, which has ten points. According to Senator Mike Enzi from Wyoming, it is the only state with the code. Each year he introduces a resolution to designate a "National Day of the Cowboy," which is celebrated annually on July 27. Sen. Enzi said, "We are the Cowboy State, and our values reflect those that made America what it is today."[5]

During the trail era and the early twentieth century, the innovative idea of heritage tourism and its benefits emerged on the vast plains. Wyoming became the center of the nascent tourism industry with the help of President Theodore Roosevelt's advocacy of national parks. He recognized the importance of promoting natural resources for people's enjoyment while conserving it for future generations. Known as the conservation president, Roosevelt said, "I recognize the right and duty of this generation to develop and use the natural resources of our land; but I do not recognize the right to waste them, or rob, by wasteful use, the generations that come after us."[6] These thoughts are cogent today, as our nation and national parks become more congested. One of the GWT project goals, promoting heritage tourism, was in harmony with Roosevelt's ideas.

The trail era, often depicted as an idealistic era, had its darker side. Evidenced sporadically along the trail was a smoldering political and financial conflict for land ownership between open-range ranchers and small ranchers/homesteaders. In Wyoming, the conflict became violent in 1892. A cattle-rustling dispute ignited the violence that became known as the Johnson County War. Several small ranchers were murdered, thus escalating the violence. The wealthy ranchers with political connections that reached to the White House hired gunmen from Texas. Their hit list targeted small ranchers who then formed a large posse of some two hundred men. The US 6th

Cavalry intervened by capturing the hired gunmen. Eventually, all charges were dropped. The range war became prominent in the history and movies of the American West. Movie plots revolving around range wars, such as the one for *Shane*, captivated silver-screen audiences and became a classic of the Western genre. The violence served to bring Wyoming and the conflict to the attention of a larger national audience. It helped to preserve that period of time but also to counterbalance the idealism with realism.

Writers who chronicled the Johnson County War in Wyoming have viewed it from both sides of the issue. The cattle barons, who organized as the Wyoming Stock Growers Association and socialized at the Cheyenne Club, had connections with Scottish and English syndicates. The numbers of small ranchers/homesteaders in Johnson County had increased because of the Homestead Law of 1862. The range war started when Ellen "Cattle Kate" Watson and store owner James Averill, who had staked claims on ranch country, were hanged—actually lynched—for cattle rustling without benefit of judge or jury.[7] In June 1891 Tom Wagoner of Newcastle was found hanged from a cottonwood tree. He was said to have been pulled from his horse by three men. Some sources said he had a herd of stolen horses with him when he was caught.[8] Like a mindless mob, violence moved across the rolling grassy hills of this part of America, destroying everything that got in its way.

The violence stirred Asa Shinn Mercer to use the power of his pen to expose the guilty parties. In *Banditti of the Plains or the Cattlemen's Invasion of Wyoming in 1892 (The Crowning Infamy of the Ages)*, also titled *The Powder River Invasion*, Mercer called out by name those who had killed two men and had ridden to finish off the others. Mercer's book was burned. A few copies escaped destruction to be reproduced in the twentieth century.[9] The results are a study in the destruction and resolution of violence between cattle barons, small ranchers/homesteaders, the government, and the law. The violence has been replayed in books and movies, and it still smolders between the Tom Wagoner family and those on the other side of the conflict.

The GWT research project combined the past on the Great Plains with the present. Asa Shinn Mercer, a major player in the Johnson County War, had ties to Vernon, Texas. Mercer, an educator, writer, and newspaper publisher, also helped settle early-day Seattle. In the 1860s he brought marriageable women, called the Mercer Girls, from the US East Coast to the western territories. He was the first president of the Territorial University of Washington and a member of the Washington State Senate. Mercer moved to Wyoming by way of Texas during the GWT days. In North Texas, he had established six newspapers.[10] His tenure in 1883 as Vernon *Guard* publisher lasted only a few months. Then he moved to Wyoming where he founded the *Northwest Livestock Journal*.[11] His newspaper experience in Texas had given him knowledge of the commerce and culture of the ranching and trail era.

Johnson County Range War Issues Still Hot in the Twenty-First Century

The Johnson County War and Mercer's early connection to Vernon brought me into a conversation with Vernon resident Beth Ekern. She and her husband had ranched in Montana at an earlier time near a rancher/neighbor named Mercer. After learning that the *Vernon Daily Record* editor Jimmy Carr and publisher Larry Crabtree had no record of Asa Mercer having established that newspaper, it motivated further inquiry. A call to a college rodeo friend, Butch Bratsky, senior banking executive for Stockman Bank in Billings, Montana, led to my connecting with an employee who was married to a Mercer. Through him, I talked to John Mercer, a rancher in the Big Horn Mountains of western Wyoming. He verified that Asa Shinn Mercer, his great-grandfather, had established and owned the Vernon paper in 1883 for approximately nine months before moving to Wyoming.[12]

This Mercer research led to even more unresolved conflict. Rhonda Sedgwick Stearns of Newcastle, Wyoming, connected me with Colleen Pollat, a Wyoming author who wrote about the Johnson County War in *Secrets: The Tom Wagoner Story*. The author lives on land in Wyoming that her ancestors had homesteaded during the Johnson County War era. She wrote, "The wall of silence that surrounded Tom Wagoner's death by hanging is only now understandable." Pollat told of the hanging on June 4, 1891, of Thomas Jefferson Wagoner II, who owned a large horse ranch in northeastern Wyoming. His estate, valued at $100,000, was seized and "most likely used to finance their invasion of Johnson County in April 1892." In 1992, descendants of the Johnson County War held a reunion in Buffalo, Wyoming, "hoping to heal the last of the old wounds."[13]

At that reunion, Tom Smith, grandson of another Tom Smith who was a hired gunman, said to Glen Wagoner, "I believe my grandfather killed your grandfather."[14] This catalyst and unanswered questions in the court documents from the *State of Wyoming vs. Wagoner* sparked the Wagoner family's search for answers. Pollat's attempt to set the record straight resulted in her book published in 2007 about Tom Wagoner. The Wagoner family, eight generations later, was working to assuage their sense of outrage that Tom Wagoner was remembered in history as a rustler, a common horse thief.[15]

The GWT project brought to light the decades of the 1880s and 1890s on the Great Plains, which revealed a composite of cowboy ethics based on survival of the fittest. Nonetheless, the cowboy ethic was coupled with a world that included murders, mayhem, and violence. This code for survival engendered strong-willed people experienced in self-reliance, supported by a weapon strapped to the hip. As we traveled up the trail and continued to read about the trail era, it became evident that humanity at its best and worst had been active on the Great Plains during the trail era.

No matter how profoundly different the Western stage, people of the West could not escape an American perspective; they were captive to its good and its ill. For all the good of the American experience, there is another side, a side of rowdy, almost gratuitous, violence; it is a consistent, undeniable theme throughout our history. And one of the most distinctly American manifestations of that wide, rowdy streak was lynching. Lynching was almost exclusively an American phenomenon, virtually unheard of anywhere else in the world. James Elbert Cutler referred to it as "our country's national crime."[16]

Lynching, the seizure and killing of a person by a group without lawful authority, most commonly by hanging, became commonplace throughout much of the United States in the late nineteenth century. The peak year for lynching was 1892, when 230 killings took place. The nineteenth-century frontier, despite its small population, recorded 35 lynchings in Wyoming, 84 in Montana, and 43 in Colorado.[17]

Along with the violence, the GWT research project found a weather-related ferocity that created havoc on the Great Plains. The infamous blizzard during the winter of 1886–1887 caused the loss of 50 to 90 percent of the cattle across the northern plains. The bankruptcy of many large ranchers left vast stretches of the open range vacant. Small ranchers and homesteaders moved onto the land. Many of the first deeds, or United States patents, date from claims made during that time.[18] The irony of nature inserting its force into the conflict on the Great Plains between the wealthy and the commoner is a point to ponder.

Weather also brought another destructive element to the Great Plains: fire and its abetting wind. The wind could whip fire rapidly across the rolling grassy plains and burn thousands of acres in a few short moments. John

Leakey, a Texas cowboy who went to Montana and the Dakotas, recalled fire being spotted near Adobe Wall Creek, which burned some fifty thousand acres. Using fire drags made of freshly skinned cowhides, the cowboys fought it for three days and nights. Leakey said, "We killed and used them for fire-drags, a common firefighting practice in those days. Killing the biggest critter we could locate in a hurry, we skinned out half the carcass and piled dirt on the empty half of the hide. The backbone kept the hide stretched out when we tied our ropes onto the front and rear legs and dragged it along the edge of the fire behind our horses. It worked pretty good, except that the hide soon burned up, after which we'd fix another one."[19]

In spite of the weather, wind, and fire, drovers continued moving cattle up the GWT, or Texas Trail, from Wyoming into Montana along the west side of the north-flowing Little Powder River. The trail then crossed the Powder River and trailed west to Pumpkin Creek in what is now Custer County. Following that creek to the confluence with the Tongue River, the herds continued to Miles City, Montana, a trail town with the reputation and impact of Dodge City and Ogallala.[20] With Fort Keogh to the southwest and the confluence of the north-flowing Tongue River and the east-flowing Yellowstone River, Miles City was strategically located to accommodate large herds of cattle. The need for cattle in Miles City increased with the arrival of the Northern Pacific Railroad in 1881, which made it possible to ship cattle to Eastern markets. This new market added to the burgeoning need for longhorns being herded to Miles City to meet the demand for ranchers, beef for soldiers, Indians, and the Royal Canadian Mounted Police in the North West Territory.

The trail history of Miles City set the stage for the first dedication of a GWT marker in Montana on August 5, 2010. The famous little cow town located on the southeastern rolling grasslands was a composite of the past and the present. Larry McMurtry's novel Lonesome Dove and the movie of the same name had embedded Miles City into the American psyche as the place where Augustus "Gus" McRae said to his friend Woodrow F. Call, "I want to be buried in Clara's orchard in Texas by that little grove of live oaks on the south Guadalupe."[21] Call said, when burying Gus's body in that grove in Texas, "That will teach me to be more careful about what I promise."[22] Oliver Loving, the real-life trail boss who was the inspiration for Gus's character, was killed in New Mexico. Nonetheless, fiction won out over fact. Miles City is noted for being the place where Gus died.

Another book that popularized Miles City was E. C. "Teddy Blue" Ab-

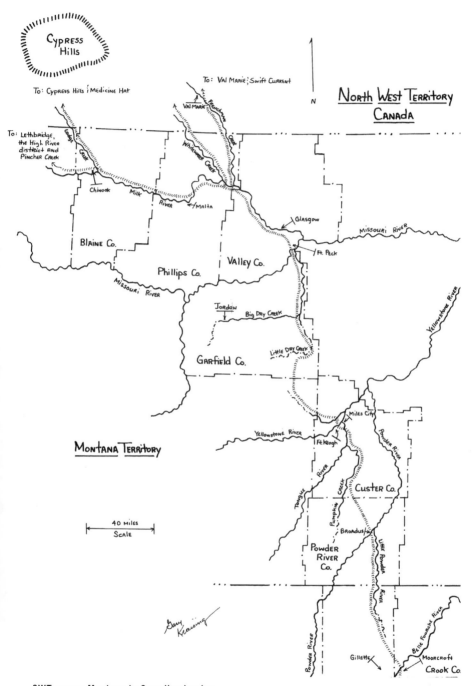

CYPRESS
Hills

To: VAl MARIE; Swift CuRRENT

To: CypRESS Hills; MEdiciNE HAt

VAl MARIE

North West TERRitoRY
CANADA

N

To: LethbRidge,
the HigH RiveR
distRict ANd
PiNcheR CReek

Chinook   Milk   RiveR   MAlta

Glasgow

BlAiNE Co.

Phillips Co.

VAlley Co.

Ft. Peck

MissOuRi RiveR

MissOuRi RiveR

JoRdAN   Big DRy CReek

GARfield Co.

Little DRy CReek

YEllowstoNE RiveR

Miles City

Ft. KeogH

MontANA TERRitoRy

YEllowstoNE RiveR

CusteR Co.

Powder RiveR

40 miles
ScAle

BRoAdus

Powder
RiveR
Co.

Gillette

MoorcRoft

CRook Co.

GWT across Montana to Canadian border

bott's book *We Pointed Them North* written in 1939. The author reminisced about citizens of Miles City, Montana. Teddy Blue said, "Granville Stuart lived on the frontier, and he did what the frontier required of him."[23] Stuart and other citizens' ethical and cultural legacy, defined in books and art, has endured through the generations that lived on the same ranches under common conditions. The quality of character admired by Teddy Blue and exhibited by Granville Stuart was still evident in citizens of Miles City, Montana, and other places along the trail as we made visits and marked the path of the Great Western Trail.

On August 5, 2010, eleven Texas Rotarians, two Missouri Rotarians, and four Oklahomans arrived in Miles City to participate in the ceremony that would be held two days later. On arrival, we stopped at the Stockman Bank to meet Stan Markuson, the bank president and past Rotary president. Stan gave us a tour of the bank and the small town. Markuson's Wrangler jeans belied his status as president of a privately owned Montana bank that had nineteen locations in Montana in 2009 and $1.7 billion in holdings.[24]

The Stockman Bank has connections to a Texas rodeo cowboy, C. M. Coffee, who went to Montana to run a ranch, which he eventually bought. Coffee is an inductee to the Montana Cowboy Hall of Fame.[25] Coffee and his wife, Virginia Nefsy Coffee, daughter of William and Lorene Nefsy, merged their ranching and banking interests and became one of the top five landowners in Montana. Today, Coffee and his wife serve on the bank board, their son William Coffee is the bank CEO, and their daughter Caren Coffee, also a bank senior officer, runs the ranching operation. The bank's statement of purpose reflects the Coffees' values, which remain rooted in the cowboy code: "Stockman is a Montana-born company built on western values, focused on creating long-lasting relationships through integrity, expertise, and results."[26]

Stockman Bank president Stan Markuson and his wife Nancy also have deep ranch roots. In 1906, Stan's family came to Ekalaka, eighty-five miles southeast of Miles City, where Stan still owns a ranch. On Nancy's side, in 1881, the W. W. Terrett family started the JO Ranch southwest of Miles City. In 1882, the JO's first cattle, Texas Longhorns, were trailed up to Dodge City and on to Miles City. The severe winter of 1886–1887 reduced the company's calf crop of one thousand to only three hundred head. They rebuilt the herd and survived the Panic of 1893. W. W. Terrett is a 2008 Montana Cowboy Hall of Fame Legacy Award Inductee. The ranch has remained in continuous operation by five generations of the Terrett family.[27]

Our tour of the Stockman Bank exemplified the pride of the bank's employees and town's citizens in their ranching heritage. Markuson, a typically low-key cowboy/rancher, responded to questions with a sense of well-placed pride. The spacious bank building showed the magnitude of the holdings, and numerous titles on office doors displayed the banks diverse operations. The art on display, by renowned photographer Laton Alton Huffman, illustrated Montana's heritage, which Markuson was proud to explain. His vast knowledge of trail and ranch history supported him well as the president of a bank in Montana named *Stockman* Bank. The strong intangible connections between Texans and Montanans became apparent as we talked to Markuson and later to Barrie Matthews, the current Rotary president, and other residents.

Art and photography played significant roles in preserving Montana's frontier and trail history. In photographer Laton Alton Huffman's relatively short life, 1879 to 1926, he made 1,300 glass and film negatives. They are invaluable records of military life, Crow and Cheyenne Indians, the slaughter of the buffalo, cattle, ranch life, and the Custer Trail Expedition. Huffman worked at Fort Keogh near Miles City as the post photographer before setting up a studio in Miles City. A Huffman photo connects Miles City to Junction, Texas, where Frederica Wyatt, the local GWT historian, displays a Huffman photo of her father's cousin, George Marshall Pearl of London, Texas. The photo verifies that drover Pearl went up the GWT from Texas to Miles City.

Another Montana connection with Texas made it possible for our group to tour Fort Keogh. Texan Rod Heitschmidt, who had worked at Fort Keogh, arranged a tour for his friend Harold Hardcastle, Vernon Rotary president. Historic Fort Keogh, a 55,000-acre USDA Agriculture Research Service for rangeland beef cattle, was established as an Army Calvary post on July 22, 1876, approximately one month after the Battle of the Little Bighorn. In 1909, it was designated as a Remount Station. Today, its research focuses on developing ecologically and economically sustainable range animal management systems. Many of the research scientists stationed there had also worked in Texas. On the tour, the Fort Keogh personnel told us about historical and research icons of the past and about their current research successes, all much to be admired.

Already immersed in the rich area history, we soon experienced even more history. On the evening of August 6, 2010, Stan Markuson and Barrie Matthews, a banker and a dentist, treated the visiting trail teams to an evening at the historic Miles City Club, the oldest social club in Montana. Founded in 1884, the club became the social center for the eastern Montana livestock industry and the informal headquarters for conventions of the Montana Stockgrowers Association. Local historian and attorney George W. Huss verified that the GWT, also called the Texas Trail and Northern Trail, provided the path for some 600,000 longhorns to Miles City. The first name in the guest registry of the Miles City Club was posted in January 1885. Huss used eight drovers' names from the registry to connect Texas cattle to Montana, some of which were then moved on into Saskatchewan.

George W. Huss's trail research recovered evidence that W. W. Terrett, Nancy Markuson's great-grandfather, came from the same area in Missouri that Ray Klinginsmith, Rotary International president, called home—Kirksville. Terrett, a member of the Miles City Club, came from Chariton County, Missouri, approximately fifty miles from Klinginsmith's home. Huss, an attorney, also provided evidence for the path of the GWT being the route that carried longhorns to Miles City. He explained the changes in eastern Montana that allowed it to become a viable cattle country. This occurred with confinement of the Indians to reservations, the elimination of the buffalo, and the arrival of a railroad in 1881. The Northern Pacific Railroad arrived first and was followed by the Great Northern and the Milwaukee. The railroads brought settlers to Montana as well as transported cattle to Eastern markets. Miles City's location on the rolling plains of southeastern Montana positioned it to be a destination town for trail cattle as well as a town where trail bosses could purchase supplies to move their herds on north across Montana into Saskatchewan.[28]

Modern Miles City emphasizes its ranching and rodeo heritage. Dedication day started Saturday morning with a breakfast at the historic 1939 Range Riders Museum. Many local ranchers attended the breakfast that morning. One was Dianne O'Neill, whose ranch south of Miles City had been in the family for 111 years. The O'Neill ranch family had a Texas relative, Larry O'Neill, who was a rancher, architect, and University of Texas college bareback national champion. Dianne's son Pat had competed at the national finals for college rodeo, and her husband, Frank, and his brother Larry O'Neill were there to watch Pat compete. I had met them at the finals that year. The rodeo-inspired signature event at Miles City is the world-famous Bucking Horse Sale held in May each year. Rodeo stock contractors purchase between two and four hundred new mounts for rodeo competition each year. In addition to being an auction, the gathering acts as a reunion, a rendezvous, and a social scene rivaling the trail-era celebrations. Much-sought-after hotel accommodations in the small town must be booked two years in advance.

With its eleven buildings, a major attraction and history collection is Miles City's Range Riders Museum. The museum displays an in-depth perspective on Montana's ranch history. Bob Barthelmess, the historian/executive director, brought our attention to the 875 photos that lined the banquet room walls—pioneers who had settled Montana. Bob's grandfather Christian Barthelmess contributed his work to the historical collection of photos. The 1870 immigrant from Bavaria photographed the frontier life of soldiers, Plains Indians, ranchers, and homesteaders. Christian's history was recorded in the book *Photographer on an Army Mule*. Three other famous Montana photographers had displays: Evelyn Jephson Flower Cameron, a British expatriate; Robert Morrison, a buffalo hunter and wagon trail guide, and L. A. Huffman.[29] The museum lost a vast reservoir of Montana history when Bob Barthelmess died in 2011.[30] The GWT trail team lost a valued friend.

Miles City Range Riders Museum
Miles City Range Riders Museum historian/executive director Bob Barthelmess explained the history of the area during the museum tour he gave to GWT team members, Stan Markuson of Miles City, Jim Aneff of Abilene, Texas, and Bill Huskinson of Vernon, Texas.

First GWT Marker Dedicated in Montana, Miles City, 2010

The first GWT marker dedication in Montana at Miles City on August 7, 2010, at the Range Riders Museum, illustrated the commitment of project volunteers—some drove more than a thousand miles to attend the one-hour ceremony. Keynote speaker Ray Klinginsmith, Rotary International president, traveled from Missouri. Barrie Matthews, Miles City Rotary Club president, recognized Paul Broughton of Arkansas and Don Gatzke of western Montana for their initial Montana Rotary GWT leadership. Michael Babb of Oklahoma sang his original song, "Great Western Trail." (back, l-r) Ian Toms, Canada; Paul Lucas, Texas; Broughton; Gatzke; Jim Aneff, Texas; Sylvia Mahoney, Texas; Klinginsmith; John Barton, Oklahoma; Jim Ozbun, North Dakota; Phil McCuistion, Texas; (front, l-r) Gene Griffith, Canada; Matthews; Dave Mason, Texas; Harold Hardcastle, Texas; Dennis Vernon, Oklahoma.

August 7, 2010, Miles City, First GWT Dedication in Montana

On August 7, 2010, in the shade of towering trees next to the Tongue River at Riverside Park, some thirty-eight out-of-state Rotarians and trail partners joined a large group of Montana Rotarians and local citizens. Miles City's Stan Markuson said, "Marking the GWT brought Miles City the honor of being the first town in Montana to attract the Rotary International President Ray Klinginsmith."

The crowd moved from the park to the Range Riders Museum for the dedication ceremony. Rotary leaders and historical society members came from Regina, Saskatchewan, North Dakota, Texas, and Oklahoma. Bilingual greetings from the Matamoros, Mexico, trail partners were read. Two Montana Rotary leaders, Don Gatzke and Paul Broughton, now of Arkansas, were recognized for their early and continuing efforts to recover evidence to mark the trail in Montana. In honor of this international event, Rotarians were presented longhorn Rotary pins from Jose Luis Diaz del Lie of Leon, Mexico. Michael Babb of Oklahoma sang his original song, "Great Western Cattle Trail." Keynote speaker Ray Klinginsmith emphasized four points: the networking of Rotary members that made the project possible, the importance of preserving GWT history, promoting heritage tourism especially in small towns, and the Cowboy Code, a standard of ethics applicable for drovers then and for people today.

After tours, talks, and the dedication, the visitors were invited to experience an evening of cowboy entertainment. The Montana Bar, a building on the National Register of Historic Places, provided a place to experience the past. In 1893, it was a saloon; from 1900 to 1907, it was Charles Coggshall's saddle making business. In 1908, James Kenney moved his Montana Saloon there. In 1912, a Missouri River steamboat brought in a new bar with a brass railing, a back bar, a liquor cabinet, horsehide-covered booths, and a walk-in icebox. The electric paddle fans, the Italian terrazzo tiles, and a bullet hole in the front center pane added historic value in different ways. Mounted on the wall was the head of a red Texas longhorn steer that had been the lead steer in drives from Texas to Montana in the late 1880s.[31]

During the trail days, Miles City had lured many cowboys with its abundance of good times of various kinds. However, the trail itself did not stop at Miles City. The vast open-range grasslands beckoned trail bosses to continue farther north with their contracted herds to stock ranches in Canada and to provide beef for the Royal Canadian Mounted Police. From Miles City, drovers pushed the longhorns along the north side of the east-flowing Sunday Creek that joined the Yellowstone a few miles north of Miles City. From Sunday Creek, the herds were trailed into what is now Garfield County to water on Little Dry Creek. Next, the cowboys drove the animals along the north-flowing creek to the confluence with Big Dry Creek and on to the east-flowing Missouri River near Fort Peck. After a short distance on grassland, the drovers traveled northwest along the Milk River, branching into the North-West Territory of Canada, which is now Saskatchewan and Alberta. The first herds to leave the Milk River going into Canada followed Frenchman Creek to Val Marie, Swift Current, and Moose Jaw, Saskatchewan.[32]

Other herds entered Saskatchewan from Montana via the next river going north, Whitewater Creek. Farther west was another entry point for drovers going to Maple Creek. Some trail bosses bypassed the entry to Maple Creek and continued along the Milk River across northern Montana beyond Fort Belknap. At Lodge Creek, others left the Milk River and moved the longhorns north into Cypress Hills, bordering Alberta. Some continued to Medicine Hat in Alberta to supply longhorns for open-range ranching there. Yet another route went up the Milk River to ranches in Alberta at Lethbridge, Pincher Creek, the High River District, and Calgary, home of the famous Calgary Stampede.[33] Since 1912, the Stampede has united professional cowboys and cowgirls from America and Canada in rodeo and other competitions.

The Canadian research teams surveyed two provinces in Canada to recover evidence regarding the length of the trail. The initial contact in Canada was with a Regina, Saskatchewan, Rotarian. After explaining the reason for the call, William "Bill" Whelan responded to the proposal with these words: "I never was a cowboy, but I always wanted to be one." His answer epitomized the driving force that motivated people to volunteer to join the project. This conversation occurred two years prior to the dedication in Miles City. Bill had promised that when a marker was dedicated in Miles City, he would be there. However, when the time arrived, Bill's health was fragile, and he was using a walker. But he remained determined to make the 450-mile trip to meet the Rotary International president and to keep his promise to attend the Miles City dedication. Combining Bill's cowboy spirit with the caring spirit of his club members, Bill made it to Miles City.

That same spirit flowed through the Regina Rotary Club. When Doug Mortin, Rotary district leader, asked the Regina club to consider joining the GWT project, the board formed a committee: Gene Griffith, Ted Turner, Bill Whelan, and Doug Alexander. They invited two others to join the committee: Jason Pollock, manager/CEO of Canadian Western Agribition, the premier livestock show in Canada, and Bill Small, "one of the most respected livestock producers in Canada."[34]

The Regina research committee used several methods to recover evidence. One was to research the history of the cattle that came up the Great

Western Trail into Saskatchewan. They knew that South Texas longhorn cattle had arrived in southwest Saskatchewan and southeast Alberta, so the dates and the specific routes were the focus of the research. Ted Turner, Bill Whelan, and David Stewart worked to corroborate the path of the trail, also called the Texas Trail or North West Trail. The three men found an official Parks Canada publication and two Regina Public Library books that gave the history of ranchers and ranches that were established between 1872 and 1896 and an additional one in 1902. Two maps they found "coincided with those defined by GWT historian Gary Kraisinger of Halstead, Kansas."[35]

As elsewhere along the trail, the research focused on the number and breed of cattle, the known path for cattle, and the years of arrival. "It is becoming more clear day by day that Texas longhorns came into Canada with the Northwest Mounted Police (Royal Canadian Mounted Police today) supervising their entry at various points from Montana into Saskatchewan at a point near Frenchman's Creek to Wood Mountain." The number of longhorns increased from ten thousand to forty or fifty thousand head by 1900.[36]

Soon, information was being sent to me to corroborate the time period, the number of cattle, the breed, and the Texas cowboys who stayed in Canada. One descendant, Willard Nelson of Beaumont, California, sent the Jesse Day Jr. family history. A. J. "Tony" Day managed the Turkey Track Ranch for a large American company, Creswell Cattle Company. It was located near the present-day site of Vanguard, Saskatchewan. Tony Day, born in South Texas in 1848, was Nelson's uncle. Nelson's mother, Cora Alice Day, had married Benjamin Franklin Austin from Belle Plain, Texas, which is on the GWT.[37]

Another valuable book, *Beyond the Range*, by Boyd M. Anderson is a definitive history of the Saskatchewan Stock Growers Association and early-day ranches. That history was verified by two respected historians and additional reviewers: Thelma Poinier; Pete Perrin, stock grower; and John Archer, past president of the University of Regina, author, and archivist. Thelma, who has written books on Maple Creek and Wood Mountain and who worked with the Rodeo Ranch Museum in Wood Mountain, Saskatchewan, conveyed many details about the longhorns from Texas.[38]

After the Canadians verified the trail, the Regina Rotarians sent an invitation to attend the first dedication in Canada. The GWT did *not* extend north all the way to Regina, Saskatchewan. Nonetheless, the Canadian trail team consulted with several livestock organizations and ranchers on possible locations. The location for the first marker dedicated in a state, county, or province was one of prominence. They selected the Canadian Western

Agribition Center, the second-largest livestock exhibition in North America, second only to the one in Denver, to be the marker's permanent home.

July 28, 2008, Regina, First GWT Marker Dedication in Canada

On July 28, 2008, at Regina, the Queen City of the Plains, the first Great Western Trail marker in Canada was dedicated. It was a symbolic dedication, however, as a marker was not physically placed in the soil. The well-laid plans of the Regina Rotary Club went awry when a labor dispute at the center kept our group from dedicating the first marker in Canada at its permanent location. The dedication ceremony was held at a hotel overlooking the city of 199,000 residents. Rick Mitchell, the club president, surprised then inspired the listeners when he said that at first he was not too eager to be involved with the "Marking the Trail" project. However, he, like many others, gave his support when he learned the significance of marking the trail from Mexico to Canada. He later made the 450-mile round-trip to the Val Marie, Saskatchewan, dedication.

At the symbolic dedication in Regina, two Royal Canadian Mounted Police (RCMP) greeted us at the hotel—one was wearing an original uniform. They helped the president unveil the GWT history plaque that "recognized the significance of the role played by the Trail in supplying meat and horses to the RCMP and breeding stock to the territorial ranches." Doug Alexander, master of ceremonies, introduced many Texas and Canadian dignitaries, including the Province of Saskatchewan Hon. Laura Ross and Regina Councillor Sharron Bryce. The group exchanged flags, exchanged proclamations from state and national officials, listened to cowboy poetry, and recounted the purpose of the GWT project. The (Texas) Red River water used to dedicate the post was matched with Red River water from Saskatchewan. The list of dignitaries introduced is included in the Appendix.

Once again, Canadians and Texans discovered connections between the two places. At lunch, Jason Pollock, Canadian Western Agribition Center Manager/CEO, mentioned that his brother had competed on the Vernon College, Texas, rodeo team. Jason is also a rancher. In 2011, he returned to his ranch roots to continue the family's ranch operations at Maple Creek, once a destination for South Texas longhorns. Another Canadian/Texas connection showed the diverse commonality of the two places. Ted and Mel Turner invited Texan Larry Crabtree to attend a Saskatchewan Rough Riders game, part of the Canadian Football League Western Division. Ted told a story about his nephew Ian, the third generation to live on the Mitchell ranch on Battle River thirty miles south of Lloydminster. Ian's son, Tristan, a 4-H member, called his show steer Reggie Hunt, named for the former Texas Christian University (Fort Worth) linebacker who played for the Rough Riders. Ted had yet another Texas connection. Their ranch land had been originally selected by a Texan named Lockwood.[39] Ted's support of the grassroots trail project is emblematic of his leadership role of an agrarian political action and wheat farmers' cooperative, the Saskatchewan Wheat Pool, that became "the world's largest grain cooperative" that "maximized member democratic input and control."[40]

Canadian similarities to Texas continued. Rancher Bill Small and his wife Agnes gave us a tour of ranches, cattle, and land that were similar to Texas ranch country. As so often occurs in Texas, that evening a tornado touched down near where we had earlier toured the countryside with Bill. On that afternoon's tour, it became apparent that Bill's unassuming ways belied the respect that the agriculture and cattle industries held for him. At the 40th Canadian Western Agribition, Bill was one of the first five inductees into their Hall of Fame.[41]

November 28, 2008, Canadian Western Agribition GWT Marker Dedicated

After the symbolic dedication in July, the GWT marker was dedicated on November 28, 2008, at the Canadian Western Agribition annual show. That year the livestock exhibition attracted some 150,000 paid attendees. The marker was placed at a choice spot, the main entrance to the show. More than one hundred people attended the second dedication ceremony. Shannon McArton, Canadian Western Agribition president, spoke about the Val Marie GWT dedication. Sherri Grant, chair of the Val Marie dedication, read her original GWT poem. Ted Turner, Jason Pollock, and Saskatchewan Stock Growers Association representative Doug Gillespie unveiled a granite plaque inscribed with trail history. The marker was christened with a mixture of Red River and Frenchman River water from Val Marie. The media spread the message about the longest Texas cattle trail extending into Canada.[42]

On September 20, 2008, two months prior to the dedication at the Canadian Western Agribition Center, Sherri Grant, CWAC board member, had invited everyone to Val Marie, Saskatchewan, to dedicate a marker. Val Marie's committee found evidence that GWT longhorns had been herded

GWT Marker Dedication at Canadian Western Agribition, Regina, Saskatchewan
On November 28, 2008, the third Canadian GWT marker dedication ceremony took place at the annual Canadian Western Agribition (CWA) at Regina, Saskatchewan. The show attracted 150,000 visitors. Master of Ceremony Regina Rotarian Doug Alexander (pictured with the flags of three nations), introduced CWA president Shannon McArton and Val Marie event chair Sherri Grant. GWT team member Ted Turner and Agribition CEO Jason Pollock were assisted by Saskatchewan Stock Growers Association representative Doug Gillespie in unveiling the trail marker and a granite plaque inscribed with GWT history.

up the Frenchman River from Montana to the little village of Val Marie, with a current population of 450. Three members of the Texas trail team and two from Montana traveled to Val Marie for the dedication. The airport at Billings, Montana, was the closest to Val Marie. Dave Mason and his wife, Vonda, of Abilene and I were picked up at the airport by Dave's parents, Walter F. and Allegene Mason, ages ninety-one and eighty-eight, of Bozeman, Montana.

The four-hour road trip to Val Marie was interrupted by a night spent at Malta, Montana, to wait for the international border checkpoint to open at 9:00 a.m. Dave drove, and Walter, with his phenomenal memory, explained area history and ecology as we went north. He recounted the lives of his trail-driver ancestors. Walter's early ranch life combined with degrees in

GWT Marker Dedication, Val Marie, Saskatchewan
On September 20, 2008, a Great Western Trail marker was dedicated at the Prairie Wind
& Silver Sage Museum at Val Marie, Saskatchewan, near where the trail followed the
Frenchman River from Montana into the Canadian province. Val Marie co-chair Sherri
Grant introduced Yogi Huyghebaert, MLA (state rep.) for Wood River; Dave Mason,
Texas Rotary district leader; Royal Canadian Mounted Police (NWMP) Constable Gor-
don Yetman; NWMP Sgt. Omar Murray; the Regina Rotary committee members who
donated the GWT granite plaque; Texas trail co-chair Sylvia Mahoney, and (not pic-
tured) Vonda Mason, Texas, Rotarian Walter F. and Allegene Mason from Montana.

chemistry, botany, and theology and Allegene's degree in home economics
qualified them to work in Chile at El Vergel Agricultural Institute.[43]

Citizens of the small town of Val Marie welcomed us with warm Canadian hospitality. The dedication, planned by Sherri Grant and her committee, coincided with the 44th Annual Indoor Rodeo held at the rodeo arena/
curling rink. Prior to the dedication, the group gathered west of town to travel in wagons drawn by draft horses across the beautiful rolling grasslands.
A dozen steers, twenty mounted riders of all ages, three wagons, and additional out-riders crossed hills covered with lush grass that was belly-high
to a horse. Our domiciles were separated by almost two thousand physical
miles, but it felt like Texas because of the terrain, the cowboy lifestyle, and
our common bond borne of the trail days.

Tour of 76 Ranch and Grasslands of Saskatchewan
After the group visited a buffalo jump, Dave Mason listened to rancher Jason Legault talk about the history of the 76 Ranch; Grasslands National Park pasture manager John Thibault explained the management of the grassland pastures; and historian Thelma Poinier discussed area history.

The Val Marie trail team selected the Prairie Wind & Silver Sage Museum for the permanent location for the GWT marker. The museum is housed in a former Val Marie school, built in 1927. The site is near where the trail moved along Frenchman River and turned west/northwest. David Mason of Abilene presented a resolution to David Anderson, a member of Canada's Parliament for Cypress Hills–Grasslands. The topics that Yogi Huyghebaert, MLA (similar to a state representative) for Wood River Province of Saskatchewan, used in his speech were the cattle industry and the shared trail history.

The Regina trail committee presented the trail marker and a large marble plaque inscribed with trail history to the citizens of Val Marie. Colette Schmidt of the Grasslands National Park, dressed in period clothing, presented Saskatchewan cattle-trail history. Rick Mitchell, Regina Rotary president, and Merv Timmons, RCMP and cattleman representative, removed

Cabin Where Author and Artist Will James Lived, Near Val Marie, Saskatchewan
A contributor to the legend of the cowboy, Will James, artist and writer, once lived in
the cabin on the Grasslands National Park near Val Marie, Saskatchewan. James, born
in Quebec in 1892 to French-Canadian parents, wrote twenty-three illustrated books;
his most famous is *Smoky the Cowhorse*.

steer hide that had protected the post. Don McDonald, Prairie Wind & Silver Sage executive director, and I dedicated it with Frenchman River water
and Red River water. Sherri Grant concluded the program with her original
poem, "The Legacy of the Drover." She said, "Our legacy to those who follow
is the knowing it can be done. Whatever the challenge, step forward, and,
yes, your goal will be won."

Following a chuck wagon chili lunch at the Community Curling Rink,
rancher Jason Legault gave us a tour of the old 76 Ranch. We saw the first
line shack on the ranch and listened to the passion in Jason's voice as he
explained why he admired the old cowboys. Historian Thelma Poinier and
Grasslands National Park pasture manager John Thibault continued the tour
of the vast ranch country, which is divided into 90-section pastures. From a
high bluff, we viewed a "buffalo jump" over which Indians stampeded them
to secure meat. Later, we continued on a self-guided tour of the west block
of the Grasslands National Park, where we saw the cabin of artist and writer

Will James, born in Quebec in 1892 to French-Canadian parents. James's book, *Smoky the Cowhorse,* became the most famous of his twenty-three illustrated books. After the tour, it was time for the group to attend the Val Marie 44th Annual Indoor Rodeo, a semi-pro rodeo that boasted an attendance of approximately 500 people in a town with a population of only 450.

Although the Vernon Rotary research team did not make contact with Rotarians or ranchers in Alberta, evidence shows that the GWT delivered longhorns to Alberta. The Alberta Texas Longhorn Association verified the first herd of longhorns arrived in 1876. A census taken of cattle in 1884 estimated the number of longhorns to be forty thousand head. Another identifying factor for the longhorn was their durability and stamina that enabled them to help stock the open-range land some two thousand miles from their initial home.[44]

Edward Brado's book, *Cattle Kingdom: Early Ranching in Alberta,* verified that longhorns were found at Pincher Creek in 1881. A friend, Julie Swanson was raised on a ranch west of Pincher Creek in the Beaver Mines area. Julie recounted memories of riding her horse to school and her grandfather and uncle "passing on good advice about handling and understanding horses." She also talked about the cattle that came from Texas. The Texas connection continued with this Alberta native who married a Montana rancher: their daughter, a professional barrel racer, married a Texas professional team roper. They moved to Texas to compete and to continue the generational knowledge of training horses.

When the trail research teams reached the terminus in Canada, they recognized that across the Great Plains, much was still the same as in the trail days. Transportation had become more diversified, and communication was more rapid. Even with these changes, horses, cattle, ranches, and rodeo competition kept people close to the land. They were aware of the fickle effects of nature, a capricious economy, and the benefits of having a good neighbor. With generations of the same families living on the same land using the same skills, much remained as it once was. Documentation of the GWT in Wyoming, Montana, Saskatchewan, and Alberta verified the terminus of a trail that originated in Mexico some two thousand miles away, lasted the greatest number of years, and therefore must have carried more cattle than any other trail.

CHAPTER 10
The Trail Home: A Living History

After seven years, the goal to verify the route of the Great Western Trail at its local roots had been completed from Mexico to Canada. Some states, however, are continuing to identify the path with additional posts. Evidence showed that the trail was the longest (two thousand miles), lasted the greatest number of years (nineteen), and carried the most cattle (said to be seven million horses and longhorns). More than two hundred trail markers stand as reminders that the path of the trail went through that area. Trail teams shared on-site dedication experiences that added a second dimension to the project: it rekindled the spirit of the trail era. The trail research project recovered primary sources for historians to consider in continuing efforts to give the GWT its rightful place in historical documents. In addition, trail volunteers initiated studies, created organizations, and started projects to preserve the recovered evidence for the trail's route and to sustain the spirit of the GWT, a spirit that unified communities and fostered international camaraderie.

Of vital importance to the authenticity and stature of GWT history was Congressional approval for a three-year Federal Feasibility Study to determine whether the trail, along with the Chisholm Trail, should be designated as a National Historic Trail. During the trail-verification process, community trail teams contacted their Congressional representatives and senators to request that they co-sponsor or support a bill to designate the Great Western Trail and the Chisholm Trail as National Historic Trails. The study, approved on March 30, 2009, was included in the Omnibus Public Land Management

Act of 2009 (P.L. 111.11). One section called for the secretary of the interior to study the Chisholm and Great Western Trails for their potential to be designated as National Historic Trails. On June 25, 2007, Oklahoma Representative Tom Cole introduced H.R. 2849, legislation in the House to approve a feasibility study for the two trails' possible designation. Six legislators cosponsored the bill—three from Oklahoma and one each from Texas, Colorado, and Kansas.[1] On October 30, 2007, Senator Kay Bailey Hutchison (R-TX) introduced a bill, S. 2255, to the Senate requiring the federal government to conduct a feasibility study. Sen. John Cornyn (R-TX) and Sen. James Inhofe (R-OK) were original cosponsors of the bill.[2]

The Congressional Feasibility Study historians held town hall meetings in states that fell within the Study boundaries. To document the *significance* of the two trails, a criterion for the study, National Park Service Superintendent Dr. Aaron Mahr and lead research historian Dr. Frank Norris collected comments, questions, and information at town meetings. They assimilated the information into their study. The Study and the meetings raised awareness of the GWT and the need to recover primary sources to verify its history. At a town hall meeting in Albany, Texas, three noted Texas Tech University historians, Dr. Monte Monroe, Dr. Tai Kreidler, and Dr. Paul H. Carlson provided evidence they had recovered for the GWT's path. Dr. Monroe announced the designation of a Great Western Trail Special Collection at the Texas Tech Southwest Collection/Special Collections. Dr. Monroe also said that they would conduct oral interviews of trail descendants and collect data.

After months of town hall meetings, the assimilation of the information, and additional research, the next step in the approval process started on May 16, 2012, in Washington, DC. At the Landmarks Committee of the National Park System Advisory Board meeting, Dr. Norris, research historian for the Study from the "NPS National Trails Intermountain Region Office," Intermountain Region, Santa Fe, New Mexico, presented a well-documented case for the two trails becoming National Historic Trails. The committee, composed of various cultural-resource professionals from across the nation, scrutinized the proposal for national significance. Jim Aneff, Roland Jaz (Rotary youth exchange student from Slovakia), and I attended the meeting. Dr. Norris introduced Jim and Roland, and he asked me to introduce the committee to the GWT grassroots research project. Several of the committee members expressed interest in this unique endeavor. The committee members gave positive reinforcement to Dr. Norris for his proposal and voted unanimously to forward the proposal to the next level, the National Park Service Advisory Board meeting in Denver the following week. The full National Park Service Advisory Board recommended that the finalized research study be presented to the Secretary of the Interior. The final step will be approval by Congress, possibly in the late fall of 2015.

The Congressional Feasibility Study bill, approved in 2009, limited the study to the segments of the GWT trail that carried the largest number of cattle to two railheads: Dodge City, Kansas, and Ogallala, Nebraska. More than half of the cattle trailed to northern states for reservations, military troops, and open-range ranchers were not included in the study. Thus, the funding for research was limited to the parameters established in the bill for its length. When the Congressional bill was written, the lack of documentation at the time for the length of the GWT from Mexico to Canada limited the route for the study to four trail states instead of nine states. If a drover called the trail anything, it was the name of the next supply point. The GWT had many names from Mexico to Canada: Matamoros Trail (Texas and Mexico border), Western Trail (a short segment leaving San Antonio), Fort Griffin, Doan's, Fort Supply, Dodge City, Ogallala, Texas Trail (north of Ogallala into Canada). The short segment called the Western Trail was used in popular fiction to differentiate it from the Eastern Trail, now named the Chisholm Trail.

The Congressional study's limiting the length of the Great Western Trail constrained the trail to historical inaccuracies. The study defined the path of the trail as the following: "The Great Western Trail (also known as the 'Dodge City Trail'), from the vicinity of San Antonio, Texas, north-by-northwest [to] Oklahoma, north through Kansas to Dodge City, and north through Nebraska to Ogallala."[3] Chris Jefferies, former executive director of the Chisholm Trail Heritage Center at Duncan, Oklahoma, said, "We didn't include a longer Great Western Trail in the original draft legislation simply because we were finding it difficult to get support for the project and wanted to keep it as straight-forward as possible. In hindsight, that was probably a mistake."[4]

The Draft Study, however, included a proviso for the study of the trails south of San Antonio and the possibility of including feeder routes in the historical trail designation. The draft included details: "Given the multiplicity of routes that have been historically linked to these trails, however, these significance-related questions need to be answered on a trail-by-trail and a segment-by-segment basis."[5] The question about the GWT origin south of

San Antonio, as stated in the bill, said: "The Secretary of the Interior shall identify the point at which the trail originated south of San Antonio, Texas."[6] Feeder routes have the possibility of being included as a part of the National Historical Trail designation. "Feeder trails and connecting trails may indeed qualify for status as a nationally significant trail; what is important is that any feeder trail or connecting trail that is deemed nationally significant—just as a trail's 'trunk route'—needs to be shown to have witnessed the passage of a large, significant number of cattle over a significant number of years."[7]

Thus, a segment of the GWT trail, south of San Antonio to Kingsville, was verified by the study historian and an independent researcher, so that segment is included in the official designated path of the GWT. The study statement says that the designation is based on "the passage of a large, significant number of cattle over a significant number of years." The GWT South Texas volunteers recovered evidence that not only did longhorns go north from the King Ranch, but that the Brownsville area and the Matamoros area supplied vast numbers of longhorns. Someday, when an academician taps the newspaper archives in Matamoros and other local and area primary source archives, the path of the GWT will be officially extended from San Antonio south to Brownsville and Matamoros.

When the draft copy of the Feasibility Study was completed, it was placed online for public comment for sixty days—from January 5, 2015, to March 6, 2015. The comment period gave individuals a voice in the approval of the content of the extensive research study and its conclusions that would ultimately become the "verified" history of the two trails. On the second page of the 163-page draft, the Great Western Trail teams, who had placed more than two hundred GWT markers from Mexico to Canada, were shocked to find that once again the Great Western Trail's name was at risk; the trail name was recommended to be designated as just "Western Trail."

The *Draft Chisholm and Great Western National Historic Trail Feasibility Study/Environmental Assessment*, says, "The name 'Great Western' does not have strong historical associations. National Park Service (NPS) and independent research has led to an understanding that the 'Great Western' trail should be more appropriately referred to as the 'Western Trail.'"[8] The name of the Congressional bill and the draft study both used "Great Western Trail" in the titles. Chapter 1 of this book provides details for the first academic study of the trail and reasons for the lack of an academic study until 1965. The Draft reference section has one hundred sources, with forty-three about Native Americans, four for trails (one was written in 1875, one year after the first herd went up the GWT), and four books on the Chisholm Trail. Jimmy M. Skaggs's definitive 1965 academic study was not included as a reference. The only reference, a defining study, for the GWT was Gary Kraisinger and Margaret Kraisinger's 2004 book, *The Western: The Greatest Texas Cattle Trail 1874–1886*. Gary, a cartographer, provided accurate maps and details on the trail from Fort Supply in Indian Territory (Oklahoma) to Dodge City, Kansas, on to Ogallala, Nebraska. Research for Gary's maps of the complete length of the GWT from Mexico to Canada was not completed until after the GWT research projects started. They are used to illustrate the path of the GWT in each chapter of this book.

The Draft Study statement: "'Great Western' does not have strong historical associations" could be compared to the evolution of the name for the Chisholm Trail. Enough years have passed so that Chisholm Trail has become commonly used; however, its name was once highly disputed by many Texas trail historians. The first definitive GWT academic study by Jimmy Skaggs in 1965 was needed in the Congressional Study to offset the proliferation of the name *Western Trail* used in popular fiction. The GWT grassroots historical research project that started in 2003 recovered primary sources to verify that the Great Western Trail extended from Matamoros to Saskatchewan. The name *Great Western Trail* is historically significant to three nations marking the path of the trail. More than two hundred GWT markers stand along the two-thousand-mile path to verify that the name is GWT.

A major part of the one thousand comments made during the public comment period included international citizens from Canada and Mexico, as well as US citizens, supporting the designation of the trail name as *Great Western Trail*. The comments from citizens in three nations and with some eighteen hundred people participating in the marking of the GWT should work in favor of the name *GWT* being considered historically significant. From the first definitive study in 1965 to 2015, the evolution of usage of the name Great Western Trail for the complete trail has become common in the media and other public forums. However the Skaggs' academic research and the grass-roots research studies have not been recognized as historically significant. The study has relied on books that briefly mention the name Western Trail that is common to popular fiction and early trail popularizers.

The Draft writers included statements supporting the various reasons that the GWT name is in dispute. "Neither of these trails gained their present name until they had been used for a number of years, and no name seems to have predominated during the period in which the trails were active." They acknowledge that ". . . both popular fiction and the efforts of early trail popularizers played a role in applying the 'Chisholm Trail' name to other trails as well, most specifically to the Western Trail."[9] As in this comment, popular fiction continued to determine the name.

The final draft for the congressional study has not been completed, so, as is said, "the jury is still out," about what will become the official designated name for the Great Western Trail. If GWT is not selected, it must become yet another project for historians, one that could leave a mark on history. They could set the record straight by on-site primary research using the sources listed in this book to secure a national designation name change. History has shown that the name of the GWT has been besieged by those who have not taken time to corroborate the sources they have used.

A second issue surfaced during the Draft Study comment period: the United States Cattlemen's Association and the Texas, Oklahoma, and Kansas Farm Bureaus sent comments disapproving the designation of the trails during the public comment period. Asserting that they did not know about the study until the public comment period, they requested an extension of the public comment period; a two-week extension was granted. They specified that government regulations regarding the trail designation might cause problems for the private and public land owners.

The old issue of ownership of private property and the role of government overrode the pride in historic cattle trails. The issue of land ownership during the trail era created violence between open-range ranchers and homesteaders. Later, the leasing of federal land for ranching under the regulations of the Bureau of Land Management (BLM) created some abrasive relationships that promoted concerns, without substance, for owners of private land. Some trail states have a large percentage of federally owned land, such as Wyoming (48.2 percent) and Montana (28.9 percent). Other trail states have small amounts of federally owned land, such as Kansas, only 0.6 percent; Nebraska, 1.1 percent; Oklahoma, 1.6 percent; and Texas, 1.8 percent.[10] When conflict occurs between the government and land owners, sometimes the message leaves out the fact that the land issue is not always private property, but federal land leased by ranchers and administered by the BLM. Of course, eminent domain continues to be a major issue between the state and private land owners.

Whatever the cause, the friend of an Oklahoma rancher sent this message to other ranchers during the comment period. My friend . . . owns and operates the historical Stuart 7S Ranch with her sons. The National Park

Service is threatening to steal their ranch and anybody else's property that this trail runs through. Please contact your Oklahoma House of Representatives by March 6th and let your voice be heard. Tell them NO. No more land grabs. It's not American."[11] The president of the United States Cattlemen's Association supported this stand. In a letter to the National Park Service, Danni Beer said, "The potential use of eminent domain in securing land involved with these trails is especially concerning to our membership whose operations subsist off of both public and private lands. USCA opposes the designation of the Chisholm Trail and Great Western Trail. Protecting private property rights is a priority of USCA and we will continue to advocate on these rights as this issue moves forward toward any potential designation."[12]

National Park Service trail research historian Dr. Frank Norris said that the study did not include funding for land acquisition, and the agency, in administering National Historic Trails for thirty-plus years, had not purchased any land. He said,

(The El Camino Real de los Tejas bill from 2004, for example, states that "The United States shall not acquire for the trail any land or interest in land outside the exterior boundary of any federally-administered area without the consent of the owner of the land or interest in land.") While this bill (above) states a prohibition against an unwilling transfer of land, the historical reality is that the NPS has purchased no land—at all—in relation to its administration of the various national historic trails.[13]

Many ranchers along the trail, especially the Great Western Trail, had joined the GWT research project, placed markers on their ranches, and worked to promote designation of the two trails as National Historic Trails.

There are two major steps to the completion of this project. The first will be the National Park Service's assessment of the public comments, determining if any substantive changes are needed (hopefully, designating the official name as GWT), then, preparing the final study, and sending it to the regional office to be signed. Then, the transmittal to Congress going first to the National Resources Committee will move it toward the Congressional Liaison office. A committee hearing may be required before the bill is written and submitted to Congress for consideration.

The GWT needed publicity to overcome the obscurity of its name and

RI President Ray Klinginsmith's International Photo Shoot, Brownsville, Texas
On December 10, 2009, at the International Photo Shoot in Brownsville, Texas, held at the request of Ray Klinginsmith, Rotary International president, Rotarians from three nations attended. Rotary leaders pictured are (l-r) Jerry Klinger, Brownsville; Norma Nelly Aguilar, Matamoros, Mexico; Jose Alfredo Sepulveda, RI director, Hidalgo, Mexico; Noel Bajat, RI director, Louisiana; Sylvia Mahoney, Vernon, Texas; Klinginsmith, Missouri; Jose Luis Diaz del Castillo Lie, Leon, Mexico; and Rotary district leaders Dennis Roberts, Brownsville (front), Jim Aneff, Abilene; and Dave Mason, Abilene. Not pictured are Regina, Saskatchewan, Rotary GWT committee members Gene and Catherine Griffith.

to raise awareness of its newly verified length. An international goodwill event in South Texas provided a venue to raise the awareness of the GWT while creating a sense of community. In October 2009, Ray Klinginsmith, the president of Rotary International, proposed a photo shoot at the GWT marker at Brownsville near the US border with Mexico. On December 10, 2010, Rotarians from the United States, Canada, and Mexico joined the president and two international Rotary directors, Noel Bajat from Louisiana and Jose Alfredo Sepulveda from Hidalgo, near Mexico City. Gene and Catherine Griffith, a Rotary trail team from Regina, Saskatchewan, traveled two thousand miles to present the Canadian flag during the one-hour ceremony. Brownsville and Matamoros Rotarians presented the US flag and the Mexican flag. Jose Luis Diaz del Castillo Lie of Leon, Mexico, provided Rotary Longhorn pins he had designed and produced to commemorate

Jose Luis Diaz del Castillo Lie of Leon, Mexico, Presented Longhorn Rotary Pins
Jose Luis Diaz del Castillo Lie of Leon, Mexico, presented Longhorn Rotary pins to all Rotary trail research project volunteers to recognize the good will created among the three nations recovering primary sources to document the GWT from Mexico to Canada.

the three-nation GWT research project. José Alfredo Sepulveda, wearing a magnificent Charro suit, expressed the mission of the trail project that volunteers working together would document the complete length of the GWT, and so doing, it would unify the trail's segments into one trail. He said, "Trails lead us away, and trails bring us back again."[14] Sepulveda noted an important result for the volunteers' efforts. He said, "I have the firm conviction that this path is the key to further promote good will between our three countries."[15]

Another international venue for the GWT brought recognition to its name and its history. The international fascination with the American cowboy drew attention to the GWT presenters at the Rotary International Convention on May 21–25, 2011, in New Orleans. During the convention, attended by some twenty thousand Rotarians from approximately two hundred countries, a South African choir of high school students sang "Happy Trails" and "Home on the Range." Their songs primed the audience for our presentation about the Great Western Trail. Our boots, jeans, hats, and denim trail shirts brought approving comments from attendees about our "native costumes." Members of the international audience listened as I summarized the GWT Rotary research project and as Dr. Michael Babb sang his original song, "Great Western Cattle Trail."

The general sessions at the convention were infused with the president's chosen theme: the cowboy code and its use. When Ray Klinginsmith gave his farewell speech, incoming president Kalyan Banerjee from India pointed to a picture on the huge screen of Cowboy Klinginsmith and of himself, Indian Banerjee. He said, "If there is anything better than a cowboy, it is a cowboy and an Indian." Again, memories were refreshed and formed about the range of values supported by the legend of the cowboy and the importance of promoting cultural understanding. Moreover, within the framework of Rotary, those values are being promoted among the international community.

While Dr. Babb sang "Great Western Cattle Trail," it noticeably resonated among the convention attendees. Despite international language differences, the whole audience responded to the rhythm of the song. Babb's song was the product of Ray Klinginsmith's request that someone write and record a Great Western Trail song. While researching details for the song, Babb discovered that as a child he had lived on the trail in Oklahoma. He found real and mythical information about the life of a trail driver in E. C. "Teddy Blue" Abbott's book, *We Pointed Them North*. Babb wrote, "I was born in the East and destined for the West. I am a cowboy." His song includes stampedes, rustlers, Indians, grifters, burning sun, quick-flowing rivers, and twisters. The cowboy's reward came when he delivered "the entire herd." His song lyrics moved from trail days to modern times. "All things must change. The trail is but a memory in the heart of every cowboy on the Great Western Trail."[16] The CD recording of the song, played worldwide on four hundred syndicated radio stations, reached #32 on the European Country Chart in Norway. It aired 123 times in Australia. Babb designated the profit to one of Rotary's international projects—the eradication of polio.[17]

During the research process, a number of people asked why Rotarians were so dedicated to recovering evidence to verify the path of the trail. Part of the answer lies in the fact that both cowboys and Rotarians have similar codes of ethics. Paul Harris founded the world's first service organization three years after Owen Wister wrote *The Virginian*, which helped define the Cowboy Hero. In 1905, Harris, an attorney in Chicago, a destination town

Michael Babb Sings "Great Western Trail" at RI Convention, New Orleans, Louisiana
Michael Babb sang his original song, "Great Western Cattle Trail," at the 2011 Rotary International Conference in New Orleans. With twenty thousand Rotarians from two hundred countries, some who listened did not understand the words, but they responded to the rhythm of the music and to Babb's "native costume."

for many of the trail cattle, established Rotary for businessmen. Harris wrote that he saw a need to create the same friendly spirit he had felt in the small towns of his youth. This organization would help support public-service efforts in communities. In Harris's 1915 article, "Passing Our Tenth Milestone," he traced his ideals of service to America's promise of life, liberty, and the pursuit of happiness. "Philosophy is at the bottom of almost everything. It is the foundation of permanent happiness, and it lies way down beneath the very laws of the land."[18]

Harris's new service club had much in common with the cowboy legend. Not only should a person, especially a businessperson, be truthful, fair, create goodwill, and make his [or her] efforts be beneficial to others, he [or she] should spread that philosophy around the world promoting a fertile environment for life, liberty, and the pursuit of happiness. Rotarians embraced that idea. The cowboy code of ethics and Rotary's Four-Way Test have a common foundation for expected outcomes. Both codes, the legendary cowboy and Rotary, have attracted interest as well as membership worldwide. Rotary International has 1.2 million members in some two hundred countries.

As awareness of the trail research project expanded, people provided new primary evidence from their family's history collections, sometimes serendipitously. While visiting friends, Gussie Allmer mentioned John Leakey, her trail-driver grandfather. He had trailed cattle from Texas to Montana. She offered an out-of-print book he had written about his trip from South Texas near Uvalde to eastern Montana and western North Dakota. As many Texas drovers did, Leakey had stayed in North Dakota to ranch.

That trail-era autobiography, *The West That Was*, captured the trail-era memories of drover John Leakey. He carved out a life in North Dakota that led to his induction into the North Dakota Cowboy Hall of Fame. Leakey was honored for being a founder and first president of the North Dakota Stockgrowers Association.[19] One incident in Leakey's life illustrated the spirit of the trail. He told of his effort to honor a friend by marking his grave. The Leakey family ranch in South Texas had joined King Fisher's ranch. Fisher, a notorious person associated with the Nueces Strip, had become a famous local sheriff. On March 22, 1884, Fisher and US Marshall Ben Thompson were killed in San Antonio in the line of duty, in an incident later known as the Vaudeville Theater Ambush. After a large funeral, Thompson was buried in Austin. Fisher was buried on his ranch near Leakey, Texas.[20]

After ranching for sixty years in North Dakota, John Leakey returned to Texas to search for Fisher's grave. He found Fisher's unmarked grave in Pioneer Cemetery in Uvalde. He cleaned the overgrowth of weeds and placed a marker on it.[21] Given Leakey's honors in North Dakota and the many years that had passed since he left Texas, his return to Texas to mark Fisher's grave seemed unusual. South Texas rancher King Fisher had lived on both sides of the law. However, he had been a neighbor and friend. The trail culture seemed to inspire a need for cowboys to be buried in a marked place in the earth near a place they called home and to have friends who would honor that need for a burial spot.

John Leakey's history had another twist. At the 2011 National Cowboy Symposium and Celebration in Lubbock, Leakey's history, North Dakota, and Teddy Roosevelt came together. Two noted Roosevelt experts addressed the subject in a panel discussion, *Teddy Roosevelt: How the Dakotas Years Influenced His Political Legacy and Still Influences National Issues Today*. One of the panelists, Darrell Dorgan, North Dakota Cowboy Hall of Fame executive director, based his portion on Roosevelt's Dakota years. The other pan-elist, Dr. Richard Slatta, North Carolina State University history professor, addressed the national issues and the political legacy. They were a well-rec-ognized team: Dorgan's documentary, *Theodore Roosevelt: A Cowboy's Ride to the White House*, had been nominated for an Emmy Award. Slatta's nine books on the cowboy era often included Roosevelt, who had adopted a cow-boy persona. Both panelists described efforts by Roosevelt that had helped bring national recognition to the cowboy, especially including his friend-ships with Western author Owen Wister and Western artist Frederick Rem-ington.

The panelists discussed Teddy Roosevelt and North Dakota, which re-lated to the trail. The Leakey, Texas, connection, however, followed the con-clusion of the formal discussion. The Celebration's chuck wagon cook-off was in progress on a large grassy area outside the convention center. The chuck wagon was originally designed by cattle-trail boss Charles Goodnight as a portable kitchen for a cook to serve drovers. The teams at the chuck wagon cook-off, arranged in a horseshoe design, were ready to serve their meals of chicken-fried steaks, beans, and cobbler.

Darrell Dorgan had chuck wagon tickets and invited me to go. While deciding which wagon would get our two tickets, Darrell stopped to visit the Hawk's Nest chuck wagon group from Leakey, Texas. He inquired about any knowledge of kin of drover John Leakey. One woman with biscuit flour on her apron, a large smile, and a robust voice said she, Linda Kirkpatrick, was kin to him. Darrell forged North Dakota to Texas connections related to John Leakey. I took a photo of Linda and Darrell. The photo of Gussie's long-lost Leakey relative was included in the book when I returned it to her. These examples of trail-era kinship and relationships were common at on-site locations along the trail. The trail history chronicled in this book is personal, memorable history for so many individuals.

In a wonderful flight beyond our original expectations for the project to mark the trail, our efforts brought forth ancillary, sustainable, and heart-warming responses in communities along the trail. Below are some exam-ples that heightened the public's awareness of the Great Western Trail and reinforced their fascination with the romanticized West.

A retiree proposed an idea to sustain the GWT recognition project. Paul Noack of Austin, Texas, volunteered to take photos and chart the global po-sitioning system (GPS) coordinates for the markers. Starting at the south-ernmost point on the trail, Paul continued across Texas, Oklahoma, and

Kansas, stopping in Ogallala, Nebraska. After returning home, he created a cyber-herd drive with daily photo e-mail postings on the Internet. Each day his cyber-herd stopped at a GWT marker. As the trail boss, he gave reports on the terrain, the herd, the drovers, the dangers, and the troubles. He reported meeting famous and infamous drovers, gunslingers, and lawmen in trail towns.

When Paul Noack's cyber-herd arrived at Ogallala, Nebraska, he sent his 119th daily photo and report from the GWT marker location at Boot Hill Cemetery. In the photo, the statue, *Trail Boss*, could be seen near the grave of W. T. "Bill" Campbell. In 1877, Bill died in a shoot-out with a Texan on Front Street. Two brothers from Texas, Andy Moye and Iverson "Babe" Moye, had hired on with Bill Butler from Karnes County, Texas, to trail a herd to Ogallala. In what bystanders said was a fair fight, Andy shot Bill Campbell, who was "half drunk and spoiling for a fight." The crowd witnessed the fight, but unfortunately for Andy, Campbell was a local man. Andy and Babe, being outliers to the town, understood that frontier justice, augmented with a grand jury comprised of local citizens, might not take too kindly to their reducing the local population. The two brothers left for Texas, luckily, unharmed.[22]

Paul Noack returned to Texas to search for the Moye brothers' final resting places. After a few phone calls, he located Bill Moye at Warren in Tyler County. Mr. Moye, a highly regarded history teacher, remembered two trail drivers in his family, but the Ogallala incident was fresh news to him. Later, Moye sent Noack the birth and death dates of both drovers, the location of their graves, and he verified that Andy and Babe had been drovers.[23] The trail project added to their family history.

Another project to maintain interest in the GWT was the organization of the National Great Western Cattle Trail Association (GWCTA-National). The initial group met in Baird, Texas, at the historic 1911 Texas and Pacific Depot, now the Baird Visitors Center and Transportation Museum. Tommie Jones, Baird Chamber of Commerce manager, volunteered to help with the trail event. Bandera's David and Heather Burell had initiated the meeting. After several meetings, the group established a national board, and state trail teams organized chapters in Texas, Oklahoma, Kansas, Nebraska, South Dakota, and North Dakota.

Young people benefited from several trail-team projects that would help sustain the GWT project efforts. On January 8, 2011, in Lubbock, Texas, Ray Klinginsmith's talk about the Great Western Trail at a dinner fundraiser helped send two hundred international youth exchange students to the international convention in New Orleans. Another youth event was organized in 2011. The Great Western Cattle Trail Association-Texas Chapter initiated a Young Texas Trail Blazer Award. The criteria to be an award winner, for students eighteen years or younger, was to collect oral histories of trail descendants, maintain trail markers, or take on other trail-related projects. The award would be presented at the National Cowboy Symposium and Celebration in Lubbock.[24]

A young man with North Dakota roots started another trail event. In June 2011, Ken, the son of A. Jay Grantier, rode his bicycle more than one thousand miles from Medora, North Dakota, down the trail to Texas. He took the same path south that his grandfather had taken north. The Grantiers are descendants of Jay Newman Grantier, who made two cattle drives from Texas, stayed to become a cattleman and rancher, and was inducted into the North Dakota Cowboy Hall of Fame.[25]

Art had helped sustain trail history through the years, and in 2011, the Western Trail Art Association was organized to promote artists who live and work along the Great Western Trail. The Museum of the Western Prairie in Altus, Oklahoma, hosted the premier art exhibit, opening to a sellout crowd in 2012. Among the board members of the Art Association, five were noted area-artists, including the president, Mary Ann McCuistion—museums and galleries readily scheduled the organization for an exhibit.[26]

Yet another effort to promote the legacy of the trail was the use of the trail's name for businesses or nonprofit organizations. The Western Trail Chapter of the National Society of Daughters of the American Revolution (DAR) was officially organized in Vernon on October 9, 2010. The chapter regent, Judy Ditmore, said, "We wanted to unite our Texas heritage with our national heritage, and the Trail connects with our DAR-Texas theme: Preserving the past, our gift to the future."[27]

The interaction among communities that sponsored GWT marker dedications inspired another commemorative historical project. Dr. Holle Humphries, in September 2011, attended a Great Western Cattle Trail board of directors meeting representing the Texas Plains Trail Region (TPTR). This group is a component of the Texas Historical Commission's cultural heritage trail group. She said, "The effort to mark the Great Western Trail has provided us all with a template to show how it is possible for anyone in any community to find a way to mark a cultural heritage trail with a physical marker in their own communities and regions. I learned that placing a marker in

Club Matamoros Rotario Members Co-Sponsored Photo Shoot
Along the GWT, evidence demonstrated the changing role of women. The Club Matamoros Rotario members, all businesswomen, illustrated the increasing numbers of women who owned businesses or were in career positions in businesses along the trail into Mexico. They co-sponsored the RI International's Photo Shoot at Brownsville on December 10, 2009.

the ground makes the trail "real." The TPTR is marking a fifty-two-county region with a twenty-one-foot arrow to create a Quanah Parker Trail. The arrows will educate others about the Native Americans, who had last lived free on the region's frontier before the arrival of Anglo settlers in the 1870s.[28]

The trail, the cowboy culture, and ranches originating during the trail days continued to attract international visitors to trail communities. The Vernon trail team met with several Chinese entrepreneurs in 2008. The Red River, made famous by John Wayne, was their first stop. In Beijing, an emerging horse culture was creating investment opportunities. One visitor owned a large equestrian center for Chinese citizens to be weekend cowboys. The diverse opportunities for Chinese investors ranged from importing horses for brood mares and publishing an equestrian magazine, to promoting the growing interest in the Western way of life on Chinese national TV. With the group was Nina Wang, a famous host and producer for CCTV movie channel, Beijing, China. Her program claims an audience of 800 million. Her camera crew filmed her riding a horse with the Waggoner cowboys on their legendary ranch. The cowboy culture has also taken root in several other countries: Germany, Sweden, Japan, and Norway.

At the marker dedication in 2009 at the North Dakota Cowboy Hall of Fame (NDCHF) in Medora, the Texas and North Dakota groups bonded as they toured the museum and learned how many activities and interests they had in common. Numerous honorees were from Texas originally. An evocative moment connecting with the past happened in 2010 in Lubbock, Texas, at the National Cowboy Symposium and Celebration. Phil Baird, president of the NDCHF, had come to Texas along with Darrell Dorgan, the executive director, and thirteen other board members to accept the national 2010 American Cowboy Culture Award for Outstanding Museums. The NDCHF focuses on Native Americans, ranching, and rodeo.

Phil Baird, a Rosebud Sioux, and I had a chance to reminisce while he and his group were in Lubbock. Phil spoke of talking with the leaders of his tribe about his transporting Sitting Bull's headdress from one exhibit place to another. He spoke of the honor of being responsible for its safety and security. His passion showed when he expressed what it meant for him to be responsible for the tribes' spiritual leader's eagle-feather headdress. His words symbolized all that was good and right for leadership, for enriching the intangible human spirit. Baird said, "There are no coincidences." I understood as I listened to Phil. I thought about the past times when his people and mine met and mingled on the Great Western Trail. Standing in the shade of a West Texas elm tree with my trail friend, our personal contact enriched my spirit with appreciation for that past . . . and gratitude for this present time. Bonding on the trail project, another unexpected result, was much more than preserving history, it was celebrating the human spirit.

A Pause for Reflection

The drover, that independent cowboy who created a worldwide legend, might not utter such a philosophical statement as there are no coincidences. However, with the Great Western Trail now being celebrated in three nations, with its history being presented to an international community, with a Congressional bill in place to recognize its importance, it seems appropriate to take one more look at the significance of the trail, of its economic impact on the southwest, and its continuing influence on those living along the trail.

The Great Western Trail stretched more than two thousand miles across parts of three nations. The seemingly unforgiving land supported the largest migration of cattle in history. The cowboys quickly learned that sufficient water and adequate grass would support herds. In spite of being confronted by a diversity of hazards while moving the cattle north, hundreds of cowboys signed on for the job. All the while, they were establishing a new industry made possible by the new era of railroad transportation. The cattle-trail industry employed previously jobless Civil War veterans and others who were short on cash but long on spirit. It provided opportunities for the drovers, mostly young men, to become entrepreneurs. For a brief period, the trail drivers pursued their trade outside of the encumbrances of traditional ideologies and beyond the reach of law enforcement. The wealthy and the workers violently challenged each other for possession of the open-range land, but this conflict eventually resolved itself in a way that their legacy changed some age-old traditions, helping equality and ethics to gain precedent across the vast grassland prairies. The composite of these elements coalesced to initiate a way of life that keeps people living on the Great Plains stable, happy, and willing to continue there for generations.

The grassroots research project became a study of the social, cultural, and economic influences of the trail era that made the America of the West an icon of strength and integrity. The research helped provide an understanding of the historical analogy between the cowboy culture and an international service club. With Rotarians reminding members of the value of speaking the truth, promoting fairness and goodwill, with beneficial results for all, the cowboy code under the guise of the Four-Way Test continues today. This code serves as a guide to the national and international community under the flag of Rotary International.

According to award-winning author Elmer Kelton, being a cowboy is a state of mind, a spirit deep-rooted in values and implemented through hard work, bonding people together to a common cause. That state of mind resonated in the response of Bill Whelan, Canadian Rotarian, when asked whether he was a cowboy. He said, "I always wanted to be a cowboy." The statement supports a testament to the ongoing popularity of the legacy of the cowboy, his work ethic, and his sense of responsibility and integrity.

This book is a record of those community volunteers, who gave selflessly to verify the length of the trail, and thus rescued it from obscurity. Their efforts showed a living spirit, a common collective memory of the trail era. Along the two-thousand-mile trail, the cattle and horse-related businesses and competitions have kept people connected. Their sense of community is embedded in the commonality of cowboy ethics. Volunteers expressed their passion for trail research as it related to the land they call home. Their recovery of data supporting the Great Western Trail's name and length was a phenomenal twenty-first-century historical grassroots effort to set the record straight. In the process, trail teams discovered the far-reaching effects of the trail on the American economy and on popular culture.

APPENDIX

Trail-Team Volunteers

Thanks to the people whose names are on this list. All volunteered to search for primary sources, help organize dedication ceremonies, and/or provide valuable services needed for the grassroots research project.

Vision: Visionary & Mold Maker for Marking the Great Western Trail
Bob Klemme, Enid, OK

Challenge to the Rotary Club of Vernon, Texas
Dennis Vernon & John Yudell Barton, Altus, OK
Chris Jefferies, executive director, Chisholm Trail Museum, Duncan, OK

Project
"Marking the Great Western Trail from Mexico to Canada"
Rotary Club of Vernon Centennial Project 2004–2011

Vernon Rotary Co-Chairs, "Marking the GWT"
Sylvia Gann Mahoney & Jeff Bearden

Vernon Rotary Marker Makers
Phil McCuistion, Rick Jouett, & Paul Hawkins

Red River Valley Museum
GWT Events & Collection, Vernon, Texas
Mary Ann McCuistion, executive director

Maps in this Book
Gary Kraisinger, cartographer; Gary & Margaret Kraisinger, authors
The Western: The Greatest Texas Cattle Trail 1874–1886

Vernon Rotary Trail Team: Attended Trail Dedications
Jeff & Mary Bearden, Dr. Ed & Jean Clark,
Larry & Judy Crabtree, Michelle Everett
Harold & Peggy Hardcastle, Paul Hawkins

Bill & Ann Huskinson, Rick & Patti Jouett
Sylvia G. Mahoney, Dr. Doug & Missie Matthews
Phil & Mary Ann McCuistion, Dr. Marvin & Patsy Sharp

Vernon Sponsors of Markers

AEP, Jeff & Mary Bearden, Mr. & Mrs. Gary Chapman, Choice Wireless, Inc.,
Dr. & Mrs. Lewis E. Clark, Mr. & Mrs. Garland Gibbs, Paul & Sunny Hawkins,
Bill & Ann Huskinson, King, Moore, Truelove & Pharis CPAs, Sylvia G. Mahoney,
Osborne's Distributing Co., Red River Farm Supply—Mr. & Mrs. David Singleton,
Santa Rosa Telephone Cooperative, Inc., Joe Chat Sumner III,
Vernon Veterinary Clinic, in memory of E. C. True,
Wilbarger County Historical Society

Rotary Events—GWT

2005 Rotary Zone Institute

Corpus Christi, Texas, Oct. 21–24, 2005, Other Trail States Requested GWT Project
Rotary International President-Elect Bill Boyd, New Zealand
Rotary International Director Ron Burton, Norman, OK (later RI president)
Texas DG 5790 Jim Aneff, Abilene, TX
Nebraska DG 5630 William (Bill) E. Ballou, Kearney
Nebraska DG 5630 Cloyd Clark, McCook
Texas DG 5930 Jorge Verduzco, Laredo
Texas District 5840 Doug Whinnery, Kerrville
Texas Assistant DG 5790 Sylvia Gann Mahoney, GWT Trail co-chair

2009 Rotary International Photo Shoot

Brownsville, Texas, GWT Marker, Dec. 10, 2009
Requested by Rotary International President Ray Klinginsmith
Rotary International Director Zone 21 Jose Alfredo Sepulveda, Hidalgo, Mexico
Rotary International Director-Elect Zone 22 & 27 Noel A. Bajat, Abbeville, Louisiana
Canada Rotary GWT committee, Gene and Catherine Griffith, Regina, Saskatchewan
Longhorn Rotary Pins—José Luis Diaz del Castillo Lie, Leon, Mexico
Club Rotario Matamoros Profesional President Norma Nelly Aguilar &
Past-President Melida Buntello
Brownsville Sunrise Rotary Club President Hector Hernandez
Brownsville Sunrise Rotary Club Albert Perez, Assistant Governor
Brownsville Sunrise Rotary Club Andy Hagan, Lieutenant Govenor
Brownsville Sunrise Rotary Club Past-President Jerry Klinger
Texas DG 5930 Dennis Roberts, Texas 5930 DGE Gilbert Serna
Harlingen Rotary Club President Bill Reagan
2010 Lone Star President-Elect Training (PETS)

DFW Airport Hotel, March 20–21, 2010
Rotary International President Ray Klinginsmith
Premiered Original "Great Western Cattle Trail" Song
Dr. Michael Babb, Cushing, OK

2005 National Cowboy Symposium & Celebration, Lubbock, TX
Rotary District 5790 Leadership Award to President Alvin G. Davis presented for providing a venue to connect people to promote the Western way of life, specifically the Great Western Trail. DG Jim Aneff presented award, September 3, 2005.
Texas Trail Team & Oklahoma Trail Team attended.

2006 National Cowboy Symposium & Celebration, Lubbock, TX
Panel Discussion: Great Western Trail & Chisholm Trail, September 8, 2006
Moderator: Sylvia Gann Mahoney, Texas GWT co-chair
Panelists:
Texas GWT co-chair Jeff Bearden; Oklahoma GWT co-chairs Dennis Vernon & John
  Barton; Kansas historian Dr. Jim Hoy; Oklahoma Chisholm Trail historian Bob
  Klemme

2011 Rotary International Convention
New Orleans, Louisiana, May 21–26, 2011
20,000 Rotarians attended from nearly 200 countries
Rotary International President Ray Klinginsmith
invited Dr. Michael Babb to sing his original GWT song on stage at the House of
  Friendship and Sylvia G. Mahoney to talk about the GWT research project.
PDG Jim Aneff, Abilene, TX; Montana DG David Kinsey;
Helen Reisler, New York City Rotary Past-President
Miles City Rotary President Barrie Matthews, Montana; PDG Dr. Tamie Babb
Gathering hosted by Enoch & Fran Dawkins, New Orleans

Texas Rotary District 5790 Governors—Dedications
Thanks to PDG Jim Aneff and PDG David Mason
Their vision opened doors to expand GWT efforts and their willingness to travel supported commitments to attend dedications, which included traveling across nine
  US states and into Mexico and Canada.
PDG Jim Aneff, 2005–06; PDG David & Vonda Mason, 2007–08
DG Paul & Monica Lucas, 2010–11; PDG Tom Sheriff, 2004–05

Texas District 5790 Rotary
Printed Proclamations—Will Speight, Abilene, TX
Support *Past Rotary International Director—Don Mebus*
PDG Jerry Parr, PDG Dan Morales, PDG John Miller

GWT Programs & Club Program Chairs

Mineral Wells Rotary Club, Feb. 6, 2008, PDG Janet Holland, Mike Holland

Rotary Club of Fort Worth, Jan. 26, 2007, Janelle Kavanaugh, Ted Paup

Abilene Rotary Club, 2005, PDG David Stubbeman

Abilene Southwest Rotary Club, June 2, 2009, PDG David Mason

Altus Rotary Club, June 9, 2009, Holly Urbanski & Dennis Vernon

Arlington, Texas, Rotary Clubs, June 7–8, 2007
Arlington Sunrise, Ed Peters; Lisann Peters, Arlington North

March 14–16, 2005, Rotary Club Programs & Contacts
Sylvia G. Mahoney

Baird Chamber of Commerce, Coleman, Texas

Brady, Texas; Menard Chamber of Commerce, Texas

May 24–27, 2005, George West, Texas; Alice, Texas, Falfurrias, Texas; Edinburg, Texas; Brownsville, Texas

October 22, 2009, Ray Klinginsmith, RI president, GWT PowerPoint presentation

October 5, 2010, William "Bill" & Lorna Boyd, New Zealand, RI president
GWT Video for Rotary International Past President

2007 Rotary District 5790 Conference
Westlake, Texas, GWT Display
José Luis Diaz del Castillo Lie, Leon, Mexico, helped set up the GWT display and sent longhorn Rotary pins for all Rotary trail team volunteers

Texas Rotary District 5930—Dedications
DG Jorge & Olga Verduzco, 2005–06
DG Dennis & Migdalia Roberts, 2009–10, DG Gilbert & Deya Serna, Jr., 2010–11

2011 Texas Rotary District 5730

Presidential Dinner fundraiser, Lubbock, TX, January 8, 2011
South Central Rotary Youth Exchange (SCRYE), 200 students
RI President Ray Klinginsmith, speaker
Dr. Michael Babb, GWT song; Sylvia G. Mahoney, GWT history
DG 5790 Jim Aneff, Abilene, TX
J. B. Roberts, Plainview, TX; Monte Montgomery, Lubbock, TX

GWT Recognized at Texas State Capitol, Austin, TX, May 17, 2005
Resolutions sponsored in House and Senate by Rep. Rick Hardcastle and Sen. Frank
Madla in recognition of Great Western Cattle Trail and its importance to the

recovery of the post–Civil War economy in the state and continuing to current times. Honored Oklahoma Senator Robert Kerr and his wife Robbie Kerr for their support. GWT display approved for the lower level of the Rotunda set up by Mary Ann McCuistion, executive director Red River Valley Museum, Vernon. Fifty GWT team leaders attended.

Jan. 26, 2006, Dedication, Western Trail Heritage Park, Bandera, Texas
Dave Burell, Heather Burell, and Rudy Robbins, movie star

Rotary International Public Relations Award: GWT Project
Staley Heatly & Clayton Henry—Vernon Rotarians wrote proposal
Welder of GWT Metal Molds—Gene Nessel, Vernon College Welder
GWCTA Logo—Jim Carothers, Perry, OK

GPS Locations & Photos of GWT markers—Paul & Connie Noack, Austin, TX

Red River Water in Mason Jar for Dedications—Grant Smith, Vernon, TX

Research: Asa Shinn Mercer—Butch Bratsky, Bart Aby, Billings, MT
John Mercer, Hyattville, WY, Rhonda Sterns, & Colleen Pollat, Newcastle, WY

Media Support for GWT

Vernon Daily Record—Publisher Larry Crabtree & Editor Jimmy Carr

Video of Events and Interviews—J. L. Courtney & Elaine Courtney, Oklahoma City, OK

Video Design & Production—Jerry McClain, Vernon, TX

History of the GWT Research & Dedication Project Marking the GWT
Co-Partners: Red River Valley Museum & Vernon Rotary Club

Great Western Cattle Trail song, Dr. Michael Babb, Nashville, TN
"Great Western Trail," song, Leroy Jones, original song award, National Cowboy and Western Heritage Museum
Video of Russian Rotary Exchange Student—Yulia Chrnova up the GWT from Texas to the Dakotas and Montana to present to her fellow students in Mozhga, Russia. Made by Texas District 5790 DG David & Vonda Mason, Abilene.

PBS *History Detectives:* National TV
"Did Longhorns from the South Texas Border Travel Up the same path on the Great Western and Chisholm Trail?" Interviewed:
Laura Lincoln, executive director, Donna Hooks Fletcher Historical Museum
Sylvia G. Mahoney, Vernon Rotary GWT project co-chair

Congressional Feasibility Study—2009–2015

Thanks to the following for the supporting research to designate the GWT and the Chisholm Trail as National Historic Trails.

National Park Service Superintendent Dr. Aaron Mahr; Historian—Dr. Frank Norris; Chief of Planning—Gretchen Ward; Texas State Historical Deputy Commissioner Dr. Terry Colley

First Step Toward Approval, Washington, DC, May 2012

Dr. Frank Norris presented "Findings of Trail Research" to Congressional Appointed Committee of Cultural Professionals; Sylvia G. Mahoney presented an overview of the GWT project. Texas DG Jim Aneff and Slovakia exchange student Roland Jaz attended.

Thanks to everyone on the trail who contacted his/her Congressional representatives and senators to support the bill. It is scheduled for a vote in 2015.

Texas Tech University Southwest Collection/GWT Special Collection

Thanks to the following for establishing the GWT Special Collection & Research for the Feasibility Study, Dr. Monte Monroe, Dr. Tai Kreidler, Texas Tech Professor Dr. Paul Carlson
Robert Weaver, oral history interviews

2008 Great Western Cattle Trail Association (GWCTA)

Organized Baird, Texas, April 8, 2008
Host Baird Chamber of Commerce, Tommie Jones, exec. dir.
Initiated first meeting, David & Heather Burrell, Bandera, Texas
Attending
Jill Campbell, Texas Lakes Trail Region regional director
Dr. Don Frazier, McWhinney Research Foundation, McMurray University, Abilene, TX
Vernon Chamber of Commerce manager, Sheri Morriss; Sheila Barrow, journalist
Seymour Chamber of Commerce manager, Myra Busby; Richard Burney, Bandera, TX
Sylvia G. Mahoney, Vernon GWT project co-chair

Great Western Cattle Trail Association
GWCTA-National Chapter President Myra Busby; Texas Chapter President Tina Hodge
Kansas Chapter President Jim Sherer; Oklahoma Chapter President John Yudell Barton
North Dakota Chapter President Darrell Dorgan; South Dakota Chapter President,
Senator Betty Olson

Western Trail Art Association, Founders & Officers, President Mary Ann McCuistion

Laura Gillis, Dr. Beth Robinson, Mary Bearden, Su McMahen

Bicycle trip down the trail from Medora, North Dakota, to Texas
Ken Grantier, son of A. Jay Grantier, GWT descendant

South Texas Trail Partner, Betty Sue "Susie" Gann Potter, Houston, TX

Dedication Ceremonies—Canada & Mexico

Canada—Saskatchewan

District 5550 Rotary Club of Regina, GWT Marker Dedication,
Regina, July 28, 2008
Note: (The GWT did not go to Regina.) The marker was located at the Canadian Western Agribition Center, second largest livestock show in North America, with a large marble plaque inscribed with the history of the GWT.
Doug Alexander, Rotary Master of Ceremonies; DG Doug Mortin; Rick Mitchell, president; David Stewart, past president; Regina Rotary GWT Committee: Gene (Catherine) Griffith; Ted (Mel) Turner; William "Bill" Whelan; Doug Alexander
Jason Pollock, GM/CEO Canadian Western Agribition Center; Bill Small—rancher
The Hon. Laura Ross, Province of Saskatchewan; Regina Councillor Sharron Bryce
John Dawes, Assistant Rotary Governor, Regina; Vernon Mayor Jeff Bearden
Vernon City Commissioner Phil McCuistion, Texas flag on behalf of Texas Rep. Rick Hardcastle; Vernon newspaper publisher Larry Crabtree, US flag, on behalf of
US Senator Kay Bailey Hutchison of Texas; Bill Huskinson, US flag flown over the US Capitol to Shannon McArton, President, Canadian Western Agribition Center
John Dawes, Rotary Asst. Governor District 5550; David Mason, Governor District 5790, Abilene, TX; Gene Griffith, Regina GWT project chair, and Sylvia G. Mahoney, Vernon GWT project co-chair, presented Red River water

Val Marie, Saskatchewan, September 20, 2008
Sherry & Lynn Grant, Dedication Chair; Val Marie Committee Members:
Betty Waldner, Don McDonald, Colin Schmidt; January Legault, Jason & Cathy Legault;
John Thibault; Yogi Huyghebaert, MLA (state rep.) for Wood River;
NWMP Sgt. Omar Murray; RCMP Constable Gordon Yetman;
Tom Reardon, *Canadian Cowboy Country* magazine journalist
Texas DG 5790 David & Vonda Mason, Abilene, TX
Montana Rotarian Walter F. & Allegene Mason, Bozeman, MT
Texas GWT Co-Chair Sylvia G. Mahoney, Vernon, TX
Rick Mitchell, Regina Rotary president
Jason Pollock, manager/CEO Canadian Western Agribition
Lynn Grant, Saskatchewan Stock Growers Association
Regina Rotary GWT Committee Members:
Gene Griffith, Ted Turner, Doug Alexander, Bill Whelan; CEO Canadian Agribition CEO Jason Pollock; Bill Small, cattleman/rancher

The committee donated the GWT marker and a large marble plaque with the history of the GWT inscribed on it. Original poem for GWT dedication, "The Legacy of the Drover," by Sherri Grant

Mexico

Matamoros, June 3, 2006, Dedication; Club Rotario Matamoros Profesional
President Norma Nelly Aguilar; Edith Mercedes Angulo
President-elect Melida C. Buentallo; Hilda Corina; Irma G. De Gonzales; Isabel Gomez
District 5930 Governor Jorge & Olga Verduzco, Laredo, TX;
District 5790 Governor-Elect David & Vonda Mason; Vernon Rotary Trail Team

Dedications in US States

Colorado
Julesburg Rotary Club Dedication, June 23, 2007, Jim Fender,

GWT dedication chair, Terry Hinde, president; Colo. State Rep. Jerry Sonnenberg
Sedgwick County Commissioner Gene Bauerle; Colo. Congresswoman Marilyn Musgrove's
representative Deb Carlstrom; PDG District 5440 Nancy Pettus, Jackson Hole, WY
PDG District 5440 William F. Pettus, Jackson Hole, WY;
DG Tom and Janet Kraus, Ogallala, NE; Jack Pollack, Ogallala Rotarian, GWT historian
Sylvia Mahoney, Vernon Rotary GWT project co-chair, TX;
David & Heather Burell, Bandera, TX

Kansas
Dedication in Dodge City, Oct. 23, 2004
KS State Rep. & Dodge City Rotary Pres. Jan Scoggins-Waite
Kim Goodnight, Ford County Commissioner; Jim Sherer—GWCTA Kansas Chapter
President
Kansas authors Gary & Margaret Kraisinger; PDG Virgil Howe, Rotarian
Chuck Couch, Boot Hill Museum Board of Directors
Vernon Trail Team; Oklahoma Trail Team; Bandera Trail Riders

Montana
Rotary District 5390. Miles City GWT Dedication, August 7, 2010
Rotary International President Ray Klinginsmith
Miles City Past President Stan Markuson; President Barrie Matthews
Montana PDG Paul & Pam Broughton; Montana PDG Donald A. Gatzke
Montana DGE David Kinsey; Rotarian Walter F. & Allegene Mason, Bozeman, MT
Rotarians Gene Griffith and President-Elect Ian Toms, Regina, Saskatchewan
North Dakota Past District Governor Jim Ozbun; Texas PDG 5790 David & Vonda
Mason
Texas PDG 5790 Jim Aneff, Texas; DG 5790 Paul Lucas
Oklahomans Dennis Vernon and Yudell Barton;

Vernon Rotary Past-President Harold & Peggy Hardcastle
Rotarian Michael & PDG Tami Babb of Cushing, OK
Sylvia G. Mahoney, GWT project co-chair, Vernon, TX
Vernon Marker Maker Phil McCuistion & RRVM executive director Mary Ann McCuistion

Parade of Flags: Three Countries & Nine US States
US—Bill Huskinson, Vernon Rotary; Canada—Gene Griffith, Regina Rotary
Mexico—David Mason, PDG 5790, Abilene, TX; Montana—Barrie Matthews and
Stan Markuson; District 5390 Secretary Ellen Robinson; North Dakota—DG 5580 Jim
Ozbun
Oklahoma—PDG Tamie Babb and Maurice King; Texas—Mary Ann McCuistion
Colorado, Kansas, Wyoming—Neal Fitzgerald & grandsons Josh and Ryan Fitzgerald,
Texas

Nebraska

Rotary District 5630; Culbertson
Rotary PDG Cloyd Clark, McCook, NE; DG William R. "Bob" Stetter, Valentine;
DG Tom Kraus, Madrid, NE; Neb. State Rep. Mark Christensen;
Rotary President Jeanette Miller; Mayor Roma Sense; Rancher Roland Miller
Marla Makin, Hill City, KS

Ogallala, Nebraska, May 6, 2006
PDG William E. "Bill" Ballou; DG Tom & Janet Kraus
Ogallala Rotary President Don W. Andrews; Ogallala Rotarian and Historian Jack
Pollock
District 5440 Governor John & Jin Patton, Gillette, WY
Rotarian Bill Patton, Gillette, WY; Rotarian Eric Scalzo, WY
Colorado Rotarians Jim Fender, Daphne Davis, and Ken Hodges
North Dakota DG Jim & Sonja Ozbun, Dickinson; National Little Britches Rodeo
Queen Anita Moorhead; Haythorn Ranch, Craig & Jody Haythorn

Ogallala Dedication Ceremony; PDG William E. "Bill" Ballou
Ogallala Rotary President Don Andrews; TX DG 5790 Jim Aneff, Abilene; TX;
DG 5790 David Mason, Abilene, TX; Vernon Rotary GWT Co-Chair Jeff & Mary
Bearden;
GWT Co-Chair Sylvia G. Mahoney, Dedication with Red River Water
Flag Presentation
Canada, Vernon Rotarian Larry Crabtree; North Dakota, DG Jim Ozbun
South Dakota, Vernon Rotarian Bill Huskinson; Montana, Texas DG Dave Mason
Wyoming, Eric Scalzo; Nebraska, DG Tom and Janet Kraus; Colorado, Jim Fender;
Kansas, Bob Klemme; Oklahoma, Dennis Vernon; Texas, Vernon Honorary
Rotarian Rick Jouett; Rotary Interact Breanne Wehmeyer, trumpet, "The Star-Spangled
Banner;" Ogallala Rotary President Don Andrews led the Pledge of Allegiance;
John Carter, Historian; Wayne & Roxanne Eatinger, Thedford, NE

GWT Nebraska Drover Descendants

Harry Haythorn's granddaughter Beldora Haythorn

Harry Haythorn's great-granddaughter Sally Haythorn-Mayden

Haythorn Ranch owner/manager Craig & Jody Haythorn

Douglas Parks, Ogallala, grandson of Walter E. Baker

Rita Shimmin, Ogallala, granddaughter of George B. Melvin

Kendra Melvin Homola, descendant of George B. Melvin

Dick and Mary Ellen Bacon, Longmont, Colorado, great-granddaughter of

Samuel David "Lep" Sanders; Brent & JoEllen Lewis, Minden, Nebraska, great-grandson

of Thomas Dalton Lewis; Terry P. Brown, his daughter Peggy and Jay Petersen,

Harrisburg, descendants of Christopher Streeks

North Dakota

Bowman, ND—Rotary

Chris Peterson; Ron Petrowski

PDG 5790 David and Vonda Mason, Abilene, TX;

Yulia Chrnova, Rotary Youth Exchange Student, Russia

Medora at North Dakota Cowboy Hall of Fame & Rotary, May 1, 2008

ND DG 5580 Jim & Sonja Ozbun; ND Governor John Hoeven

North Dakota State Rep. C. B. "Buck" Haas; North Dakota Cowboy Hall of Fame

Exec. Dir. Darrell Dorgan; Medora Mayor Doug Walker; NDCHF President Phil Baird

Texas Rotarians: Sylvia G. Mahoney, Jim Aneff, David Mason

Mary Ellen Engle, Medora

Oklahoma

Altus, Oklahoma State Sen. Robert & Robbie Kerr; John Yudell & Anelle Barton;
Dennis & Ilena Vernon; Joe & Linda Harkins; Maurice King; Helon LeGree; Tal Odin
Other Oklahomans: Jim Peck, Vici; LeRoy Jones, Jim Carothers, Lawrence & Jean LeVick

South Dakota

High Plains Western Heritage Center, executive director, Peggy Ables, Spearfish, SD

SD Senator Betty Olson, Museum Board & SD GWT Chapter President

Lance Russell, Museum Board & SD GWT Chapter Legal Adviser

Texas

Abilene—Rotary District 5790; Dedication April 28, 2006

DG Jim Aneff; President Peter Fox; Texas State Rep. Bob Hunter;

DG Lee Hamilton; DG David J. Mason; DG David Stubbeman

Will Speight, parchment proclamations with gold letters

Frank Dlugas; Bruce Bixby; Ken Musgrave

Alice—Rotary Dedication, March 17, 2006

President Jim Doughty; Past-President Homer Anderson

County Commissioner Lawrence Cornelius; Charles Hoffman; George Hoffman;
Roger Hoffman; Tom Donald; Bill Findley; Dean Kruckenberg; Tom Donald;
Sheriff Oscar Lopez; Alice Chamber of Commerce Director Mike Smith;
Juan Navejar Jr.; South Texas Museum executive director Joyce Dunn

Baird, July 3, 2005
GWT Dedication
Chair & Callahan Co. Historical Com. Pres. Reggie & Suzi Pillans
Chamber of Commerce manager Tommie Jones; Baird Mayor Jon Hardwick
Tom Ivey, trail descendant; Bill Hatchett, trail descendant
Callahan County Sheriff's Posse: Jeff Burleson and Mike Walker
Misty Oliver, Baggage House Restaurant; Anita Mays, Baird, TX
Abilene Rotarians: President Lee Hamilton, DG 5790 Jim Aneff,
Past-President David Stubbeman; Vernon Rotarians: President Paul Hawkins,
Dr. Marvin & Patsy Sharp, Bill & Ann Huskinson, co-chairs
Jeff Bearden & Sylvia Mahoney, Phil & Mary Ann McCuistion

Bandera Dedication, September 6, 2004
Texas Sen. Frank Madla; Texas Rep. Carter Casteel
Friends of the Trail Pres. David & Heather Burell; Historical Society Pres. Peggy Tobin;
Mayor Denise Griffin; Bandera County Judge Richard Evans;
Bandera Chamber President Bob Click;
Celebrate Bandera and Celebrate the Western Trail Pres. Dan Wise
Bandera County Regional Foundation President Dave Demers
LH7 Ranch owner, Maudeen Marks; Barbara Merrell
Rudy Robbins, movie star; Sudie Burditt, Kerrville Convention and Visitors Bureau;
Trail Boss Suzie Heywood; Assist. Trail Boss Richard Burney

Boerne—Rotary Dedication, Sept. 2, 2007
Ron Cisneros, Rotary Trail Team & Historical Association
Rotary Trail Team, Robert Cisneros, John Krause

Brady, Nov. 16, 2008
Mark Day, Trail Team chair, rancher and attorney
Senior District Judge V. Murray Jordan, Bluff Pens Ranch
Bill Derrick; Jim Ross, rancher; Heart of Texas Historical Museum Pres. Chris Leifeste
Donated money, allowed a marker on their property or assisted:
Heart of Texas Historical Museum, VFW Post 3234, Bobby Hurd, Kevin Dodds,
Robert Evans, Bert Broad, Dan and Betty Gandy, Kiwanis Club of Brady, Brady Butane,
Dayton Boren (for the Brady Rotary Club), Troy Syfrett, Juanice Cavin Owens, and
Donald Owens, The Woodrow Kothmann Estate, the late Pauline Jordan Parker,
V. Murray Jordan, Chris Leifeste, Paul Jensen

Brownsville—Rotary Dedication June 2, 2006
District Governor 5930, Jorge Verduzco, Laredo, TX

Brownsville Sunrise Rotary President Hector Hernandez
Rotary Assistant Governor Albert Perez Jr., Trail co-chair
Bill Stirling, Trail co-chair; Andy Hagan, lieutenant governor
DG Jerry Klinger; DG 5790 Jim Aneff, Abilene, TX;
DG-Nominee 5790 David Mason, Abilene, TX
Cameron County Judge Gilberto Hinojosa
Orive Park co-chair, Gale Armstrong; Mrs. Prax Orive Jr.
Portia Belmont, sister lives in Regina, Sask.

Coleman—Rotary Dedication, Oct. 31, 2005
President Joe Rose; Past-President Charles Chessier
Heath Hemphill, Rotarian and Trail Descendant;
Coleman County Judge Jimmie Hobbs;
Bill Castleberry; PDG Jim Aneff and DG David Mason, Abilene, TX
Paul Hawkins, Vernon Rotary President;
Sylvia G. Mahoney & Jeff Bearden, Vernon Rotary Trail Co-Chairs
Mickey Sharp, Phil McCuistion, Rick Jouett, Vernon Rotary

Donna, June 2, 2006
Donna Hooks Fletcher Historical Museum—Exec. Dir. Laura Lincoln
Hazel H. Anderson, Museum Board President; Donna Rotary Pres. Jay Seiver

Edinburg—Rotary Dedication, June 2, 2006
Rotary President Mark Peña; Tamara Sanchez
Texas State Rep. Aaron Peña; County Judge Ramon Garcia
Precinct 4 Commissioner Oscar Garza
Museum of South Texas History—Exec. Dir. Shan Rankin
DG 5930 Jorge Verduzco and his wife Olga, Laredo, TX
DG 5790 Jim Aneff, Abilene, TX; Rotary Club President Dr. David Fridie;
Rotarians: Michael Minor; Mark Fryer; Ella Delarosa
Daniel Perry, *The Monitor* (Edinburg, TX)

Falfurrias—Rotary Dedication, March 17, 2006
Rotary President Robert R. Scott Jr.; Rotary President-elect Adela Barker;
Mayor Wesley Jacobs; Dr. Bill Tinnell;
Heritage Museum President Lisa Ann Molina-Montayo; Raul Guiterrez;
Rolando Carrasco; Randy Fugate, Texas Parks & Wildlife; Honorary Rotarian
Lourdes Trevino-Cantu; Museum Board member Constable Joe Garza;
Alice Rotary President Constable Jim Doughty; County Commissioner Raul Ramirez
David and Heather Burell, Bandera, TX; Rotary President Paul Hawkins, Vernon, TX
Jeff and Mary Bearden, Vernon, TX. Phil and Mary Ann McCuistion, Vernon, TX
DG-Elect 5790 David and Vonda Mason, Abilene, TX; Bill Huskinson, Vernon, TX;
Sylvia G. Mahoney, Vernon, TX
Falfurrias High School Students/Historians;

Gustavo Berrera, exec. dir., Falfurrias Chamber of Commerce

Fort Griffin State Historic Park, September 18, 2004
Lester Galbreath, park & Longhorn herd manager
Mitch Baird, Site Manager; Will Cradduck, Longhorn herd manager
Vernon Rotary Trail Team
George West & Three Rivers Rotary Dedication, June 2006
DG 5930 Jorge Verduzco; Rotary—Robert Galloway
Chamber of Commerce—Becky West
Mary Margaret Campbell; Rodger Glenn

Kerrville—Rotary Dedication, Kerr County, Jan. 12, 2007
Rotary Trail Team Leader Sue Whinnery; PDG District 5840 Doug Whinnery
Rotary President Bob Waller; Past-President Mike Hunter; Mayor Gene Smith;
Judge Pat Tinley; City Council Scott Gross; Richard Assunto, curator,
Museum of Western Art; Sudie Burditt, Kerrville Convention and Visitors Bureau;
Griff Carnes, Former Museum of Art Director
Vernon Rotary Trail Team

Old Ingram Loop, Kerr County, Jan. 13, 2007
Harold & Judy Wunsch
Sudie Burditt, Kerrville Convention and Visitors Bureau
Vernon Rotary Trail Team

Y.O. Ranch, Kerr County, Jan. 13, 2007
Gus & Lori Schreiner, ranch owners; DG 5840 Bruce Flohr
Clarabelle Snodgrass, Kerr County Historical Commission; Vernon Rotary Trail Team

London—Rotary Club of Junction, August 4, 2006
Frederica Wyatt, Rotary & Kimble County historian
Rotary President Derrick Ard; Past Rotary President Lisa & Alan Herring
Joe & Ginger Andrews; Vernon Rotary Trail Team
Trail descendants/trail landowners; Jaydeen Young and other Peril family members;
Gene and Gayle Ake; Gwen and Sammy Plumley; Col. William George Hahn

Menard Chamber of Commerce, August 3, 2006
Tina Hodge, Menard Chamber Manager & GWCTA-Texas Chapter President
Menard Judge Richard Cordes; Mayor Johnny Brown; Steve Self
Wanda Hitzfelder, regional director for US Representative Mike Conoway;
Pat Focazio, represented Harvey Hildebrand, Texas House of Representatives;
Margaret Hoogstra, regional coordinator, Texas Forts Trail;
Col. Richard McTaggert, Presidio Board VP & Pres. of Friends of Ft. McKavett;
    Carleton Kothmann, Menard historian; Menard County Historical
    Commission Chair
Lois Sikes Beirschwale, Sierra and Sheridan Hodge
Cowboy Craig and Oreo, the Longhorn & Crisp and Working Cowboys
Vernon Rotary Trail Team

2009 Menard 1st Annual "Around the Campfire on the GWT"
At the Stock Pens Crossing on the Sabine River
Menard Chamber of Commerce Manager Tina Hodge

Moran, Oct. 27, 2007
Bennie Parker—GWCTA—Texas Chapter Secretary
Ted & Nancy Paup, Fort Worth, TX; Lester Galbreath; Joe Parker, rancher
James & Sarah Shelton; Morris D. Snyder & Cowboys; Vernon Rotary Trail Team
Pleasanton—Rotary Odis White; PDG Gene Clements
Jeff Bearden, Vernon co-chair

San Antonio—Rotary Dedication, September 3, 2007
District 5840 PDG Bruce Flohr; Witte Museum Pres./CEO Marise McDermott
Old Time Trail Drivers Assoc. Pres. Pat Halpin; Alamo Heights Rotary—Cliff Borofsky
District 5840 PDG Jayson D. Fritz, trail descendant;
Rotarian Ed Dylla; Michael Austin, trail descendant
Bexar County Commissioner Tommy Adkinsson, Prec. 4
Marco Barros, Pres./CEO, San Antonio Tourism Council, Rotary Exchange Student
Bruce Shackelford, consultant and appraiser, known for *Antiques Roadshow;*
San Antonio Mission Trail Rotary Past-President, Richard Arias
Jim Doughty, Alice; Jack & Evelyn Kingsbery, Crystal City, drover descendants;
Rudy Robbins, Bandera, movie star; Dave & Heather Burrell, Bandera, TX
Vernon Rotary Trail Team

Seymour, September 27, 2004
Myra Busby, Chamber of Commerce manager; Judge Butch Coltharp;
John Gaither, ninety-year-old working cowboy;
State Rep. Rick Hardcastle; Seymour ISD Superintendent Dr. John Baker
Vernon Rotary Trail Team

Throckmorton, September 25, 2004
Terry Armstrong—*Throckmorton Tribune*
Trey Carrington; Jack Fauntleroy; Ted Paup, Chimney Creek Ranch
Bandera Chamber President Bob Click; Vernon Trail Team
Friends of the Trail president Dave Burrell, Bandera, TX

Vernon

2004 Dedication, First Marker in Texas
May 1, 2004, Doan's Adobe
Vernon Rotary Club & Altus, Oklahoma Western Trail Historical Association
Master of Ceremony Ann Huskinson; Texas State Rep. Rick Hardcastle
Oklahoma State Senator Robert Kerr
Dennis Vernon & John Yudell Barton, Oklahoma trail project co-chairs
Jeff Bearden, Texas trail project co-chair; Sylvia Gann Mahoney, Texas trail project co-
chair
Vernon Rotary Club President R. C. Babione; Wilbarger County Judge Gary Streit;

Vernon Mayor Kelly Couch; Joe Harkins, Altus, OK; Maurice King, Altus, OK

Altus Rotary Club President Rev. Buddy Dugan; Dodge City Council Kim Goodnight

Vernon Santa Rosa Palomino Club—Ambassadors on Horseback

Bandera Trail Riders president Dave & Heather Burell

Bandera Riders Trail Boss Suzie Heywood; Assist. Trail Boss Richard Burney

2007 Final Texas GWT Marker Dedication

May 5, 2007, Red River Valley Museum & Vernon Rotary Club
Welcome—Gary Chapman, Vernon Rotary President
Master of Ceremony, Jeff Bearden

PARADE OF 12 FLAGS
Vernon Santa Rosa Palomino Club—Ambassadors on Horseback

Flags of Three Countries
U.S.A.

—PDG Tom Sheriff, Wichita Falls, TX, &

Rotarian Janelle Kavanaugh, Fort Worth, TX

Mexico—DGE Dave Mason, Abilene, TX & Bill Huskinson & Mickey Sharp, Vernon Rotarians
Canada—PDG Doug & Sue Whinnery, Kerrville, TX

Flags of Nine States

State flags presented in order from north
Montana—PDG Paul Broughton, Longview, TX
Wyoming—PDG Jim Aneff, Abilene, TX
Colorado—PP Jim Fender, Julesburg, CO
North Dakota—DGN Jerry Parr, Gainesville, TX
South Dakota—Rotarian Jack Pollack, Ogallala, NE
Nebraska—DG Tom & Janet Kraus, Ogallala, NE
Kansas—Assistant Governor Don Ferrell, Arlington, TX
Riderless Horse Ceremony in Memory of Oklahoma Sen. Robert Kerr

Riderless Horse led by John Barton, Altus, OK
Texas—Rep. Rick Hardcastle, Vernon, TX
Oklahoma—Dennis Vernon, Altus, OK
Texas flag—Larry Crabtree, Vernon Rotarian
Oklahoma flag—Paul Hawkins, Vernon Rotary Past-President

Dedication Ceremony

Recognize Elected Officials, Rotarians, Dignitaries, Friends of the Trail

District Attorney Staley Heatly; Wilbarger County Judge Greg Tyra & County Commissioners

Vernon Mayor Ed Garnett & City Commissioners;

Wilbarger County Historical Society—Jimmy Anderson;

Red River Valley Museum Executive Director Mary Ann McCuistion;

RRVM President of the Board Joe Rogers; David & Heather Burell, Bandera, TX

Recognition of All Rotarians; Recognition of All Descendants
Trail Music—Larry Drennon
Charles & Molly Goodnight Re-enactors

Lanny Joe Burnett and Cindy Baker, Bonham, TX
Great Western Trail History
Remarks—Alvin G. Davis, President, National Cowboy Symposium, Lubbock, TX
Remarks—Rotary District Governor Nominee, Tom Kraus, Ogallala, NE
Proclamation for Dennis Vernon & John Barton, Altus, OK
By Rotary District 5790 PDG Jim Aneff
Proclamation for Bob Klemme, Enid, OK
Introduction of Bob's son, Mike Klemme, Official Oklahoma Centennial Photographer
By Vernon Rotary President Gary Chapman
Vernon Mayor Ed Garnett Proclamation for Texas Rep. Rick Hardcastle &
Oklahoma Sen. Robert Kerr
Honoree: Texas Rep. Rick Hardcastle
By Sylvia G. Mahoney, Vernon Rotary Project Co-Chair
Honoree, Posthumous, Okla. Sen. Robert Kerr; By Jeff Bearden;
Remarks by Mrs. Robert Kerr; Kerr children: Robert Kerr, Brad & Robin Kerr Wenk;
Rodger & Tamra Kerr & five grandchildren

Dedication of the Trail Marker; Vernon Rotary Co-Chair, Sylvia G. Mahoney
Phil McCuistion & Rick Jouett, Marker Makers

United Supermarkets $1 million incentive pledge
For a Western Trail Heritage Center at the Red River Valley Museum
Alan Smith, United Supermarket manager, Vernon, TX
Dr. Mickey Sharp & Jeff Bearden, development directors

Book Signing at Red River Valley Museum
Texas authors Robert and Jean Flynn of San Antonio, once of Chillicothe;
Historians Gary and Margaret Kraisinger, Halstead, KS, *Western: The Greatest Texas
    Cattle Trail*; Gary's Kraisinger's GWT maps used in this book
Sylvia Gann Mahoney, *College Rodeo: From Show to Sport*

2007 Doan's Picnic & Crowning of the King and Queen
King Dillon Lynn Koch, son of Sherri and Ricky Koch
Queen Lindsey Kaye Lockett, daughter of Joni and Richard Lockett
2007 Man and Woman of the Year at Doan's Picnic
Irl Holt and Aneita Riggins

September 14, 2004, Marker Dedicated Third Wilbarger Co. Marker
Courthouse Lawn; Rotary; Texas State Rep. Rick & Nancy Hardcastle
Rotary Club of Vernon; *See twenty—Rotary Trail Team above*
Mayor Kelly Couch; R. C. Babione; Bob Cochran; Larry Cheshier;
Dr. Ed and Jean Clark; Hub & Beth Colley; Terry Graf; Todd Greenwood; Jim Gunn;
Dave Hardin; Staley Heatly; Clayton Henry; Bill & Ann Huskinson; Curtis Johnson;
Sheri Morriss; Jim Murray; Dina Neal; Don Pittman; Dr. Mark Reynolds;
Sean Stockard; Gary Streit; James & Pat Streit; Eric Shelton;

Joe Chat Sumner; Lewis Templeton; Henry Yao; John B. Hardin III
Other Trail Team Members: Clay Bearden, Dr. Don Robinson, Doug & Lana Tolleson
Oklahoma Trail Team

Vernon, Texas, Businesses
Vernon Daily Record, Larry Crabtree, publisher
Vernon Daily Record, editor in chief, Jimmy Carr
KVWC Radio, Mike Klappenbach
Doan's Picnic Association, Pat Mints, Tip Igou, Grant Smith
Wilbarger County Historical Association, Jimmy Anderson
Vernon Chamber of Commerce, Jessica Holton; Wilbarger County Commissioners
Vernon City Commissioners

Wyoming; Working on the project
Thanks to Texas Rotarians, chambers of commerce, museums, and
historical associations that staged twenty-four post dedications in Texas and thirteen
more from Mexico to Canada. Thanks to the volunteer trail-teams in Oklahoma,
Kansas, Nebraska, Colorado, North Dakota, South Dakota, Montana, Regina and
Val Marie, Saskatchewan, and Matamoros, Mexico, who offered national and international friendship as we worked together. Thanks to some 720 people who actively
participated in the dedications. Thanks to some 1,800 who attended the dedications.

Thanks to the GWT descendants who provided primary sources from their family
history collections and other documents that corroborated the path of the trail.
Thanks to all who love history and did trail research to promote trail history accu-
racy. May this bond of friendship and community efforts to preserve and promote
our shared trail history continue to promote the truth, good will, better friendship,
and benefits for all concerned.

*ROTARY TITLES:
AG—Assistant Governor
Director—Rotary International Board of Directors
DG—District Governor
DGE—District Governor Elect
LG—Lieutenant Governor
PDG—Past District Governor
RIP—Rotary International President

SOURCES AND FURTHER READINGS

Abbott, E. C. "Teddy Blue," and Helen Huntington Smith. *We Pointed Them North: Recollections of a Cowpuncher.* Norman: University of Oklahoma Press, 1939, 1955.

Abernethy, Francis E. "Dobie, James Frank." *The New Handbook of Texas.* Vol. 2. Austin: Texas State Historical Association, 1996.

"About the Texas Longhorn Marketing Alliance." Texas Longhorn Marketing Alliance. Accessed July 2, 2011. http: www.thelonghornalliance.com/default.asp?contentID=583.

Abstract of Title No. 7571. The Vernon Abstract Company, 4.

Adams, Paul. "Fisher, John King." The Handbook of Texas Online. Accessed Nov. 29, 2011. http://www.tshaonline.org/handbook/online/articles/ffi20.

Adams, Ramon F. *Burrs Under the Saddle: A Second Look at Books and Histories of the West.* Norman: University of Oklahoma Press, 1964.

Ainsworth, Len, and Kenneth W. Davis, eds. *The Catch-Pen: A Selection of Essays from the First Two Years of the National Cowboy Symposium and Celebration.* Lubbock, TX: Ranching Heritage Center, Texas Tech University, 1991.

"Alice." *South Texas Traveler Magazine*, May 2005, 4.

Allen, Frederick. *A Decent Orderly Lynching: The Montana Vigilantes.* Norman: University of Oklahoma Press, 2004.

Alvarez, Elizabeth Cruce, ed., "Bexar County, San Antonio," *Texas Almanac 2008–2009.* Dallas, TX: Dallas Morning News, 2008.

Amberson, Mary Margaret McAllen, James A. McAllen, and Margaret H. McAllen. *I Would Rather Sleep in Texas.* Austin: Texas State Historical Association, 2003.

Anders, Evan. "Wells, James Babbage, Jr." *The New Handbook of Texas.* Vol. 6. Austin: Texas State Historical Association, 1996.

Anderson, Boyd. "Beyond the Range." Excerpt in "Super Issue." *The Saskatchewan Stockgrower.* September 2005, 53–54.

Anderson, Frank W. *Chief Joseph and the Cypress Hills.* Humbolt, Saskatchewan: Gopher Books, 1999.

———. *Fort Walsh and the Cypress Hills.* Humbolt, Saskatchewan: Gopher Books, 1999.

———. *Riel's Saskatchewan Rebellion.* Humbolt, Saskatchewan: Gopher Books, 1999.

Anderson, Gary Clayton. *The Conquest of Texas: Ethnic Cleansing in the Promised Land, 1820–1875.* Norman: University of Oklahoma Press, 2005.

Anderson, H. Allen "Hashknife Ranch." The Handbook of Texas Online. Accessed Jan. 29, 2012. http://www.tshaonline.org/handbook/online/articles/aph01.

———. "Blocker, John Rufus." The Handbook of Texas Online. Accessed Aug. 2, 2011. http://www.tshaonline.org/handbook/online/articles/fb\27.

Anderson, Ian. *Sitting Bull's Boss: Above the Medicine Line with James Morrow Walsh.* Surrey, British Columbia: Heritage House, 2000.

Angulo, Edith Mercedes. "GWT Dedication Speech." Public speech. Museo del Agrarismo Mexicano, Matamoros, Mexico. June 3, 2006.

Ashton, John, and Edgar P. Sneed. "King Ranch." The Handbook of Texas Online. Accessed Nov. 21, 2011. http://www.tshaonline.org/handbook/online/articles/apk01.

Atherton, Lewis. *The Cattle Kings.* Lincoln: University of Nebraska Press, 1961.

Babb, Michael. "Great Western Cattle Trial." *GWCT: Songs for the Cowboy in All of Us.* Nashville, TN: Magic Yellow Bird Publications, 2010.

Bailey, Jack. *A Texas Cowboy's Journal up the Trail to Kansas in 1868.* Edited by David Dary. Norman: University of Oklahoma Press, 2006.

"Balance Sheet." *2009 Annual Report.* Miles City, MT: Stockman Financial Corp.

Banister, Margaret White. "Banister, Emma Daughtery." The Handbook of Texas Online. Accessed Jan. 4, 2012. http://www.tshaonline.org/handbook/online/articles/fbacq.

Barrett, Neal, Jr. *Long Days and Short Nights: A Century of Texas Ranching on the YO 1880–1980.* Mountain Home, TX: YO Press, 1980.

Bearden, Jeff. "Marking the Great Western Trail: A Centennial Project of the Rotary Club of Vernon, Texas." Brochure, n.d.

Beer, Danni. Letter. March 20, 2015. Official Comments and Communications, United States Cattlemen's Association. Accessed April 18, 2015. http://www.uscattlemen. org/Templates/Official_Comments_And_Communications/2015_Official-Comments/3-20USCA-Comments-Chisholm-Trail.pdf.

"Bevo." University of Texas at Austin. Accessed Sept. 27, 2011. http://www.utexas.edu/alumni-friends/ut-traditions/bevo.

Blake, Michael. *Indian Yell: The Heart of an American Insurgency.* Flagstaff, AZ: Northland, 2006.

Bodnar, John. *Remaking America: Public Memory, Commemoration, and Patriotism in the Twentieth Century.* Princton, NJ: Princeton University Press, 1992.

Bonner, Robert E. *William F. Cody's Wyoming Empire: The Buffalo Bill Nobody Knows.* Norman: University of Oklahoma Press, 2007.

Borland, Hal. *When the Legends Die.* New York: Bantam Pathfinder Editions, 1963.

Bradley, James. *The Imperial Cruise: A Secret History of Empire and War.* New York: Back Bay Books, 2009.

Brado, Edward. *Cattle Kingdom: Early Ranching in Alberta.* Vancouver, BC: Douglas & McIntyre, 1984.

Brayer, Garnet M., and Herbert O. Brayer. *American Cattle Trails, 1540–1990.* Bayside,

NY: Western Range Cattle Industry Study in cooperation with the American Pioneer Trails Association, 1952.

Brown, Dee. *American West.* New York: Touchstone, 1994.

Brown, John Earl. *Yesteryears of Texas.* San Antonio, TX: Naylor, 1936.

Burgess, Tamela J. *The Big Muddy Badlands. Past to Present.* Moose Jaw, SK: Grand Valley Press, 2007, 2009.

Butala, Sharon. *Old Man on His Back: Portrait of a Prairie Landscape.* Toronto, ON: HarperCollins, 2002.

Campbell, Mary Margaret Dougherty. "The West Boys from Sweet Home: Trail Drivers, Cattlemen." Paper presented at the National Cowboy Symposium and Celebration, Lubbock, TX, Sept. 9, 2011.

Capps, Benjamin. *The Trail to Ogallala.* Fort Worth, TX: TCU Press, 1964, 1985.

Carlson, Paul M., and Tom Crum. *Myth, Memory, and Massacre: The Pease River Capture of Cynthia Ann Parker.* Lubbock: Texas Tech University Press, 2010.

Carr, Jimmy. "First Blair Witch, Now Doans Ghosts?" Town Crier column. *Vernon Daily Record* (TX), Nov. 16, 1999, 1–2.

Carter, Samuel, III. *Cowboy Capital of the World: The Saga of Dodge City.* Garden City, NY: Doubleday, 1973.

Cashion, Ty. *A Texas Frontier: The Clear Fork Country and Fort Griffin, 1849–1887.* Norman: University of Oklahoma Press, 1996.

Cattle Brands. Julesburg, CO: Fort Sedgwick Historical Society, 2001.

"Cattle Trail Marker Dedicated at Moran." *Albany News* (TX), Nov. 1, 2007, 5.

Chrisman, Harry E. *Lost Trails of the Cimarron.* 2nd ed. Norman: University of Oklahoma Press, 1998.

Clark, Walter Van Tilburg. *The Ox-Bow Incident.* New York: New American Library, 1940.

Clayton, Lawrence, *Chimney Creek Ranch: An Historical Account and Personal View of a Shackelford County Ranching Heritage.* Booklet. 2011.

———. *Clearfork Cowboys: Contemporary Cowboys along the Clear Fork of the Brazos River.* Abilene, TX: Cowboy Press, 1985.

———. *Contemporary Ranches of Texas.* Austin: University of Texas Press, 2001.

———. "Fort Griffin Fandangle." The Handbook of Texas Online. Accessed Jan. 14, 2012. http://www.tshaonline.org/handbook/online/articles/kkf02.

———. "Fort Griffin, TX." The Handbook of Texas Online. Accessed Jan. 15, 2012. http://www.tshaonline.org/handbook/online/articles/hnf35.

Clayton, Lawrence, and Joan Halford Farmer, eds. *Tracks Along the Clear Fork: Stories from Shackelford and Throckmorton Counties.* Abilene, TX: McWhiney Foundation Press, 2000.

"C. M. Coffee," Montana Cowboy Hall of Fame. Accessed October 9, 2011. http://www.montanacowboyfame.com/151001/380760.html.

Cole, Burna, and Bart McClenny. "Altus, Oklahoma." Museum of the Western Prairie. Accessed Feb. 16, 2012. http://en.wikipedia.org/wiki/Altus,_Oklahoma.

Collins, J. E. "Doan Family Among County's Earliest Pioneers." *Early-Day History of Wilbarger County*. Wilbarger County Historical Society, n.d.

"Colorado Central Railroad." Utah Rails.net. Last updated May 9, 2013. http://utahrails. net/up/colorado-central.php.

"Col. Prentiss Ingraham: King of the Dime Novels." The Department of Archives and Special Collections, The University of Mississippi. Accessed May 24, 2012. http:// www.olemiss.edu/depts/general_library/archives/exhibits/past/ingrahamex/ ingraham.html.

Combs, Vernon. "Buffalo Bill as a Pony Express Rider." Pony Express Gazette, April 1999. Quoting from Ivan J. Barrett, *Eph Hanks* (Covenant Communications, 1990). Accessed May 10, 2012. http://www.xphomestation.com/vcombs.html.

Cords, Nicholas, and Patrick Gerster. *Myth and the American Experience*. Vol. 2. 2nd ed. Encino, CA: Glencoe, 1973, 1978.

Cox, Matthew Rex. "Roosevelt's Wolf Hunt." Encyclopedia of Oklahoma History and Culture. Accessed April 15, 2015. http://www.okhistory.org/publications/enc/entry. php?entry=RO026.

Crimm, Ana Carolina Castillo, and Sara R. Massey. *Turn-of-the-Century Photographs from San Diego, Texas*. Austin: University of Texas Press, 2003.

Dary, David. *Cowboy Culture: A Saga of Five Centuries*. New York: Alfred A. Knopf, 1981.

Davis, John W. *Goodbye, Judge Lynch: The End of a Lawless Era in Wyoming's Big Horn Basin*. Norman: University of Oklahoma Press, 2005.

Day, William Mark, "The Western Trail Through McCulloch County, Texas." Unpublished article, n.d.

DeArment, Robert K. *Bravo of the Brazos: John Larn of Fort Griffin, Texas*. Norman: University of Oklahoma Press, 2002.

"Descendants of Trail Drivers to Be Recognized." *Keith County News* (Ogallala, NE), May 1, 2006.

"Development and Patterns of Euro-American Settlement in the White River Badlands (AD 1880s–1960s)." In *Discovery and Re-Discovery in the White River Badlands: Historic Resource Study*, Badlands National Park, John Miller Associates, July 2006.

Dickinson, Darol. "Seven Families of Texas Longhorns." International Texas Longhorn Association. Accessed February 11, 2006. http://www.itla.com/SevenFamilies.htm.

"A Different Kind of Association." International Texas Longhorn Association. Accessed August 12, 2011. http:www.itla.net/ITLA-Information/index.cfm?con=history.

Ditmore, Judy. Speech at the Meeting of Western Trail National Society of Daughters of the American Revolution Chapter, Vernon, TX, Jan. 13, 2011.

Dobie, J. Frank. Letter to Mr. Clarence Snider. Brady, Texas. April 23, 1947.

———. *The Longhorns*. Austin: University of Texas Press, 1997.

———. *Prefaces*. Austin: University of Texas Press, 1975.

———. *Some Part of Myself*. Austin: University of Texas Press, 1980.

———. *Tales of Old-Time Texas*. Edison, New Jersey: Castle Books, 1928, 1955.

Draft Chisholm and Great Western National Historic Trail Feasiblity Study/Environmental Assessment. National Park Service. US Department of the Interior. December 22, 2014.

Drago, Sinclair. *Great American Cattle Trails: The Stories of the Old Cow Paths of the East and the Longhorn Highways of the Plains*. New York: Bramhall House, 1965.

Durham, George, as told to Clyde Wantland. *Taming the Nueces Strip: The Story of McNelly's Rangers*. Foreword by Walter Prescott Webb. Austin: University of Texas Press, 1962.

Enzi, Mike. "Country, Patriotic Pride." John Wayne Collector's Edition 2014, *American Cowboy*, Special Issue, 43.

"Ex-State Senator, Relative Die in San Antonio Fire." *Houston Chronicle*. Accessed Aug. 16, 2011. http://www.chron.com/disp/story.mpl/front/4357475.html.

"The Faith Healer of Los Olmos: Biography of Don Pedrito Jaramillo: 1829–1907." 4th ed. Brooks County Historical Survey Committee, August 1990.

Faulk, Odie B. *Dodge City: The Most Western Town of All*. New York: Oxford University Press, 1977.

"Federal Land Ownership: Overview and Data." Congressional Research Service, February 8, 2012. Accessed April 18, 2015. https://fas.org/sgp/crs/misc/R42346.pdf.

Fenin, George N., and William K. Everson, eds. *The Western: From Silents to the Seventies*. New York: Grossman, 1974.

Fife, Austin E., and Alta S. Fife. *Cowboy and Western Songs: Comprehensive Anthology, 200 Songs with Music Lines and Guitar Chords*. New York: Bramhall House, 1982.

Fink, Tiffany Marie Haggard. "The Fort Worth and Denver City Railway: Settlement, Development, and Decline on the Texas High Plains." PhD diss., Texas Tech University, 2004. http://repositories.tdl.org/ttu-ir/handle/2346/19677.

Flanagan, Sue. *Trailing the Longhorns: A Century Later*. Austin, TX: Madrona Press, 1974.

"Fort Supply History." Oklahoma Historical Society, Military Sites. Accessed Feb. 19, 2012. http://www.okhitoryy.org/sites/fshistory?full.

Frantz, Joe B., and Julian Ernest Choate Jr. *The American Cowboy: The Myth and the Reality*. Norman: University of Oklahoma Press, 1955.

Frazer, Robert W. *Forts of the West*. Norman: University of Oklahoma Press, 1972.

Frazier, Ian. *Great Plains*. New York: Farrar, Straus and Giroux, 1989.

Galbreath, Lester, and Glenn Dromgoole. *Learning from Longhorns*. Albany, TX: Bright Sky Press, 2004.

Gard, Wayne. *The Chisholm Trail*. Norman: University of Oklahoma Press, 1954.

———. *Rawhide Texas*. Norman: University of Oklahoma Press, 1965.

Garza, Alicia A. "Brooks County." The Handbook of Texas Online. Accessed May 2, 2014. http://www.tshaonline.org/handbook/online/articles/hcb16.

Gerhardt, Karen, and Laura Lincoln. *Images of America: Donna, Texas*. Chicago: Arcadia, 2002.

Gillispie, Emalyn (Sam). "Head 'em up . . . move 'em out." *Fort Griffin Fandangle Souvenir Program*, June 2006, 33-A-11-A.

Givens, Murphy. "Up the Trail from Texas." *Corpus Christi Caller Times*, Feb. 16, 2000, A13–A14.

Goodwyn, Frank. *Life on the King Ranch*. College Station: Texas A&M University Press, 1951, 1993.

Grantier, A. Jay. *Tracks of Sand . . . Our Family History*. Dickinson, North Dakota: Quality Quick Print, 2001.

Graves, John. *Texas Rivers*. Austin: University of Texas Press, 2002.

Graves, Lawrence L. "Baylor County." The Handbook of Texas Online. Accessed Jan. 28, 2012. http://www.tshaonline.org/handbook/online/articles/hcb04.

Gray, James H. *Red Lights on the Prairie*. Toronto: McMillian of Canada, 1971, 1986, 1995.

Great Western Trail Drive. Brochure. Vici, OK.

Guthrie, Woody, and Jack Guthrie. "Oklahoma Hills." Arlo.net. Accessed Aug. 8, 2011. http://www.arlo.net/resources/lyrics/oklahoma-hills.shtml.

Haley, J. Evetts. *Charles Goodnight: Cowman and Plainsman*. Norman: University of Oklahoma Press, 1935, 1949.

———. *Focus on the Frontier*. Amarillo, TX: Shamrock Oil & Gas Corp., 1957.

"Hall of Fame." Canadian Western Agribition. Accessed March 23, 2012. http://www.agribition.com/Show_Information/Hall_of_Fame//Hall_of_Fame/.

Halsell, H. H. *Cowboys and Cattleland: Memories of a Frontier Cowboy*. The Chisholm Trail Series. Fort Worth, TX: TCU Press, 1937, 1983.

Harger, Charles Moreau. *Cattle-Trails of the Prairies*. Scribner's Magazine, 1892. Six Flags Series. Limited Edition. Dallas, TX: Highlands Historical Press, 1961.

Harris, Jim. "Building Community: Physical, Economic, and Educational Substructures." History Notebook column. *Lovington Leader* (NM), October 19, 2010, 3.

———. "History and the Arts." History Notebook column. *Lovington Leader* (NM), Oct. 10, 2006, 3.

Harris, Paul. "The Life and Times of Paul Harris." Accessed April 23, 2012. http://www.rotary.org/en/AboutUs/History/paulharris/Pages/ridefault.aspx.

Havins, Thomas Robert. *Belle Plain, Texas: Ghost Town in Callahan*. Brownwood, TX: Brown Press, 1972.

Haywood, C. Robert. "Potter-Blocker Trail." The Handbook of Texas Online. Accessed Jan. 6, 2012. http://www.tshaonline.org/handbook/online/articles/ayp01.

Headley, Jeff. "Pollock Adds to Legacy with Award." Write to the Point column. *Keith County News* (Ogallala, NE), n.d.

Heisch, John D. "Old Greer County," Encyclopedia of Oklahoma History and Culture. Accessed April 14, 2015. http://www.okhistory.org/publications/enc/entry.php?entry=GR025.

Hemphill, Joe Morris. "Press D. and Carrie Morris." *History of Coleman County and Its People*. Vol. 2. Coleman, TX: Coleman County Historical Commission, n.d.

"The Hero: Buffalo Bill and the Dime Novel Western." Dime Novels and Penny Dreadfuls. Accessed May 23, 2012. http://web.stanford.edu/dept/SUL/library/prod//depts/dp/pennies/cover.html#boys.

Hinton, Harwood P. "John Simpson Chisum." *The New Handbook of Texas*. Vol. 2. Austin: Texas State Historical Association, 1996.

"History." Texas Longhorn Breeders Association of America. Accessed Aug. 12, 2011. http://www.tlbaa.org/tlbaa/history.html.

"History." W. T. Waggoner Ranch. Accessed Jan. 30, 2012. http://www.waggonerranch.com/images/WaggHist.htm.

Hoig, Stan. *Jesse Chisholm: Ambassador of the Plains*. Norman: University of Oklahoma Press, 2005.

Holden, Frances Mayhugh. *Lambshead Before Interwoven: A Texas Range Chronicle 1848–1878*. College Station: Texas A&M University Press, 1982.

"Homestead Act." Public Documents of American History. Accessed Oct. 7, 2011. http://local.gov/rr/program/bib/ourdocs/Homestead/html.

Horstman, Dorothy. *Sing Your Heart Out, Country Boy*. Nashville, TN: Country Music Foundation Press, 1975, 1996.

Horton, David M., and Ryan Kellus Turner. *Lone Star Justice: A Comprehensive Overview of the Texas Criminal Justice System*. Austin, TX: Eakin Press, 1999.

Hoy, Jim, and Jerald Underwood. *Vaqueros, Cowboys, and Buckaroos*. Austin: University of Texas Press, 2001.

Hunter, J. Marvin. *The Trail Drivers of Texas*. Austin: University of Texas Press, 1985.

"Initial Point of Oklahoma." Oklahoma Society of Land Surveyors. Accessed Feb. 15, 2012. http://www.osis.org/displaycommon.cfm?an=1&subarticlenbr=25.

Izzard, Bob. *Heroes Here Have Been: The Red River United the United States*. Amarillo, TX: Tangleaire Press, 1993.

Jacobs, Marilynne Howsley. "Albany, Texas." The Handbook of Texas Online. Accessed Jan. 14, 2012. http://www.tshaonline.org/handbook/online/articles/hja01.

Jameson, Sheilagh. *Ranches, Cowboys, and Characters: Birth of Alberta's Western Heritage*. Glenbow, Alberta: Glenbow-Alberta Institute, 1987.

Jary, Roland S. "Saunders, George Washington." The Handbook of Texas Online. Accessed Oct. 7, 2011. http://www.tshaonline.org/handbook/online/articles/fsa38.

"Jay Newman Grantier." North Dakota Cowboy Hall of Fame. Accessed March 2, 2011. http://northdakotacowboy.com/?id=67&form_data_id=89.

"Jim L. Ozbun Biography." President Jim L. Ozbun Papers, University Archives. North Dakota State University, Fargo.

"John Leakey." North Dakota Cowboy Hall of Fame. Accessed March 7, 2011. http://northdakotacowboy.com/Hall_of_Fame/Ranching/leakey_john.asp.

Johnson, E. H. "Edwards Plateau." The Handbook of Texas Online. Accessed October 27, 2011. http://www.tshaonline.org/handbook/online/articles/rxe01.

Johnson, Marilynn S. *Violence in the West: The Johnson County Range War and the Ludlow Massacre, a Brief History with Documents*. Boston: Bedford St. Martin's, 2009.

Jones, Daryl. "The Hero: Buffalo Bill and the Dime Novel Western." *The Dime Novel Western*. Bowling Green, OH: Bowling Green State University Popular Press, 1978.

Jones, Sylvia, ed. "Cattle Drives and Trail Drivers." *Wilbarger County History*. Lubbock, TX: Wilbarger County Historical Commission, 1986.

———. "Doan's, The First Settlement." *Wilbarger County History*. Lubbock, TX: Wilbarger County Historical Commission, 1986.

Jordan, Terry. *North American Cattle-Ranching Frontiers: Origins, Diffusion, and Differentiation*. Albuquerque: University of New Mexico Press, 1993.

———. *Trails to Texas: Southern Roots of Western Cattle Ranching*. Lincoln: University of Nebraska Press, 1981.

Kelley, Leo, ed. "Up the Trail in '76: The Journal of Lewis Warren Neatherlin." In *The Chronicles of Oklahoma*, Vol. 67, No. 1 (Spring 1988): 22–51. Reprint of article only, Altus, OK: Western Trail Historical Society, n.d.

Kelsey, Terry. *Texas Gold*. Fort Worth, Texas, in Smithsonian Art Inventory Sculptures. http://www.waymarking.com/waymarks/WM7GK3_Texas_Gold_Fort_Worth_Texas.

Kelton, Elmer. *The Good Old Boys*. New York: Bantam Books, 1995.

Kinzie, Graig. "Great Western Trail Marker Dedicated." *Keith County News* (Ogallala, NE), May 8, 2006, 1–2.

Kitzhaber, Albert R., Stoddard Malarkey, Barbara Drake, Donald MacRae, Jacqueline Snyder, eds. *Literature V: The Oregon Curriculum / A Sequential Program in English*. New York: Holt, Rinehart & Winston, 1970.

Kraisinger, Gary. *Map of North of Ogallala, Showing the Location of the Western Cattle Trail, the Upper Portion of This Great Trail That Ran from South Texas to Canada*. Halstead, KS: Mennonite Press, n.d.

———. *Map of a Portion of Kansas Showing the Location of the Western Cattle Trail, Also Called the Texas Cattle Trail, Ft. Griffin–Ft. Dodge Trail, Dodge City Trail*. Halstead, KS: Mennonite Press, n.d.

———. *Map of Texas: Western Cattle Trail Showing the Texas Portion of This Great Trail That Ran from South Texas to Canada*. According to Jimmy Skaggs. Halstead, KS: Gary Kraisinger, n.d.

Kraisinger, Gary, and Margaret Kraisinger. *The Western: The Greatest Texas Cattle Trail, 1874–1886*. Newton, KS: Mennonite Press, 2004.

Lasater, Dale. *Falfurrias*. College Station: Texas A&M University Press, 1985.

Leakey, John. *The West That Was: From Texas to Montana*. As told to Nellie Snyder Yost. Lincoln: University of Nebraska Press, 1965.

Leffler, John. "Throckmorton County." The Handbook of Texas Online. Accessed May 22, 2012. http://www.tshaonline.org/handbook/online/articles/hct05.

———. "Wilbarger County." The Handbook of Texas Online. Accessed May 24, 2012. http://www.tshaonline.org/handbook/online/articles/hcw09.

LeJeune, Keagan. *Always for the Underdog: Leather Britches Smith and the Grabow War*.

Extra Book No. 23. Denton: Texas Folklore Society, University of North Texas Press, 2010.

"LH7." The Handbook of Texas Online. Accessed October 8, 2010. http://www.tshaonline.org/handbook/onlinearticles/LL/aplts.html.

"Longhorn History." Texas Longhorn Marketing Alliance. Accessed August 12, 2012. http://www.thelonghornalliance.com.

Lovell, Dyson, and Simon Wincer. Based on Larry McMurtry's book *Lonesome Dove*. 2-disc collector's edition DVD. Made for TV. Insert. 2008 RHI Entertainment Distribution. Genius Products.com.

Mackowiak, Matt. "Sen. Hutchison Protects Chisholm and Great Western Trails." News Release, Oct. 30, 2007.

Mahoney, Sylvia Gann. GWT research files. Lubbock: Texas Tech University Southwest Collections/GWT Special Collection, 2012.

Marking the Great Western Trail in the 21st Century: A Centennial Rotary Project by the Rotary Club of Vernon, Texas. DVD. Rotary Club of Vernon and Red River Valley Museum, April 2010.

"Marks and Brands Registry." Vol. 1, 1881 to 1885. Wilbarger County (TX) Courthouse.

Massey, Sarah R., ed. *Texas Women on the Cattle Trails*. College Station: Texas A&M University Press, 2006.

Matamoros: Gateway to Mexico. Matamoros: Municipal Government, 2005.

Matthews, Sallie Reynolds. *Interwoven: A Pioneer Chronicle.* College Station: Texas A&M University Press, 1982.

McClellan, Kathy. "John Wayne Movies Dominate List of 1960s Favorites." Here's My Take column. *Vernon Daily Record* (TX), October 23, 2010.

McClenny, Bart. Script. Calendar. Museum of the Western Prairie, 2011.

McCoy, Joseph G. *Historic Sketches of the Cattle Trade of the West and Southwest.* Lincoln: University of Nebraska Press, 1939, 1966.

McCubbin, Robert G. *The Life of John Wesley Hardin as Written by Himself.* Norman: University of Oklahoma Press, 1961.

McMurtry, Larry. *Lonesome Dove.* New York: Simon & Schuster, 1985.

McNamara, Robert. "Ned Buntline," About.com, About Education. Accessed May 23, 2012. http://history1800s.about.com/od/dimenovelsandmagazines/fl/Ned-Buntline-biography.htm.

Mercer, Asa Shinn. *The Banditti of the Plains or The Cattlemen's Invasion of Wyoming in 1892 (The Crowning Infamy of the Ages).* Norman: University of Oklahoma Press, 1954.

Merchant, Lawrence. *The San Simon.* Carlsbad, NM: Nichols Printing, 1975.

Merriman, Walter W. *Once Upon a Time in Throckmorton.* N.A. 1996.

Miles City: Visitors' Guide 2010. Miles City, MT.

Miller, Nyle H., and Joseph W. Snell. *Why the West Was Wild.* Norman: University of Oklahoma Press, 1963, 2003.

Minor, David. "Mercer, Asa Shinn." The Handbook of Texas Online. Accessed Feb. 3, 2012. http://www.tshaonline.org/handbook/online/articles/fme22.

Monday, Jane Clements, and Frances Brannen Vick. *Letters to Alice: Birth of the Kleberg-King Ranch Dynasty.* Edited and annotated by authors. College Station: Texas A&M University Press, 2012.

———. *Petra's Legacy: The South Texas Ranching Empire of Petra Vela and Mifflin Kenedy.* College Station: Texas A&M University Press, 2007.

"Moran, Texas." The Handbook of Texas Online. Accessed Jan. 13, 2012. http://www.tshaonline.org/handbook/online/articles/hlm85.

Morris, Edmund. *The Rise of Theodore Roosevelt.* New York: Modern Library, 2001.

Nance, Joseph Milton. "Mier Expedition." The Handbook of Texas Online. Accessed Sept. 23, 2011. http://www.tshaonline.org/handbook/online/articles/qym02.

Nardone, Joe. "Pony Express National Historic Trail." Speech given at Dedication of the Great Western Trail marker, Julesburg, Colorado, June 23, 2007.

Nimmo, Joseph. "The American Cow-Boy." *Harper's New Monthly Magazine.* Vol. 73, June to Nov., 1886. New York: Harper & Bro., 1886, 880.

Nix, Susan J. "Buffalo Gap, TX." The Handbook of Texas Online. Accessed Jan. 17, 2012. http://www.tshaonline.org/handbook/online/articles/hlb60.

Norris, Frank. "Cattle Trails—Statement of Significance." Following Academic Peer Review/SHPO Review. Preliminary Working Draft. March 20, 2012. http://www.nps.gov/nhl/news/LC/spring2012/CattleTrails.pdf.

"Old Newspaper Story Relates History of Wilbarger in 1899, From the 'Vernon Guard.'" *Vernon Daily Record* (TX), June 22, 1958.

Olick, Jeffrey K, Vered Vinitzky-Seroussi, and Daniel Levy, eds. *The Collective Memory Reader.* New York: Oxford University Press, 2011.

Olmsted, Frederick Law. *A Journey Through Texas or, A Saddle Trip on the Southwestern Frontier.* New York: Dix, Edwards, 1857.

O'Neal, Bill. *The Johnson County War.* Austin, TX: Eakin, 2004.

Owen, James P. *Cowboy Ethics: What Wall Street Can Learn from the Code of the West.* Ketchum, ID: Stoecklein, 2004.

Pace, Robert F., and Donald S. Frazier. *Frontier Texas: History of a Borderland to 1880.* Abilene, TX: State House Press, 2004.

Padgitt, James T. Talk given in Coleman City Park. In *Coleman County Chronicle* (TX), *Coleman's Diamond Jubilee,* newspaper insert, 1951.

Parkinson, Michael, and Clyde Jeavons. *A Pictorial History of Westerns.* New York: Hamlyn, 1974.

Pearce, W. M. *The Matador Land and Cattle Company.* Norman: University of Oklahoma Press, 1964.

Pittinton, Harwood. "John Simpson Chisum." *The New Handbook of Texas.* Vol. 2. Austin: Texas State Historical Association, 1996, 91–92.

Pitts, Lee. "Great American Ranches-Haythorn Ranch." Haythorn Land and Cattle Co. Accessed Feb. 29, 2012. http;//www.haythorn.com/history.shtml.

Pollat, Colleen. *Secrets: The Tom Wagoner Story.* www.booksurge.com, 2007.

Porter, Roze McCoy. *Electra II: Electra Waggoner Biggs, Socialite, Sculptor, Ranch Heiress.* Dallas, Texas: Taylor, 1995.

———. *Thistle Hill, The Cattle Baron's Legacy.* Fort Worth, Texas: Branch-Smith, 1980.

Pruitt, Freya. "Lori Schreiner." *Country Woman.* 2007 Anniversary Edition.

Putnam, Robert D. *Bowling Alone: The Collapse and Revival of American Community.* New York: Simon & Schuster, 2000.

Rabon, Carolyn. "The Western Trail." Interview with Forman Fowler, *Coleman County Chronicle* (TX). n.d., 1958.

"R. A. Brown Ranch Hosts Legacy Sale." *Progressive Cattleman,* Nov. 4, 2013. Accessed January 19, 2013. http://www.progressivecattle.com/sales-results/5880-ra-brown-ranch-hosts-legacy-sale.

Randall, Isabel. F. *A Lady's Ranch Life in Montana.* Norman: University of Oklahoma Press, 2004.

Rath, Ida Ellen. *The Rath Trail.* Wichita, KS: McCormick-Armstrong, 1961.

Reavis, Dick. "The Cattle Drives." *Coleman County Chronicle* (TX). n.d., 1958.

"Relative Values - US." Measuring Worth. http://www.measuringworth.com/uscompare/relativevalue.php.

Richardson, Rupert N., B. W. Aston, and Ira Donathan Taylor. *Along Texas Old Forts Trail.* Denton: University of North Texas Press, 1990.

Rodenberger, Lou, ed. *31 by Lawrence Clayton.* Abilene, TX: McMurry Foundation Press, 2002.

Rollins, Philip Ashton. *The Cowboy: An Unconventional History of Civilization on the Old-Time Cattle Range.* Norman: University of Oklahoma Press, 1997.

Roosevelt, Theodore. "The New Nationalism." Osawatomie, KS, August 31, 1910.

———. *Winning of the West.* 4 vols. New York: B. P. Putnam's Sons.

Ross, Charles P., and T. L. Rouse. *Official Early-Day History of Wilbarger County.* 2nd ed. Vernon, TX: Vernon Daily Record, 1973.

Rouse, John E. *Cattle of Europe, South America, Australia, and New Zealand.* Vol. 1. Norman: University of Oklahoma Press, 1970, 1972.

Sanchez, Mario. L., ed. *A Shared Experience: The History, Architecture and Historic Designations of the Lower Rio Grande Heritage Corridor.* 2nd ed. Austin: Texas Historical Commission, State House Printing, 1994.

Savage, William W., Jr. *The Cowboy Hero: His Image in American History and Culture.* Norman: University of Oklahoma Press, 1979.

Scott, Jeanie. "About Bud and Temple." Bud and Temple: The Abernathy Boys of Oklahoma. Accessed June 23, 2012. http://budandtemple.com/content/bud-and-temple-jeanie-scott.

Sepulveda, Jose Alfredo. Speech given at Rotary Photo Shoot at Great Western Trail Marker, Brownsville, TX, Dec. 10, 2009.

Sheffield, William J., Jr. *Historic Texas Trails: How to Trace Them.* Rev. ed. Spring, TX: Absey, 2002.

Siringo, Charles L. *A Texas Cow Boy or Fifteen Years on the Hurricane Deck of a Spanish Pony*. Chicago: M. Umbdenstock, 1885.

Sizemore. Deborah Lightfoot. "LH7 Ranch." The Handbook of Texas Online. Accessed Jan. 3, 2011. http://www.tshaonline.org/handbook/online/articles/aplts.

Skaggs, Jimmy M. "Cattle Trailing." The Handbook of Texas Online. Accessed June 29, 2011. http://www.tshaonline.org/handbook/online/articles/ayc01.

———. "The Great Western Cattle Trail to Dodge City, Kansas." Master's thesis. Texas Technological College, 1965.

———. "John Thomas Lytle." *The New Handbook of Texas*. Vol. 4. Austin: Texas State Historical Association, 1996.

Slatta, Richard. *Comparing Cowboys & Frontiers: New Perspectives on the History of the Americas*. Norman: University of Oklahoma Press, 1997.

———. *The Cowboy Encyclopedia*. New York: Norton, 1994.

———. *Cowboy: The Illustrated History*. New York: Sterling, 2006.

———. "TR: First Modern President, Progressive, Conservationist, Historian, Rancher." Panel presentation at the National Cowboy Symposium and Celebration, Lubbock, TX, September 10, 2011.

Slotkin, Richard. *The Fatal Environment: The Myth of the Frontier in the Age of Industrialization, 1800–1890*. Norman: University of Oklahoma Press, 1985.

Smith, Julia Cauble. "Loving, Oliver." The Handbook of Texas Online. Accessed April 28, 2014. http://www.tshaonline.org/handbook/online/articles/flo38.

Smith, Ruby L. "Early Development of Wilbarger County." *West Texas Historical Association Year Book*, 1938.

Sonnichsen, C. L. *From Hopalong to Hud: Thoughts on Western Fiction*. College Station: Texas A&M University Press, 1978.

South Platte River Trail in Northeast Colorado: Julesburg, Ovid, Sedgwick. Brochure. Colorado Scenic and Historic Byways Commission, n.d.

"State of Wyoming: Women's Equality Heritage." State of Wyoming. Updated 2013. Accessed April 15, 2015. http://www.wyo.gov/about-wyoming/wyoming-history.

Stephens, A. Ray, and William M. Holmes. *Historical Atlas of Texas*. Norman: University of Oklahoma Press, 1989.

"Stockman Bank." StockmanBank.com. Accessed October 10, 2011. https://www.stockmanbank.com/ContentDocumentHandler.ashx?documentId=26086.

Streeter, Floyd B. *Prairie Trails & Cow Towns: The Opening of the Old West*. New York: Devin Adair, 1963.

"Super Bowl." Postcard. Barnesville, OH: Dickinson Publishing Co., n.d.

"Teddy Roosevelt's Visit Is High Point for Vernon." *The Vernon Daily Record* (TX), Sec. 4, p. 2, 1958.

The Texas Longhorn: A Living Legend. Brochure. Austin: Texas Parks and Wildlife Dept., Nov. 1982.

"Texas Trail Canyon." Road Sign. Nebraska Historical Marker.

Tippette, Giles. "Roughriding Rover Boys." May 17, 1976. Accessed Feb. 11, 2012. http://sportsillustrated.cnn.com/vault/article/magazine/MAG1091099/index.htm.

Tobin, Peggy. "Bandera Pass." *The New Handbook of Texas*. Vol. 1. Austin: Texas State Historical Association, 1996, 366.

———. "Bandera, Texas." *The New Handbook of Texas*. Vol. 1. Austin: Texas State Historical Association, 1996, 363–364.

"Trail Blazer Nominees Being Sought." *Vernon Daily Record* (TX), July 8, 2011, 1.

Turner, E. K. *Beyond the Farm Gate: The Story of a Farm Boy Who Helped Make the Saskatchewan Wheat Pool a World-Class Business*. Regina, SK: University of Regina Press, 2014.

Tyler, Ron. "Amon Carter Museum." The Handbook of Texas Online. Accessed Feb. 2, 2012. http://www.tshaonline.org/handbook/online/articles/kla02.

Vestal, Stanley. *Queen of Cowtowns: Dodge City, The Wickedest Little City in America, 1872–1886*. New York: Harper & Bros., 1952.

Webb, Walter Prescott. *The Great Frontier*. Boston: Houghton Mifflin Co., 1952.

———. *The Great Plains*. New York: Grosset & Dunlap, 1931.

———. *The Texas Rangers: A Century of Frontier Defense*. Austin: University of Texas Press, 1995.

Wellman, Paul I. *The Trampling Herd: The Story of the Cattle Range in Texas*. New York: Carrick & Evans, 1939.

"Western Trail Art Association Holds First Meeting." *Vernon Daily Record* (TX), Oct. 23, 2011.

The Western Trail Gazette. "Friends of the Western Trail newsletter." May 19, 2004. 1–4.

Williams, Dallas. *Fort Sedgwick: Colorado Territory Hell Hole on the Platte*. Julesburg, Colorado: Fort Sedgwick Historical Society, 1996.

Wilson, Mrs. Augustus, compiler. *The Opening Session of the First National Cattle Growers' Convention. And Biographical Sketches and Portraits of Prominent Men Attending the Convention*, extracted in *Parsons' Memorial and Historical Magazine*. St. Louis, MO, 1885. Reprint note: date misprint, 1884. Bryan, Texas: Fred White Jr., Book Seller, 1970.

Wister, Owen. *The Virginian: A Horseman of the Plains*. New York: Pocket Books, 1902, 1973.

Wolz, Larry. "Belle Plain, TX (Callahan County)." The Handbook of Texas Online. Accessed Jan. 12, 2012. http://www.tshaonline.org/handbook/online/articles/hvb35.

Woods, Lawrence M. *Alex Swan and the Swan Companies*. Norman, OK: Arthur H. Clark, 2006.

———. *Asa Shinn Mercer: Western Promoter and Newspaperman, 1839–1917*. Spokane, WA: Arthur H. Clark, 2003.

"World Championship Rocky Mountain Oyster Festival." *Times Record News* (Wichita Falls, TX), May 16, 2008, 17.

Worcester, Donald E. "Chisholm Trail." The Handbook of Texas Online. Accessed Oct. 7, 2011. http://www.tshaonline.org/handbook/online/articles/ayc02.

"W. W. Terrett." Montana Cowboy Hall of Fame. Accessed April 23, 2011. http://www.
montanacowboyfame.com/151001/179590.html.

"Wyoming." *The World Book Encyclopedia*. Chicago: Field Enterprises Educational
Corp., 1968.

"The Y.O. Brand." The Y.O. Ranch. Accessed Aug. 11, 2011. www.yoranch.com/history/
yo_brand.

NOTES

CHAPTER 1

1. Terry Jordan, *North American Cattle-Ranching Frontiers: Origins, Diffusion, and Differentiation* (Albuquerque: University of New Mexico Press, 1993), 210, 308–314.
2. Ibid., x.
3. J. Frank Dobie, *The Longhorns* (Austin: University of Texas Press, 1997), 33–35, 45.
4. *The Texas Longhorn: A Living Legend* (Austin: Texas Parks and Wildlife Dept., Nov. 1982.)
5. "Longhorn History," Texas Longhorn Marketing Alliance, accessed August 12, 2012, http://www.thelonghornalliance.com.
6. Ibid.
7. "A Different Kind of Association," International Longhorn Association, accessed August 12, 2012, http://www.itla.net/ITLA- Information/index.cfm?con=history.
8. "About the Texas Longhorn Marketing Alliance," TLMA, accessed July 2, 2011, http://www.thelonghornalliance.com/default.asp?contentID=583.
9. "Longhorn History—Seven Original Families," ITLA, accessed Feb. 11, 2006, http://www.itla.net/longhorn_information/index.cfm?con=7_Families&ss=history.
10. Terry Kelsey, *Texas Gold*, Fort Worth, Texas, in Smithsonian Art Inventory Sculptures, http://www.waymarking.com/waymarks/WM7GK3_Texas_Gold_Fort_Worth_Texas.
11. Jimmy M. Skaggs, "The Great Western Cattle Trail to Dodge City, Kansas" (master's thesis, Texas Technological College, 1965).
12. Ibid.
13. Ibid.
14. Ibid., 127.
15. Frank Norris, e-mail message to author, Jan. 6, 2014.
16. Ibid.
17. Tommy Lee Jones, director, *The Good Old Boys*, movie: Turner Pictures, March 5,

1995, based on Elmer Kelton, *The Good Old Boys* (New York: Bantam Books, 1995), 170.

18. Ibid., 173.

19. Harwood P. Hinton, "John Simpson Chisum," *The New Handbook of Texas* (Austin: Texas State Historical Association, 1996), 2:91.

20. Julia Cauble Smith, "Loving, Oliver," *Handbook of Texas Online*, accessed April 28, 2014, http://www.tshaonline.org/handbook/online/articles/flo38.

21. Gary Kraisinger and Margaret Kraisinger, *The Western: The Greatest Texas Cattle Trail, 1874–1886* (Newton, Kansas: Mennonite Press, 2004), 13–14.

22. Ibid., 11.

23. Ibid., 11–12.

24. Ibid., 12.

25. Ibid., 15.

26. Ibid.

27. Jimmy M. Skaggs, "John Thomas Lytle," *New Handbook of Texas* (Austin: Texas State Historical Association, 1996), 4:354.

28. H. Allen Anderson, "Blocker, John Rufus," *Handbook of Texas Online*, accessed Aug. 2, 2011, http://www.tshaonline.org/handbook/online/articles/fb\27.

29. Donald E. Worcester, "Chisholm Trail," *Handbook of Texas Online*, accessed April 28, 2014, http://www.tshaonline.org/handbook/online/articles/ayc02.

CHAPTER 2

1. Ruby L. Smith, "Early Development of Wilbarger County" (*West Texas Historical Association Year Book*, 1938), 55–56.

2. J. E. Collins, "Doan Family Among County's Earliest Pioneers," *Early-Day History of Wilbarger County* (Wilbarger County Historical Association, n.d.), 16–18.

3. Sylvia Jones, ed. "Doan's, The First Settlement," *Wilbarger County History* (Lubbock, TX: Wilbarger County Historical Commission, 1986), 561–562.

4. Tiffany Marie Haggard Fink, "The Fort Worth and Denver City Railway: Settlement, Development, and Decline on the Texas High Plains" (dissertation, Texas Tech University, 2004), 40–41.

5. "Phil McCuistion," *Marking the Great Western Trail in the 21st Century: A Centennial Rotary Project by the Rotary Club of Vernon Texas*. DVD, Rotary Club of Vernon and Red River Valley Museum, April 2010.

6. Paul Hawkins, letter to author, Nov. 2, 2010.

7. Ibid.

8. Rick Perry, letter to Vernon Rotary Club, April 20, 2004.

9. Sue Flanagan, *Trailing the Longhorns: A Century Later* (Austin, TX: Madrona Press, 1974), 105.

10. Nicholas Rea Lehman, *2004 Doan's May Day Program*.

11. Alice Tate Smith, *2004 Doan's May Day Program*.

12. David Burrell, telephone interview with author, Oct. 18, 2011.

13. "LH7," *Handbook of Texas Online*, accessed Oct. 8, 2010, http://www.tshaonline.org/handbook/onlinearticles/LL/aplts.html.

14. Gary Kraisinger, *Map of Texas: Western Cattle Trail Showing the Texas Portion of This Great Trail That Ran from South Texas to Canada*, according to Jimmy Skaggs (Halstead, KS: Gary Kraisinger, n.d.).

15. Peggy Tobin, "Bandera, Texas," and "Bandera Pass," *The New Handbook of Texas* (Austin: Texas State Historical Association, 1996), 1:363–64, 366.

16. Jimmy M. Skaggs, "The Great Western Cattle Trail to Dodge City, Kansas" (master's thesis, Texas Technological College, 1965), 28.

CHAPTER 3

1. Jimmy M. Skaggs, "The Great Western Cattle Trail to Dodge City, Kansas" (master's thesis, Texas Technological College, 1965), 25.

2. *Matamoros: Gateway to Mexico* (Matamoros Municipal Government, 2005), 30.

3. Edith Mercedes Angulo, "GWT Dedication Speech" (public speech, Museo del Agraisamo Mexicano, Matamoros, Mexico, June 3, 2006).

4. Walter Prescott Webb, *The Texas Rangers: A Century of Frontier Defense* (Austin: University of Texas Press, 1995), 233.

5. George Durham as told to Clyde Wantland, *Taming the Nueces Strip: The Story of McNelly's Rangers*, Foreword by Walter Prescott Webb (Austin: University of Texas Press, 1962), viii–ix.

6. Joseph Milton Nance, "Mier Expedition," *Handbook of Texas Online*, accessed Sept. 23, 2011, http://www.tshaonline.org/handbook/online/articles/qym02.

7. Skaggs, "The Great Western Cattle Trail," 25.

8. Ibid., 28.

9. Alicia A. Garza, "Brooks County," *Handbook of Texas Online*, accessed May 2, 2014, http://www.tshaonline.org/handbook/online/articles/hcb16.

10. Murphy Givens, "Up the Trail from Texas," *Corpus Christi Caller Times*, Feb. 16, 2000, A13–A14.

11. John Ashton and Edgar P. Sneed, "King Ranch," *Handbook of Texas Online*, accessed Nov. 21, 2011, http://www.tshaonline.org/handbook/online/articles/apk01.

12. Evan Anders, "Wells, James Babbage, Jr.," *The New Handbook of Texas* (Austin: Texas State Historical Association, 1996), 6:877.

13. Ashton and Sneed, "King Ranch."

14. Jane Clements Monday and Frances Brannen Vick. *Petra's Legacy: The South Texas Ranching Empire of Petra Vela and Mifflin Kenedy* (College Station: Texas A&M University Press, 2007), 191.

15. Ibid., 238, 246, 254–262.

16. Francis E. Abernethy, "Dobie, James Frank," *The New Handbook of Texas* (Austin: Texas State Historical Association, 1996), 2:662–63.

17. J. Frank Dobie, *The Longhorns* (Austin: University of Texas Press, 1997), vii.

18. Mary Margaret Dougherty Campbell, "The West Boys from Sweet Home: Trail Drivers, Cattlemen" (paper, National Cowboy Symposium and Celebration, Lubbock, TX, Sept. 9, 2011).

19. Jimmy M. Skaggs, "John Thomas Lytle," *The New Handbook of Texas* (Austin: Texas State Historical Association, 1996), 4:354.

20. Ibid.

21. Paul Noack, e-mail message to author, Oct. 16, 2011.

CHAPTER 4

1. Wayne Gard, *The Chisholm Trail* (Norman: University of Oklahoma Press, 1954), 238.

2. Frederick Law Olmsted, *A Journey Through Texas or, A Saddle Trip on the Southwestern Frontier* (New York: Dix, Edwards, 1857), 274.

3. Roland S. Jary, "Saunders, George Washington," *Handbook of Texas Online*, accessed Oct. 7, 2011, http://www.tshaonline.org/handbook/online/articles/fsa38.

4. Ibid.

5. Ibid.

6. Marco Barros, e-mail message to author, Sept. 13, 2007.

7. Jimmy M. Skaggs, "The Great Western Cattle Trail to Dodge City, Kansas" (master's thesis, Texas Technological College, 1965), 27.

8. E. H. Johnson, "Edwards Plateau," *Handbook of Texas Online*, accessed Oct. 27, 2011, http://www.tshaonline.org/handbook/online/articles/rxe01.

9. Jim Harris, "History and the Arts," History Notebook column, *Lovington Leader* (Lovington, NM), Oct. 10, 2006, 3.

10. "The Y.O. Brand," The Y.O. Ranch, accessed Aug. 11, 2011, www.yoranch.com/history/yo_brand.

11. "History," Texas Longhorn Breeders Association of America, accessed Aug. 12, 2011, www.tlbaa.org/tlbaa/history.html/.

12. "Super Bowl," postcard (Barnesville, OH: Dickinson Publishing Co., n.d.).

13. Skaggs, "The Great Western Cattle Trail," 29–30.

14. Frederica Wyatt, article given to author, no title, no date, no page; and Skaggs, "The Great Western Cattle Trail," 30.

15. Skaggs, "The Great Western Cattle Trail," 30.

16. Ibid.

17. Ibid.

18. William Mark Day, "The Western Trail Through McCulloch County, Texas," unpublished article, n.d.

19. Ibid.

20. Ibid.

21. V. Murray Jordan, e-mail message to author, Aug. 24, 2010.

22. Walter Prescott Webb, *The Great Frontier* (Boston: Houghton Mifflin Co. 1952), ix.

CHAPTER 5

1. J. Marvin Hunter, *The Trail Drivers of Texas* (Austin: University of Texas Press, 1985), 409.

2. Harwood Pittinton, "John Simpson Chisum," *The New Handbook of Texas* (Austin: Texas State Historical Association, 1996), 2:91–92.

3. Carolyn Rabon, "The Western Trail," Interview with Forman Fowler, *Coleman County Chronicle* (TX), n.d., 1958.

4. Dick Reavis, "The Cattle Drives," *Coleman County Chronicle* (TX), n.d., 1958.

5. Joe Morris Hemphill, "Press D. and Carrie Morris," *The History of Coleman County and Its People*, vol. 2 (Coleman, TX: Coleman County Historical Commission, n.d.).

6. Heath Hemphill, letter to author, March 9, 2006.

7. Ibid.

8. Ibid.

9. Margaret White Banister, "Banister, Emma Daugherty," *Handbook of Texas Online*, accessed January 4, 2012, http://www.tshaonline.org/handbook/online/articles/fbacq.

10. Evelyn Bruce Kingsbery, e-mail message to author, Oct. 20, 2011.

11. Tai Kreidler, e-mail message to author, Oct. 20, 2011.

12. James T. Padgitt, Talk given at Coleman City Park, *Coleman County Chronicle, Coleman's Diamond Jubilee*, newspaper insert, 1951), 44.

13. Lee Ivey, Interview by Carol Moring (Ivey's daughter), unpublished article, Dec. 1975.

14. C. Robert Haywood, "Potter-Blocker Trail," *Handbook of Texas Online*, accessed Jan. 6, 2012, http://www.tshaonline.org/handbook/online/articles/ayp01.

15. Jimmy M. Skaggs, "The Great Western Cattle Trail to Dodge City, Kansas" (master's thesis, Texas Technological College, 1965), 31.

16. Larry Wolz, "Belle Plain, TX (Callahan County)," *Handbook of Texas Online*, accessed Jan. 12, 2012, http://www.tshaonline.org/handbook/online/articles/hvb35.

17. Thomas Robert Havins, *Belle Plain, Texas: Ghost Town in Callahan* (Brownwood, TX: Brown Press, 1972), 2, 25.

18. "Moran, TX." *Handbook of Texas Online*, accessed Jan. 13, 2012, http://www.tshaonline.org/handbook/online/articles/hlm85.

19. Ibid., accessed Feb. 7, 2012.

20. Ted Paup, e-mail message to author, Jan. 30, 2012.

21. Lawrence Clayton, *Contemporary Ranches of Texas* (Austin: University of Texas Press, 2001), 73.

22. Lawrence Clayton, "Fort Griffin Fandangle," *Handbook of Texas Online*, accessed Jan. 14, 2012, http://www.tshaonline.org/handbook/online/article/kkf2.

23. "Famous Texas Cattle Baron Dies," April 16, 1997, newspaper clipping in author's files.

24. Marilynne Howsley Jacobs, "Albany, TX," *Handbook of Texas Online*, accessed Jan. 14, 2012, http://www.tshaonline.org/handbook/online/articles/hja01.

25. Lawrence Clayton, "Fort Griffin, TX," *Handbook of Texas Online*, accessed Jan. 15, 2012, http://www.tshaonline.org/handbook/online/articles/hnf35.

26. Emalyn (Sam) Gillispie, "Head 'em up . . . move 'em out," *Fort Griffin Fandangle Souvenir Program*, June 2006, 33-A-11-A.

27. Susan J. Nix, "Buffalo Gap, TX," *Handbook of Texas Online*, accessed Jan. 17, 2012, http://www.tshaonline.org/handbook/online/articles/hlb60.

28. Robert D. Putnam, *Bowling Alone: The Collapse and Revival of American Community* (New York: Simon & Schuster, 2000), 20.

CHAPTER 6

1. Lawrence Clayton, "Chimney Creek Ranch: An Historical Account and Personal View of a Shackelford County Ranching Heritage," Booklet (2011).

2. "R. A. Brown Ranch Hosts Legacy Sale," *Progressive Cattleman,* Nov. 4, 2013, http://www.progressivecattle.com/sales-results/5880-ra-brown-ranch-hosts-legacy-sale.

3. John Leffler, "Throckmorton County," *Handbook of Texas Online*, accessed May 22, 2012, http://www.tshaonline.org/handbook/online/articles/hct05.

4. "World Championship Rocky Mountain Oyster Festival," *Times Record News* (Wichita Falls, TX), May 16, 2008, 17.

5. Jimmy M. Skaggs, "The Great Western Cattle Trail to Dodge City, Kansas" (master's thesis, Texas Technological College, 1965), 32, 33.

6. Lawrence L. Graves, "Baylor County," *Handbook of Texas Online*, accessed Jan. 28, 2012, http://www.tshaonline.org/handbook/online/articles/hcb04).

7. Ibid.

8. H. Allen Anderson, "Hashknife Ranch," *Handbook of Texas Online*, accessed Jan. 29, 2012, http://www.tshaonline.org/handbook/online/articles/aph01.

9. "History," W. T. Waggoner Ranch, accessed Jan. 30, 2012, http://www.waggonerranch.com/images/WaggHist.htm.

10. "Relative Values - US," Measuring Worth.com, http://www.measuringworth.com/uscompare/relativevalue.php.

11. "History," W. T. Waggoner Ranch.

12. Roze McCoy Porter, *Thistle Hill: The Cattle Baron's Legacy* (Fort Worth, TX: Branch-Smith, 1980), 126, 134.

13. Roze McCoy Porter, *Electra II: Electra Waggoner Biggs, Socialite, Sculptor, Ranch Heiress* (Dallas: Taylor, 1995), 308.

14. Ibid., 369, 372–373.

15. Jeff Bearden, "Marking the Great Western Trail: A Centennial Project of the Rotary Club of Vernon, Texas," brochure, n.d.

16. "Marks and Brands Registry," Vol. 1 from 1881 to 1885, Wilbarger County Courthouse, provided by Kelly Wright in e-mail to author, Nov. 14, 2005.

17. John Leffler, "Wilbarger County," *Handbook of Texas Online*, accessed May 24, 2012, http://www.tshaonline.org/handbook/online/articles/hcw09.

18. Ruby L. Smith, "Early Development of Wilbarger County" (*West Texas Historical Association Year Book*, 1938), 67.

19. Leffler, "Wilbarger County."

20. Smith, "Early Development of Wilbarger County," 67.

21. Lawrence M. Woods, *Asa Shinn Mercer: Western Promoter and Newspaperman 1839–1917* (Spokane, WA: Arthur H. Clark, 2003), 229.

22. Ibid., 140.

23. A. S. Mercer, *The Banditti of the Plains Or the Cattlemen's Invasion of Wyoming in 1892 (The Crowning Infamy of the Ages)* (Norman: University of Oklahoma Press, 1954), xx–xxiv.

24. Woods, *Asa Shinn Mercer*, 141.

25. Ibid., 142.

26. Ibid., 142–143.

27. Jimmy Carr, "First Blair Witch, Now Doan's Ghosts?" Town Crier, *Vernon Daily Record*, Nov. 16, 1999.

28. Larry Holmes, e-mail message to author, May 3, 2004.

CHAPTER 7

1. "Ex-State Senator, Relative Die in San Antonio Fire," *Houston Chronicle*, accessed Aug. 16, 2011, http://www.chron.com/disp/story.mpl/front/4357475.html.

2. John D. Heisch, "Old Greer County," *Encyclopedia of Oklahoma History and Culture*, accessed April 14, 2015, www.okhistory.org.

3. Roze McCoy Porter, *Thistle Hill: The Cattle Baron's Legacy* (Fort Worth, TX: Branch-Smith, 1980), 86–87, 92–93.

4. Matthew Rex Cox, "Roosevelt's Wolf Hunt," *Encyclopedia of Oklahoma History and Culture*, accessed April 15, 2015, http://www.okhistory.org/publications/enc/entry.php?entry=RO026.

5. "Teddy Roosevelt's Visit Is High Point for Vernon," *The Vernon Daily Record*, Sec. 4, p. 2, 1958. The newspaper clipping does not include the day of publication.

6. Porter, *Thistle Hill*, 92–93.

7. "Roosevelt's Visit Is High Point," *Vernon Daily Record.*

8. Jeanie Scott, "About Bud and Temple," Bud and Temple: The Abernathy Boys of Oklahoma, accessed June 23, 2012, http://budandtemple.com/content/bud-and-temple-jeanie-scott.

9. "Initial Point of Oklahoma," Oklahoma Society of Land Surveyors, accessed Feb. 15, 2012, http://www.osls.org/?page=25.

10. *Great Western Trail Drive*, brochure, Vici, Oklahoma.

11. Leo Kelley, ed., "Up the Trail in '76: The Journal of Lewis Warren Neatherlin," in *Chronicles of Oklahoma*, Vol. 67, No. 1 (Spring 1988): 22–51. Reprint of article only (Altus, OK: Western Trail Historical Society, n.d.), 1–33.

12. Ibid., 3.

13. Ibid., 18–21.

14. "Fort Supply History," Oklahoma Historical Society, Military Sites, accessed Feb. 19, 2012, http://www.okhistory.org/sites/fshistory.php.

15. Kelley, "Up the Trail in '76," 23–24.

16. Odie B. Faulk, *Dodge City: The Most Western Town of All* (New York: Oxford University Press, 1977), 13, 17, 34.

17. Ibid., 70, 100, 133, 172–73.

18. Ibid., 128.

19. Ibid., 91–93.

20. Mrs. Augustus Wilson, compiler, "Col. Robert D. Hunter," *The Opening Session of the First National Cattle Growers' Convention. And Biographical Sketches and Portraits of Prominent Men Attending the Convention,* extracted in *Parsons' Memorial and Historical Magazine* (St. Louis, MO, 1885). Reprint note: date misprint, 1884 (Bryan, TX: Fred White Jr., Book Seller, 1970), n.p.

21. Ibid., n.p.

22. Kelley, "Up the Trail in '76," 23–27.

23. Ibid.

24. Ibid.

CHAPTER 8

1. Leo Kelley, ed., "Up the Trail in '76: The Journal of Lewis Warren Neatherlin," in *Chronicles of Oklahoma*, Vol. 67, No. 1 (Spring 1988): 22–51. Reprint of article only (Altus, OK: Western Trail Historical Society, n.d.), 27.

2. Ibid.

3. Ibid., 27, 28.

4. Vernon Combs, "Buffalo Bill as a Pony Express Rider," *Pony Express Gazette*, April 1999, quoting from Ivan J. Barrett, *Eph Hanks* (Covenant Communications, 1990), accessed May 10, 2012, http://www.xphomestation.com/vcombs.html.

5. "The Hero: Buffalo Bill and the Dime Novel Western," Dime Novels and Penny Dreadfuls, accessed May 23, 2012, http://web.stanford.edu/dept/SUL/library/prod//depts/dp/pennies/cover.html#boys.

6. Robert McNamara, "Ned Buntline," About.com, About Education, accessed May 23, 2012, http://history1800s.about.com/od/dimenovelsandmagazines/fl/Ned-Buntline-biography.htm.

7. "Col. Prentiss Ingraham: King of the Dime Novels," The Department of Archives and Special Collections, The University of Mississippi, accessed May 24, 2012, http://www.olemiss.edu/depts/general_library/archives/exhibits/past/ingrahamex/ingraham.html.

8. "Colorado Central Railroad," Utah Rails.net, last updated May 9, 2013, http://utahrails.net/up/colorado-central.php.

9. *South Platte River Trail in Northeast Colorado: Julesburg, Ovid, Sedgwick* (Colorado Scenic and Historic Byways Commission, n.d.)

10. Joe Nardone, "Pony Express National Historic Trail" (speech, dedication of Great Western Trail marker, Julesburg, Colorado, June 23, 2007).

11. Lee Pitts, "Great American Ranches-Haythorn Ranch," Haythorn Land and Cattle Co., accessed Feb. 29, 2012, http://www.haythorn.com/history.html.

12. Lawrence Clayton, *Contemporary Ranches of Texas* (Austin: University of Texas Press, 2001), 61.

13. Graig Kinzie, "Great Western Trail Marker Dedicated," *Keith County News* (Ogallala, NE), May 8, 2006, 1–2.

14. "Descendants of Trail Drivers to Be Recognized," *Keith County News* (Ogallala, NE), May 1, 2006.

15. Jeff Headley, "Pollock Adds to Legacy with Award," Write to the Point, *Keith County News* (Ogallala, NE), n.d.

16. "Jim L. Ozbun Biography," President Jim L. Ozbun Papers, University Archives, North Dakota State University, Fargo.

17. Gary Kraisinger, *Map of North of Ogallala, Showing the Location of the Western Cattle Trail Showing the Upper Portion of This Great Trail That Ran from South Texas to Canada* (Halstead, KS: Mennonite Press, n.d.)

18. Ibid.

19. Ibid.

20. "Development and Patterns of Euro-American Settlement in the White River Badlands (AD 1880s–1960s)," in *Discovery and Re-Discovery in the White River Badlands: Historic Resource Study*, Badlands National Park, John Miller Associates, July 2006, 168.

21. Myra Busby, e-mail message to author, March 12, 2014.

22. Kraisinger, *Map of North of Ogallala.*

23. Gary Kraisinger and Margaret Kraisinger, *The Western: The Greatest Texas Cattle Trail, 1874–1886* (Newton, KS: Mennonite Press, 2004), 13–14n19.

24. David Mason, e-mail message to author, Sept. 4, 2011.

25. Edmund Morris, *The Rise of Theodore Roosevelt* (New York: Modern Library, 2001).

26. Ibid.

27. Richard Slatta, "TR: First Modern President, Progressive, Conservationist, Historian, Rancher" (panel, National Cowboy Symposium and Celebration, Lubbock, TX, September 10, 2011).

CHAPTER 9

1. Austin E. and Alta S. Fife, "Git Along Little Dogies," No. 76, *Cowboy and Western Songs: A Comprehensive Anthology* (New York: Bramhall House, 1982), 206.

2. Gary Kraisinger, *Map of North of Ogallala, Showing the Location of the Western Cattle Trail, the Upper Portion of This Great Trail That Ran from South Texas to Canada* (Halstead, KS: Mennonite Press, n.d.).

3. Sue Flanagan, *Trailing the Longhorns: A Century Later* (Austin, TX: Madrona Press, 1974), 126.

4. "State of Wyoming: Women's Equality Heritage," State of Wyoming, updated 2013, accessed April 15, 2015, http://www.wyo.gov/about-wyoming/wyoming-history.

5. Mike Enzi, "Country, Patriotic Pride," John Wayne Collector's Edition, *American Cowboy*, Special Issue, 2014, 43.

6. Richard Slatta, "TR: First Modern President, Progressive, Conservationist, Historian, Rancher" (panel, National Cowboy Symposium and Celebration, Lubbock, TX, September 10, 2011).

7. Lawrence M. Woods, *Asa Shinn Mercer: Western Promoter and Newspaperman, 1839–1917* (Spokane, WA: Arthur H. Clark Co., 2003), 133–140.

8. Ibid., 145–46.

9. Asa Shinn Mercer, *The Banditti of the Plains or The Cattlemen's Invasion of Wyoming in 1892 (The Crowning Infamy of the Ages),* Foreword by William Kittrell, 1894 (Norman: University of Oklahoma Press, 1954), xxii–xxiii.

10. Woods, *Asa Shinn Mercer*, 157.

11. Ibid., 187–188.

12. John Mercer, telephone interview with author, Feb. 8, 2009.

13. Collen Pollat, *Secrets: The Tom Wagoner Story*, Note from the Author (www.booksurge.com, 2007), 6–7.

14. Ibid., 7.

15. Ibid., 6–8.

16. John W. Davis, *Goodbye Judge Lynch: The End of a Lawless Era in Wyoming's Big Horn Basin* (Norman: University of Oklahoma Press, 2005), 99.

17. Ibid., 100.

18. Ibid., 19.

19. John Leakey, *The West That Was: From Texas to Montana*. As told to Nellie Snyder Yost (Lincoln: University of Nebraska Press, 1965), 93–94.

20. Kraisinger, *Map of North of Ogallala*.

21. Larry McMurtry, *Lonesome Dove* (New York: Simon & Schuster, 1985), 783.

22. Ibid., 840.

23. E. C. "Teddy Blue" Abbott, and Helen Huntington Smith, *We Pointed Them North: Recollections of a Cowpuncher* (Norman: University of Oklahoma Press, 1939, 1955), 137.

24. "Balance Sheet," *2009 Annual Report* (Miles City, MT: Stockman Financial Corp.).

25. "C. M. Coffee," Montana Cowboy Hall of Fame, accessed October 9, 2011, http://www.montanacowboyfame.com/151001/380760.html.

26. "Stockman Bank," StockmanBank.com, accessed October 10, 2011, https://www.stockmanbank.com/ContentDocumentHandler.ashx?documentId=26086.

27. "W. W. Terrett," Montana Cowboy Hall of Fame, accessed October 24, 2011, http://www.montanacowboyfame.com/151001/179590.html.

28. *Miles City: Visitors' Guide 2010* (Miles City, MT), 75, 77.

29. Ibid., 74.

30. Stan Markuson, e-mail message to author, August 10, 2011.

31. *Miles City: Visitors' Guide 2010*, 74.

32. Gary Kraisinger, *Map of North of Ogallala*.

33. Ibid.

34. Ted Turner, e-mail message to author, Jan. 19, 2009.

35. Bill Whelan and Ted Turner, "Land of the Prairie," The Great Western Cattle Trails Update, sent to author as e-mail attachment, n.d.

36. Ibid.

37. Willard Nelson, Family Genealogy, Death Certificate, Hand-Drawn Map of Montana & Canadian Ranches, mailed to author, Feb. 24, 2009.

38. Boyd Anderson, "Beyond the Range," excerpt in "Super Issue," *The Saskatchewan Stockgrower*, September 2005, 53–54.

39. Ian Mitchell, letter to Rotary Club of Regina, with photo and caption, Battle View Livestock, Lloydminster, Saskatchewan.

40. E. K. Turner, *Beyond the Farm Gate: The Story of a Farm Boy Who Helped Make the Saskatchewan Wheat Pool a World-Class Business* (Regina, Saskatchewan: University of Regina Press, 2014), x.

41. "Hall of Fame," Canadian Western Agribition, accessed March 23, 2012, http://www.agribition.com/Show_Information/Hall_of_Fame//Hall_of_Fame/.

42. Ted Turner, "Canadian Western Agribition Great Western Trail Dedication on Nov. 28, 2008," letter, e-mailed to author, Jan. 19, 2009.

43. David Mason, e-mail message to author, Sept. 4, 2011.

44. Gary Kraisinger, *North of Ogallala*.

CHAPTER 10

1. Bob Klemme, e-mail message to author, July 15, 2007.

2. Matt Mackowiak, "Sen. Hutchison Protects Chisholm and Great Western Trails," News Release, Oct. 30, 2007.

3. Frank Norris, "Cattle Trails—Statement of Significance." Following academic peer review/SHPO review, Preliminary Working Draft, March 20, 2012, http://www.nps.gov/nhl/news/LC/spring2012/CattleTrails.pdf.

4. Chris Jefferies, e-mail message to author and Bob Klemme, September 13, 2011.

5. *Draft Chisholm and Great Western National Historic Trail Feasibility Study/Environmental Assessment* (National Park Service, US Department of the Interior, December 22, 2014), 24.

6. Ibid., 6.

7. Ibid., 23.

8. Ibid., iii.

9. Ibid., 13.

10. "Federal Land Ownership: Overview and Data," Congressional Research Service, February 8, 2012, accessed April 18, 2015, https://fas.org/sgp/crs/misc/R42346.pdf.

11. Al Stehno, email message to Bob Klemme, March 2, 2015.

12. Danni Beer, Official Comments and Communications, United States Cattlemen's Association, March 20, 2015, accessed April 18, 2015, http://www.uscattlemen.org/Templates/Official_Comments_And_Communications/2015_Official-Comments/3-20USCA-Comments-Chisholm-Trail.pdf.

13. Frank Norris, email message to Bob Klemme, March 2, 2015.

14. José Alfredo Sepulveda, speech, Brownsville, Texas, Dec. 10, 2009.

15. José Alfredo Sepulveda, e-mail message to the author, Oct. 25, 2009.

16. Michael Babb, "Great Western Cattle Trail," *GWCT: Songs for the Cowboy in All of Us* (Nashville, TN: Magic Yellow Bird Publications, 2010).

17. Michael Babb, interview with the author, Jan. 8, 2011.

18. Paul Harris, "The Life and Times of Paul Harris," accessed April 23, 2012, http://www.rotary.org/en/AboutUs/History/paulharris/Pages/ridefault.aspx.

19. "John Leakey," North Dakota Cowboy Hall of Fame, accessed March 7, 2011, http://northdakotacowboy.com/Hall_of_Fame/Ranching/leakey_john.asp.

20. John Leakey, *The West That Was: From Texas to Montana*. As told to Nellie Snyder Yost (Lincoln: University of Nebraska Press, 1965).

21. Ibid.

22. Paul Noack, e-mail message to author, Nov. 13, 2010.

23. Ibid.

24. Mary Ann McCuistion, interview with author, March 8, 2011.

25. "Jay Newman Grantier," North Dakota Cowboy Hall of Fame, accessed March 2, 2011, http://northdakotacowboy.com/?id=67&form_data_id=89.

26. "Western Trail Art Association Holds First Meeting," *Vernon Daily Record* (TX), Oct. 23, 2011.
27. Judy Ditmore, speech, Meeting of Western Trail National Society of Daughters of the American Revolution Chapter, Vernon, TX, Jan. 13, 2011.
28. Holle Humphries, e-mail message to author, May 9, 2012.

INDEX